BEST GUNS

BEST GUNS

By
MICHAEL McINTOSH

COUNTRYSPORT PRESS
Traverse City, Michigan

©1989 by Michael McIntosh

Published by Countrysport, Inc.
P.O. Box 1856
Traverse City, MI 49685

Printed in the United States of America

2nd Printing, 1990

Library of Congress Catalog Card Number: 89-060723

ISBN 0-924357-02-9

To
Susan and Bethany
the ladies
of my life

CONTENTS

FOREWORD

There are several good reasons to buy this book. Maybe you already have and you're settling in to read it for the first time. Or maybe you've already read it and you're coming back again and noticed you missed the foreword. Maybe you found this book in the attic in the year 2047 and you have opened it out of curiosity.

Doesn't matter. You still should know something about it and about the man who wrote it – Michael McIntosh.

The book is an analysis of the very best guns ever made in the United States, and the best guns being made in the world right now. It's in two sections, and it's almost like two books in one. If you like fine guns, you can't be without it. For the gunner's library, this book is as basic to his needs as ten-inch boots; everything else is a spin-off.

But the real treasure here is Michael McIntosh. Writing about fine guns is only one of Mac's skills. His knowledge of the guns makes him one of the handful of people on earth who truly can be called "expert" on the subject. Heads of gun companies regularly consult him before they make a move. Magazines depend upon his columns and articles to give them credibility and readership.

This book represents a lifetime of studying, tinkering with, scheming to buy, and simply coveting fine guns. His first gun book, *The Best Shotguns Ever Made in America* (Scribner's, 1981), is a classic and one of the most sought-after titles on the secondary book market. You are lucky; you don't have to search. Here is triple-distilled McIntosh knowledge told in the seamless prose that is his trademark.

So much for the professional McIntosh.

The other Mac – the one I know so well – loves soft-footed little Brittany girls who climb on his lap while he's trying to write. He likes good Scotch whiskey and bawdy stories in equal portions, and he is about the only guy I know who can quote "Gunga Din" with the accent of a British Sergeant-Major. And anyone who sits down for a game of duck-camp poker with him is asking to be fleeced.

He also owns, loves, and shoots fine guns, and he shoots them well. We have chased the odd pheasant and quail, and I've never had to doubt that he would handle his end of things when the birds were up. He also functions with equal aplomb at trap, skeet, and sporting clays. He is a complete shotgunner.

Oh, we have our moments, things we don't agree on. Mac thinks woodcock are best served intact; I want the insides out. (We do agree, though, that there's no finer game bird.) Mac thinks needling the other guy about his shooting during a sporting clays tournament is fair (but only, I notice, if the other guy is me); I keep looking in the bylaws for some kind of ruling I can use to get him off me. And there was the time in Iowa, well into the night, when we worked out the logistics for a walrus shoot...but that's another story, for another time. Right now, you have a gun book to read.

So, I leave you to the devices of Michael McIntosh: gun scholar, storyteller without peer, and friend. You couldn't be in better hands.

STEVE SMITH
Traverse City, Michigan

INTRODUCTION

It feels like a long road, these twelve years since I began a series of magazine articles on great American double guns. At the time, I didn't even know it *was* a road, much less where it would lead. I was a teacher then, an English professor at a state college in Missouri, comfortable in the academic round of teaching Shakespeare and Romantic poetry, of scholarly research, seminars, and writing such literary criticism as struck my fancy.

I also was extremely fond of shooting and bird hunting, a legacy from my father that touched me deeply. There was some precedence for it – Havilah Babcock, the great writer of quail-hunting stories, was an English professor, too – but a literary academician fascinated by guns was an unusual creature in the late 1960s and early '70s. Probably still is.

If my colleagues thought me an odd sort, they were kind enough not to say so. My students were, too, although I imagine they were a bit bemused by some of my behavior during fall semesters: showing up at the last minute for early classes, hip-booted, muddy, and necklaced with duck calls; meeting afternoon seminars in field clothes, lecturing on Elizabethan tragedy while my dog waited in the car, and leaving the building with a briefcase in one hand, a gun case in the other. It all seemed perfectly natural to me, as did the shooting and hunting stories I began writing in the mid-'70s.

By the time the first gun articles were appearing in print, I was a full-time editor and writer, and in 1980 those stories formed the nucleus of a book, which was published the following year under the title that Chet Fish, my editor at Scribner's, had suggested: *The Best Shotguns Ever Made in America.* I still had no idea how thoroughly gun writing would shape my life, knew only that it was an immensely rich field to study and a wonderfully satisfying subject to write about. Nothing that's happened since has changed my mind.

Best Shotguns met with a surprisingly good reception – surprising to me, anyway – and despite the parochial indifference of the New York publishing industry toward sporting literature in general and gun writing in particular, it survived through two printings. The second printing apparently sold out last year.

The feeling a writer gets when one of his books goes out of print is a lot like the feeling that comes to a parent when children leave home: They're still yours, still a vital part of you, but they're no longer part of daily life. Some important part of them, and of you, suddenly belongs more to the past than to either the present or the future.

In this case, though, there's a brighter side. More than once over the past few years, I've wished I could have another go at *Best Shotguns*. The eight years since it was published have been eight years of continual study and research, and in the process I've written something more than a half-million words on guns. I've learned a great deal that I didn't know then. My thinking about the gun and its place in social and economic and even emotional history is, I trust, better focused and more precise than it was.

In short, I've felt increasingly certain that I could make *The Best Shotguns Ever Made in America* into a better book. So, when my old friend Steve Smith asked if I'd like to do a revised, expanded version to be among the first titles put out by Countrysport Press, I could only answer that nothing would please me more.

And now you're holding the results. Some of it goes back to the beginning, back to where this road started. In the first section, you'll find the same seven guns that were the subject of *Best Shotguns*. For each, I've kept the best of what I had to say before, discarded what was wrong or vague, rebuilt the skeleton to include such new bones as I've discovered, and have dressed the framework in a completely rewritten suit of flesh.

All of these chapters are longer than they originally were, some of them considerably so. The Fox chapter probably is the most radically different. I have developed a particular admiration for Fox guns and an endless fascination with Ansley Fox himself, both of which have prompted an immense amount of research over the past four years. Working as much as possible with original documents, I've been able to construct both a highly detailed history of the guns and an enormously rich tapestry of the busy, varied life of Ansley Fox. What you'll read here in many ways amounts to the outline of a much longer work, now well under way and due to appear in print before any of us is a great deal older.

I have attempted to recast the material of *The Best Shotguns Ever Made in America* in terms of a far broader view than I took before, seeking to place American guns in the context of the world gun trade – which in all practical terms means the European trade – and of the currents in history that have shaped the nature of the gun worldwide. Attempting to fulfill that intention created an immediate and difficult problem. The guns I consider America's best are no longer in production; their stories belong almost wholly to history. In the European trade, the picture is quite different, for many of the world's best guns are very much alive indeed, and that requires a somewhat different approach. The problem, then, has been to identify and develop the principles that unify past and present; otherwise, the two sections of this book run the risk of being largely unrelated and if not incoherent, at least disunited.

So, in defining the architecture for the project early on, I fastened upon two concepts that strike me as the keys to understanding the gun, in character, in time, and in space. One is that every best-quality gun has been either a product of evolutionary development or represents a starting-point for some later evolutionary branch. History clearly seems to bear this out.

The other is that the essential nature of best guns, both aesthetic and mechanical, is remarkably similar, no matter what the ultimate form might be. Best side-by-sides and best over-unders, in other words, are more alike than different. In understanding the similarities, we can go a long way toward understanding why best guns are "best" and why others aren't. There's a paradox here, too, because differences sometimes are equally important, equally instructive; so the exceptions sometimes prove the rules.

I have attempted to weave the threads of these two concepts throughout the fabric of this book, and that helped me solve another problem – that of deciding which guns to include in the section on the European trade and which to leave out. Omissions do not necessarily represent a judgement on quality. This book is not a complete catalogue of every best-quality gun ever built; it was never intended to be. The subject is too broad, the details too many and too interwoven for that approach to work. Instead, I've chosen those guns, both American and European, that most clearly demonstrate what a best gun is, how it's conceived, and the principles that determine how it's built. In dealing with European guns, I've included historical perspectives wherever a look into history seems to me important in understanding the present.

All this, in any case, is my intention. I'm not yet prepared to judge the extent of its success. I'm standing too close to the trees right now to know for sure whether they really do make a forest. That remains for you to decide.

•   •   •   •

So many people have contributed in one way or another to the fabric of this book that I hesitate to even start a list, for fear that some names will slip through the ever-widening cracks in my memory. Nevertheless, I am deeply grateful to all of them, for all their assistance past and present.

Many friends in the gun trade have been wonderfully helpful over the years: John Falk of The Winchester Group; the late John McMorrow of Ithaca Gun Company; Dick Dietz, L.K. Goodstal, and the late E.S. McCawley of Remington Arms; Walter Bellemore of the Sporting Arms and Ammunition Manufacturers' Institute; Greg Pogson, formerly of Ithaca Gun Company and now with Precision Sports; Jack Skeuse and Donna Eubanks of Parker Reproductions; Paul Thompson and Joseph Badali of Browning Arms; Rich Giordano of Pachmayr; Mike Evans of Loren Thomas, Ltd.; Bill Ward, John Realmuto, and Dave Cosby of Griffin & Howe; George Olson of Performance

Shells; Jim and Elke Dunne of Waverly Arms; John Allen of Game Fair, Ltd.; John Mercer of Paul Jaeger; John Robertson, formerly of Competition Arms; Jack Rowe, gunmaker; and David Trevallion, gunmaker.

Special thanks to Jim Austin of New England Arms and to Jack Puglisi of Puglisi Gun Emporium for allowing me to photograph guns from their excellent inventories.

My friends in the English trade – John and Tom Wilkes, gunmakers, Roger Mitchell, managing director of Holland & Holland, and Jack Mitchell, shooting instructor – have been ever helpful and kind.

Thanks also to Carol Klaus of *The Sporting Goods Dealer* for providing access to the magazine archives.

To my colleagues, my fellow writers and researchers, good friends ever willing to share their good work: Geoffrey Boothroyd, Terry Wieland, Bob Brister, Gene Hill, Steve Bodio, Frank Conley, Bob Elliott, Roe Clark, Pete Dickey, and Ron Keysor.

To my other colleagues and friends, the editors who shepherd my typescripts into print: Chuck Wechsler of *Sporting Classics*; Dave Wonderlich of *Shooting Sportsman* and *Game Country*; Bill Parkerson of *The American Rifleman*; and Steve Smith of Countrysport Press.

To those good friends who love and study fine guns for the sheer pleasure of it, for sharing their experience and insight: Don Beck, Dave Noreen, Joe LoPiccolo, Henry McQuade, Steve West, Bill Habein, Ted Lundrigan, Bill Paquette, Bryan Bilinski, and David Brydon.

And deepest gratitude to two fine friends, both named Bill Headrick, who are always there to listen and read, to offer good whiskey and good insights, always there to be supportive and to help focus my thinking when it starts to go fuzzy at the edges.

Jefferson City, Missouri
March 1989

Part I

AMERICA'S BEST

PARKER

The Legend of Old Reliable

It all began with $70 and a blind horse. The legend. The Parker. Old Reliable.

And it began with coffee mills, not shotguns, for Charles Parker was first a hardware man.

He was born at Cheshire, Connecticut, on January 2, 1809, the son of Steven and Rebecca Ray Parker. Details of his early life are largely unknown, but his manufacturing career began in the early 1820s, when he hired on at a button factory in nearby Southington. He worked for a time in Waterbury and then at Patrick Lewis' coffee-mill factory in Meriden. Meriden would be his home for the remainder of his life.

According to an obituary published in *The Sporting Goods Dealer* in 1902, Charles Parker's first venture as an independent manufacturer began in December 1829 with a thirteen-month contract to make coffee mills. His operating capital comprised $70 saved from earlier wages, and a blind horse, hitched to a pole sweep, was his power source.

Parker was a paragon Yankee industrialist of the Horatio Alger school – energetic, hard-nosed, frugal (the blind horse remained his only source of power for twelve years) and ultimately, vastly successful. By the time he was thirty-five, he was one of the largest hardware manufacturers in New England, his factories turning out everything from pumps and door-knockers to silverware, hinges, and waffle irons. Parker products were distributed worldwide.

With success came expansion. In 1844, Parker bought an interest in Snow and Hotchkiss, a Meriden machine factory. The company no sooner became Snow, Hotchkiss and Company when Lucas Hotchkiss sold out – presumably to Snow and Parker – and in 1845 the style changed again, to Oliver Snow and Company. Nine years later, the firm was reorganized as the Meriden Machine Company, an arrangement that lasted less than a year before becoming Snow, Brooks and Company. By 1860, it was Parker, Snow, Brooks and Company. By 1877, Charles Parker controlled at least seven major factories, including the Meriden Curtain Fixture Company, America's largest manufacturer of window shade rollers, curtains, and fringes; the Parker Clock Company; a factory at East Meriden that made cabinet locks, teaspoons, tablespoons, and basting spoons; a factory at Yalesville, Connecticut, that turned out piano stools, coffee mills, and packing boxes. And he owned Parker Brothers, the Meriden gun works that built Old Reliable.

But it wasn't Old Reliable in 1877, nor was it Charles Parker's first gun.

At the outbreak of the Civil War, the North found itself alarmingly short of military arms of any sort. Most of the U.S. Army's field artillery was in the hands of the Confederacy, and many of the first Union troops to go into action did so either with hunting rifles or with military relics left over from the War of 1812. Naturally, the government called upon the New England industrialists for arms, and Charles Parker naturally was one of them.

In 1860, Parker supplied the North Kentucky Militia with several hundred .50-caliber breechloading repeaters; they were among the first such guns built in the United States. A tubular magazine in the buttstock fed cartridges into the chamber as the action was opened and the barrel turned by hand. Although its use was not widespread, it obviously was an effective weapon, for the Confederate government issued an official request to President Lincoln, branding the gun inhumane and asking that it be withdrawn from service. Lincoln, ever the canny realist, referred the matter to The Hague International Tribunal; as he no doubt anticipated, the war ended before the court could come up with a judgement.

On September 28, 1863, Parker accepted a government contract to produce 15,000 Model 1861 Springfield rifles for Union troops. The company was paid $19 each for them and presumably made delivery according to contract specifications.

Parker produced a second breechloading repeater in 1864, also on government contract. It was of about .55 caliber. The South's surrender at Appomattox Courthouse, April 9, 1865, came before the rifle could see any but the most restricted use. All told, Parker built about 17,000 rifles between 1860 and 1865. Since this figure undoubtedly includes the Springfields, the two Parker repeaters are among the rarest of all American military weapons.

The War Between the States brought both new manufacturing ventures and more corporate shuffling. By 1865, Parker's central firm was once again operating under the style of Meriden Manufacturing Company. It also was facing the question of what to do with a sizeable inventory of rifle barrels and action parts now unwanted by the government. Charles Parker's son Wilbur suggested boring out the barrels and using the remaining parts to manufacture inexpensive shotguns. Parker liked the idea, and even though the result couldn't have been much as a game gun, the first Parker shotguns took shape.

Some features of these were built according to patents for breechloading guns issued to William H. Miller on May 23, 1865, and November 13, 1866. But Miller's patents had little to do with shotguns as we know them, and the earliest Parkers, about 5,000 guns altogether, were little more than utility smoothbores.

Still, everything begins somewhere, and the fact that the converted military guns did sell must have given Charles Parker a new appreciation for what might be possible. The great age of creativity that spawned the modern game gun was by then underway in England. Parker was no innovator; all of the hardware he made was homely, tried and true, notable more for quality than novelty. But he believed absolutely in the virtues of machine manufacture and saw that a high-quality sporting gun could be so built. What he could not have known was that he was about to create the most famous shotgun ever built in America.

It was no overnight wonder. Like many great guns, the Parker grew out of what had come before. In the mid-1860s, Daniel Baird Wesson (later of Smith & Wesson) designed one of the first breechloading double shotguns in America and in May 1867 organized the Wesson Fire Arms Company at Springfield, Massachusetts, to manufacture it. It was a fairly trim, graceful hammer gun, and the heart of it rested on three patents. The first, issued to Wesson and John H. Blaze on December 31, 1867, covered manufacturing methods and means of applying ribs and bolsters. The lockwork and bolting system were covered by a patent granted to Wesson on June 9, 1868. The gun's rebounding locks were patented by John Stokes on November 24, 1868.

The precise nature of the deal that Parker struck with Wesson never has been brought to light, but there is some evidence that Parker's first real shotgun, the first double to bear the Parker name, came on the market in the summer of 1867, a few months before Wesson's gun appeared. There is irrefutable evidence that some sort of deal was struck, though, because both guns were built on the same patents. Parkers with one-digit serial numbers still exist, and they show the three Wesson patent dates on the frames. It's curious that Wesson would sell manufacturing rights to a gun that he intended to produce himself, but that seems to be what happened.

In any case, Daniel Wesson was not destined to make his mark as a shotgun-maker. In 1870, after turning out only about 200 double guns, he closed down production in favor of handguns and sold his shotgun-making machinery and supply of manufactured parts to Parker.

Though Charles Parker was the principal figure in the ever-growing family industries, the Parker gun works primarily belonged to the second generation. In 1868, Charles Parker's three sons – Wilbur, Dexter, and Charles Parker, Jr. – organized the gunmaking end of things as Parker Brothers. Wilbur Parker was in charge, a responsibility that eventually would devolve upon his own son, Wilbur Fiske Parker, Jr.

If Charles Parker took on only a small part of the firm's day-to-day affairs, he certainly loomed large in the background. He always had insisted that high quality should characterize his products, and the gun was to be no different.

The first Parker was a 14-gauge hammer gun with barrels 29 inches long. Its appearance was not unlike that of other breechloaders of the time – which is to say that some features might strike the modern eye as decidedly odd. Early designers of break-action guns, both in Europe and in America, strove mightily with the problem of how to fasten barrels and frame so that the action could be easily operated and yet bolt up strongly enough to be durable. They tried any number of designs as the gun slowly evolved toward the now-standard underbolts or top hooks operated by a latch on top of the frame, and the early Parker is one that history eventually discarded.

The first Parker bolting system, which used a sliding underlug, was operated by a lifter-type plunger in the floor plate just ahead of the trigger guard. It is an ungainly looking device and somewhat awkward to operate, but it worked. Given a choice between aesthetic appeal and mechanical reliability, Parker chose the latter; lots of stranger-looking guns have been built, but the early Parkers show little of the grace that the later guns have. Nevertheless, the lifter latch remained part of the Parker gun for fourteen years.

In the first few years, Parkers were chambered in 8, 10, 11, 12, 14, 16, and 20 gauges. Fully self-contained shotshells were not yet in general use, and the earliest Parkers fired a transitional cartridge: a brass case containing powder, wadding, and shot, but with no primer. The gun was fitted with nipples for standard percussion caps that, when struck by the hammers, sent a spark through a flash channel in the standing breech and ignited the powder through an opening in the shell base. Although the cartridge was only a step removed from the pinfire system, there is no evidence that Parker ever built pinfire guns. The nipple-and-cap shell itself lasted only until about 1870.

The earliest grading of Parker guns came in about 1872. At that time, unlike later years, when grades were distinguished almost wholly by decoration, the differences depended upon the type of locks and the quality of the barrels. Of the six grades of lifter-action Parkers, the three higher ones were fitted with bar-action locks and the lower three with locks of back-action type. The difference is the location of action parts on the lockplate; in bar-action locks, the mainspring and sear are mounted in front of the tumbler, while "back-action" indicates that these parts are located behind. Fitting bar-action locks requires that considerable steel be milled out of the frame in order to accommodate the locks, although the result probably is a stronger gun, since back-action demands that a good deal of wood be removed from the stock; the stock, in turn, becomes more likely to break.

Parker offered barrels in various grades of Damascus twist, imported as rough blanks from Liège, Belgium. The quality of the finished barrels, more than anything else, ultimately determined the grade of the gun. Lowest-grade guns were barreled in plain twist, while the higher grades showed progressively better figure and density. The top grade was barreled in Bernard twist, an extremely strong, highly ornate Damascus.

The 1870s were revolutionary years in gunmaking the world over. In America, new designs and manufacturing techniques were almost daily events, and some of the guns created during the decade – the Winchester '73 and the Colt Peacemaker, to name only two – were destined to stand as classics. The implications of such dynamic growth in the arms industry were not lost on Charles Parker, who had built his fortune and his reputation on an ability to anticipate the need for manufactured products and to supply those needs with high-quality items. In the early 1870s, it was clear that if Parker was to compete in the gun market, it needed a first-rate designer.

The man for the job was in Springfield, Massachusetts, at the time. Charles A. King had for several years worked at Smith & Wesson and had been involved in developing the American, Russian, and Schofield revolvers that proved to be among Smith & Wesson's greatest guns. In 1874, King hired on as production superintendent at Parker.

King and Wilbur Parker took a long, hard look at the Parker gun and saw improvements to be made. Over the next thirty years, King would receive fourteen patents for breechloading gun designs, a fore-end latch, barrel-making machinery, rebounding locks, ejectors, and stocks – all on Parker's behalf. He refined the old plunger-operated bolting system immediately but

The distinctive Parker doll's-head rib extension was part of all Parkers made after 1882, except for later-production Trojan Grades.

21

recognized that the future would belong to the more conventional top-latch system. In an 1872 patent, Joseph Dane had substantially improved rebounding locks, and King applied Dane's design to the Parker hammer gun.

In June 1878, Dan Lefever earned a patent for the doll's-head rib extension and a top-hook bolting system. Lefever rightly believed it to be a particularly efficient means of fastening a break-action gun and also saw that the doll's-head helped overcome any side-to-side flex between barrels and frame. Sideclips, which a number of English and German makers used, are meant to do the same thing.

Ultimately, though, everyone realized that a barrel lump of sufficient size provides all the lateral support necessary and that the advantages of doll's-heads and sideclips are more theoretical than real. But by then the doll's-head was a Parker fixture, almost a Parker signature. When Charles King applied Lefever's idea, he chose to use the doll's-head alone, with no top hook, and for some reason also chose to give it a complex shape that must in turn have given the action filers a share of headaches. Parker made some brave claims about the doll's-head in its advertising, implying that it amounted to a secondary action bolt – all of which was nonsense, because the doll's-head serves no practical purpose at all. At the end of World War I, when Parker was looking for ways to make the manufacturing process simpler and more economical, disposing of the doll's-head was an obvious choice, but the market simply refused to tolerate a high-grade Parker without it.

By 1881, King had all but redesigned the Parker gun. The old lifter latch was gone, replaced by a top lever. The locks were new, frames more artfully filed, and the Parker hammer gun was essentially in final form. The revisions went into the production the following year.

But hammer guns were on the verge of obsolescence in the 1880s. Hammerless actions clearly were the future, and King set to work on a version for Parker. Even though the Anson and Deeley system, in which internal hammers are cocked by leverage from the barrels, already was well known both in England and America, self-cocking guns were by no means fully accepted as the ultimate approach, certainly not by a maker as conservative as Parker. Among other ideas, King experimented with a lever-cocking hammerless design, although Parker never produced it.

What the company did produce, beginning in 1889, was a hammerless action that marked the real beginning of the legend of Old Reliable. The new gun was primarily Charles King's work, and even though it wasn't the best hammerless action ever invented, it worked remarkably well. Complexity was the principal flaw. Its eighteen parts were expensive to machine and fit, and a complicated mechanism is always more liable to failure than a simple one.

Even so, Parker built it well.

Through the last decade of the nineteenth century, the product line expanded. The new hammerless guns were in full production, and the company continued to build hammer guns as well. Hammer guns, in fact, remained in production at Parker until about 1915, and they were available on special order as late as 1920.

By 1899, there were twenty-three Parker grades in all, nine hammerless and fourteen hammer guns. In some cases, grades differed from one another in only the smallest details. Grades now were identified by letter designation, and the 1899 catalogue shows the following:

HAMMER GUNS

GRADE	PRICE	GRADE	PRICE	GRADE	PRICE
AA Pigeon	$400	E	$ 85	R	$ 60
A	$300	F	$ 80	S	$ 55
B	$200	G	$ 80	T	$ 55
C	$150	H	$ 75	U	$ 50
D	$100	I	$ 70		

(F, H, S, and U grades were identical to the next grades above them except for having straight-hand stocks.)

Hammerless guns were given the same grade designations, with "H" added to indicate a hammerless model. When ejectors were put into production in 1902, an "E" was added to the grade marks of ejector guns. The "H" remained part of the Parker grading system as long as the guns were built – and long after hammer guns had been discontinued.

HAMMERLESS GUNS

GRADE	PRICE	GRADE	PRICE
AAH Pigeon	$400	EH	$ 85
AH	$300	GH	$ 80
BH	$200	NH	$ 70
CH	$150	PH	$ 65
DH	$100		

The early years of the twentieth century were largely given to refinement. Ejectors for double guns were growing popular, and Charles King had been working on designs for some years. His earliest, patented March 1, 1892, apparently wasn't to Parker's liking, but the next, designed in collaboration with James P. Hayes and patented May 7, 1901, was put into production in

1902. Like other Charles King designs, the Parker ejectors are complicated, difficult to manufacture, and a gunsmith's nightmare when they get out of time. Nonetheless, they remained as long as Parkers were built.

By the turn of the century, shotshells had reached a stage of development that made smallbore guns a viable prospect, and in 1905, Parker built the first hammerless doubles in America chambered in 28-gauge. In those days, the standard 28-gauge cartridge was 2½ inches long and held ⅝-ounce of shot and 1¾ drams of black powder. The little guns proved popular enough to remain in the Parker catalogues for nearly forty years. They were available in all lettered grades, though most of those actually built were high grades. Now, only Parkers factory-chambered for 3½-inch 10-gauge Magnum and .410-bore are scarcer items.

In all its years, Parker never had offered a gun that might truly qualify as an economy model. Even though the VH Grade sold for $37.50 in 1912, the dollar's buying power was such that a serviceable double gun could be had for as little as $10. The market, in fact, was awash with cheap guns, especially the "contract" guns, which came both from American factories and from Belgium and which sold here under a multitude of trade names. They were far from being fine items, but some offered a fair value and no doubt claimed respectable sales. In the face of this and other competition from the American trade – notably the Fox Sterlingworth, which came on the scene in 1910 – Parker began looking for a way to tap the lower end of the shotgun market.

The Parker economy gun first appeared in 1915. It was called the Trojan and sold for $27.50. The materials and workmanship were worthy of Parker, but the Trojan was different from the rest. The frame is less gracefully contoured, saving the portion of manufacturing cost taken up by cosmetic milling and filing. Early Trojans had the Parker doll's-head rib extension, but it, too, was expensive to mill and was discontinued in the 1920s.

It was strictly a production-line gun, offered only in 12, 16, and 20 gauges and with no options other than a choice of barrel length and, after 1922, a single trigger. The Trojan never was factory-available with ejectors or beavertail fore-end or as a trap or skeet gun. The fore-end latch was a tension-fastener rather than the Deeley-type latch standard on other Parkers.

The Trojan wasn't beautiful, but it was tough and it was a Parker. In the years that followed, the plain little gun accounted for as much as forty percent of Parker's annual sales and proved, in sheer numbers, to be the most popular Parker of all. As many as 50,000 were built before the Trojan was discontinued in 1939.

Charles King's original hammerless action remained in production for more than twenty years before anyone made a serious attempt at revision. In 1910,

King's son Walter, who had worked at Parker since 1889, was appointed assistant plant superintendent. Walter King succeeded his father as superintendent in 1914 and shortly after became works manager in charge of the entire operation, responsible directly to Wilbur Parker. It was clear by 1910 that for all its durability, Charles King's action represented a burdensome overhead in manufacturing expense, and Walter King looked to James Hayes for help.

Over the next few years, Hayes managed to revise the Parker action to the point where King's eighteen component parts were reduced to only four. He also brilliantly extended the life of the Parker bolting system. King's bolt, like that of nearly every other double gun, directly engaged a bearing surface on the barrel lump. Hayes simply made the bearing surface a replaceable part – a small, hardened-steel plate pinned to the lump. The bearing surfaces of both the plate and the bolt are angled at a pitch of $12\frac{1}{2}$ degrees to provide a constantly tight engagement without unnecessary friction. The locking bites and bolts of all doubles are beveled in order to compensate for wear, but only the Parker can be restored to original tolerances simply by replacing a part.

The new, simpler Parker action went into production in 1917. It was Old Reliable in its ultimate form.

It was available in ten grades: A-1 Special, AAHE, AHE, BHE, CHE, DH, GH, PH, VH, and Trojan. The A-1 Special sold for $600, the Trojan for $43.50. Ejectors were standard in the top five grades and a $20 option in the rest, except for Trojan.

The Parker single trap gun followed hard on the Trojan's heels. As trapshooting had evolved from live pigeons to clay targets around the turn of the century, it also evolved from a two-shot to a one-shot game, and a number of American makers – Lefever, Baker, and Ithaca – already had single-barrel trap guns on the market. Both Parker and L.C. Smith introduced single trap guns in 1917.

Like the Ithaca, Parker's single trap was a gun of great integrity. It would have been an easy matter to simply stick half of a double gun's locks into a scaled-down frame and to cobble together such other bits and pieces as were necessary for a one-barrel, one-trigger gun. Instead, Parker did what Emile Flues had done at Ithaca: built a single-barrel gun from the ground up, incorporating the double's most appropriate features and creating the rest to achieve an integrated, original design.

In its first appearance the Parker single was offered in five qualities, corresponding to the double-gun grades, with an added "S" designation. Grade SC was the lowest and sold for $150, followed by SB at $225, SA at $310, SAA at $450, and the lovely SA-1 Special at a price of $550. Throughout its

SC Grade single trap gun.

production history, the single was built in 12-gauge only, with a 30-, 32-, or 34-inch vent-ribbed barrel. Ejector, beavertail fore-end, and rubber recoil pad were standard. Stock dimensions and choke were a matter of the buyer's choice. In later years, Remington Arms renamed the single trap as the Parker Model 930; it remained in Remington production until 1942.

The gun soon proved itself, just as Parker doubles had done for a generation of trapshooters. Of 206 shooters who entered the Grand American in 1901, seventy-three shot Parkers, a majority by far. By 1919, Parker guns had won hundreds of trapshooting titles and had won the Grand American Handicap tournament nine times. In 1920, Fred Gilbert, one of the greatest American trapshooters of all time, used a Parker single to set a new world record of 569 registered targets without a miss.

Over the course of its life, the Parker double was chambered for every standard American shotshell and for some odd cases as well. The 10-bore was predominant when Parkers were first built and remained the most popular until the turn of the century, when improved ammunition led to the 12-gauge's ascendancy. Ten-gauge Parkers were available as long as Parkers were built, though few were made after World War I. Ten-gauges chambered for the 3½-inch Magnum shell are fewer still – only about ninety-three guns in all. Parkers were available in 8-gauge almost from the beginning and remained so until about 1917; not many were built after the turn of the century. By 1912, Parker offered 8-bore hammerless guns only in D, G, and P grades and as hammer guns only in grades D, H, and R. The selection was reduced in 1915 to D and H grade hammer guns and D and G grade hammerless.

The 14-gauge enjoyed a brief flurry of interest in the United States early in the century, and Parker built D and P grade guns in 14-bore until about 1917.

There also is good evidence that a few Parkers were chambered in 24-gauge. The story, according to Peter Johnson, is that the United States Cartridge Company asked Parker to build a dozen or so 24-bore Trojan Grade guns to be used in ballistics tests at the ammunition works. Like some other odd-sized European cartridges, the 24-gauge was momentarily popular in this country (Harrington & Richardson and Stevens built single-shot guns for it well into the 1930s), and U.S. Cartridge apparently was giving some serious thought to producing the shells here. The project never panned out.

Still, there is a minor mystery in the 24-gauge Parkers. Johnson's source for the story was Robert Hoess, a Washington bureau correspondent for CBS who owned the only surviving gun from the experimental group. In Larry Baer's book on Parker, however, there is a photograph of a Parker identified as the only surviving gun for a group of 24-gauge VH Grades made up for the Union Metallic Cartridge Company. So was it U.S. Cartridge or U.M.C.? And were they Trojans or VH Grades? Baer says he knows a man who "swears that he has seen a VHE 24-gauge," and makes no other comment. The gun in the photograph clearly is not a Trojan, but whether it really is a 24-gauge is impossible to tell.

All things considered, I suspect Peter Johnson is correct. The 24-gauge experiment almost certainly was done after World War I, long after the 1912 merger of U.M.C. and Remington Arms. It seems unlikely that a Remington subsidiary would go to another company for experimental guns. Moreover, U.S. Cartridge had a reputation for willingness to attempt manufacture of virtually any sort of ammunition. It's possible that Parker may have built other 24-gauges on special order but not very likely. In any event, if you come across a 24-gauge Parker, hang onto it.

Most Parkers naturally were built in 12, 16, and 20 gauges. The company rounded out its offerings in 1927 by introducing doubles built in .410-bore. All told, no other major American maker ever built guns in as many different gauges as Parker did.

In order to offer so many chamberings and still maintain standards of weight and balance, Parker used different frames, scaled in size and weight. There's room for confusion here, according to how you tally the numbers.

And there's even a mystery in it. The largest commonly known Parker frame is the No. 3, usually used for 10-gauge guns. I've never found mention of Parker frames larger than No. 3 in any of the literature or in any Parker catalogue, but larger ones do exist. I've seen photos of an 8-gauge hammer gun clearly marked as having a No. 7 frame. My pal Bill Headrick has closely examined a hammerless 8-gauge that also was built on a No. 7 frame. He says it's proportional to the size of 8-gauge barrels, about as wide across the fences as his fist. A No. 3 Parker frame is a hefty piece of goods; a No. 7 would be the size of a Volvo engine block – which is about the size of Headrick's fist.

Parker No. 108102 is an E Grade hammerless 8-gauge built on a frame marked No. 6; it also has thirty-six-inch barrels. Another friend, who knows Parkers inside out, recalls seeing a 10-gauge on a No. 4 frame. Presumably there was a No. 5 frame as well, but any Parker built on a frame larger than No. 3 is a rare piece. If you can shed any further light on this, let me know.

Parker's system of identifying even the more common frames is not as clear as it might be, since the typical frames came in five different sizes and seven different weights. No. 3 was used for 8-, 10-, and heavy 12-gauge guns. No. 2 is the standard 12-gauge frame before about 1917 and also was used for lightweight 10-bores. No. 1½ was the standard 12-gauge frame after about 1917; it also was used for heavy 16s. Lightweight 12s, standard 16s, and heavy 20s were built on the No. 1 frame. The No. 0 frame is for standard 20s, light 16s, and heavy 28-gauges.

Standard 28s were built on the No. 00 frame and .410-bores on No. 000. Both of these are No. 0 frames with differing amounts of steel milled out of the water tables to make them lighter. Five sizes, seven weights.

Actually, though, there is a sixth Parker frame, little known and extremely rare. It's a No. ½, smaller than a No. 1, larger than a No. 0. The only specimen I've seen is a VHE Grade 12-gauge that belongs to one of my closest friends, but we've been able to confirm the existence of a few more, all of them 12-bores. All of them bear high serial numbers and most likely were built in the early 1940s. They're unusual not only for being a frame size never, to my knowledge, mentioned in any Parker catalogue, but also for their craftsmanship. They've all been described as beautifully made; the one I've seen is even better than that. The frame-filing, barrel striking, stock fit, and case-hardening done on this gun is every bit as good as that of any gun built during Parker's golden years of the 1910s, before America entered World War I. Certainly, it's better craftsmanship by far than is typical of Parkers made in the 1930s and '40s.

Otherwise, there are more questions than answers. There's no reason to believe the No. ½-frame guns were built anywhere other than the Remington factory or made by anyone other than Remington gunsmiths. But why were they built at all? And for whom? And how many? A handful, five or six perhaps, maybe a few more. No one seems to know. Were they some sort of experiment on Remington's part, prototypes for lightweight bird guns to be manufactured after the war? Such splendid craftsmanship is seldom given to prototype guns, but it's possible.

In any event, it's a pity they weren't available sooner, because a 12-gauge Parker built on a No. ½ frame is a game gun to behold – trim, lightweight, superbly balanced, dynamic to a degree that few 12-bore Parkers are. It amounts to a 12-gauge gun on a 20-gauge frame.

A final word on Parker frames: The actual differences among the various sizes and weights aren't as pronounced as one might expect. Virtually all of the scaling-down is in the width, and there's almost no difference in depth or length between a No. 0 and a No. 3. Consequently, small-bore Parkers look somewhat disproportionate in profile, their slender barrels out of aesthetic sync with the relatively tall frame. That's also why there are precious few genuinely lightweight Parkers even among the small gauges. You'll look a long time to find a Parker .410 that weighs much under six pounds.

If you want to know which frame your Parker is built on, take the barrels off and look at the bottom of the barrel lump at the breech end; the frame number is stamped there (but not, for some reason, on the frame itself). If it says ½, you have a phenomenally rare piece.

You can learn a few other things from the stampings on both barrels and frame. The serial number will be there, on the barrel flats, sometimes on the barrel lump, and on the water table. If it's a high-grade gun with Whitworth

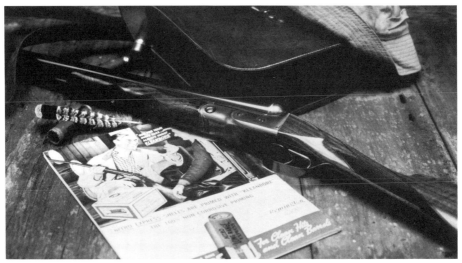

The No. ½ is among the rarest Parker frames. This VHE Grade, built on a No. ½ frame, amounts to a 12-gauge gun on a 20-gauge frame.

29

steel barrels, each barrel will have a serial number of its own, different from the serial number of the gun itself.

Grade stamps appear on the water table and often on the barrel flats. These generally are in two forms: the standard letter grades and corresponding numbers. Trojans and VH Grades don't have the numbers, but the others do, as follows:

1 = PH Grade	5 = BHE Grade
2 = GH Grade	6 = AHE Grade
3 = DH Grade	7 = AAHE Grade
4 = CHE Grade	8 = A-1 Special Grade

All of these various marks remained fairly consistent among Parkers over the years. Others – proof stamps, inspectors' marks, and the like – came and went.

Parker also frequently stamped the weight of the barrel assembly on the flats. These appear as two- or three-digit numbers; the first digit is pounds, the second (or second and third) ounces. This was done to help the factory gunsmiths match barrels and frames in assembling guns to a particular weight and balance, and the numbers refer to the weight of the barrel assembly in the rough, not as finished tubes. Despite what you may hear otherwise, weighing a set of finished barrels is not a reliable means of identifying tubes that were shortened after the gun left the factory. There are better ways of determining that, which I'll talk about in another chapter.

The thing to remember is that the weight of a set of finished Parker barrels won't necessarily match the weight that's stamped on them. It depends upon how much steel was removed when they were lapped and struck.

And while we're on the subject, Parkers show more variation in factory-original barrel length than any other American guns. In the old days of black powder and twist barrels, large-bore Parkers could have tubes up to 40 inches long. Thirty-four- and 36-inch barrels weren't uncommon on big-bores, both during the twist era and later, in the transition years when Parker used both twist and steel tubes. A lot of 20-gauges were built with 30- and even 32-inch barrels.

After the turn of the century, Parker standardized its barrels at 26, 28, 30, and 32 inches, but other lengths were available on special order at extra charge. Catalogues of the 1910s list 24-inch barrels as an available option. These also appear as late as 1937. Not very many guns were so built, but there probably were a few, so if you run across a 24-inch-barreled Parker, don't dismiss it out of hand as a hacksaw job. If it is, it should be easy to spot.

Parker barrels always were of exceptionally high quality. The Damascus tubes, like those that virtually every other American maker used, came from Belgium and England. Before World War I, Parker made a few guns with Krupp steel barrels, and before about 1925, AAHE and A-1 Special grades were fitted with the splendid English Whitworth barrels.

Parker made a practice of implying that different grades of guns were barrelled in different grades of steel. The company did so by stamping the ribs with lofty-sounding names to identify the steel from which the barrels ostensibly were made, as follows:

Trojan	Trojan Steel	CHE	Acme Steel
VHE	Vulcan Steel	BHE	Acme Steel
PHE	Parker Steel	AHE	Acme Steel
GHE	Parker Steel	AAHE	Peerless Steel
DHE	Titanic Steel	A-1 Special	Peerless Steel

Actually, with the exception of the Krupp and Whitworth tubes, all Parker barrels were made of the same stuff, regardless of what the barrel stamps say. Moreover, the grade names aren't always consistent, so you might run across a CHE with barrels marked "Titanic Steel" or a DHE marked "Acme Steel" or some similar combination.

By the beginning of the Great War, more than 160,000 Parker guns had been built and sold, and Parker's reputation reached halfway around the world. Though Major Hugh Bertie Campbell Pollard, the great English arms historian, later remarked that it was an adequate shotgun "for farmers' use," other Europeans, particularly the French, thought well of Parker. And so did Nicholas II, the tragic Czar of Russia. About 1917, Nicholas directed the Russian Consul in New York to place an order for a Parker gun. He was an enthusiastic shooter, his gun room replete with specimens of Europe's finest. The Parker was to be his only American gun.

The Czar's Parker was a 12-gauge A-1 Special, its stock trimmed in gold, the imperial Romanov eagle inlaid in gold on the trigger plate – a gun fitted and finished with all the skill and care that Parker craftsmen (and women; Mrs. Mike Hanson did the checkering) could muster.

Nicholas never saw the gun. The Bolshevik revolution plunged Russia into a nightmare of blood just after the order arrived at Parker's, and in July 1918, Nicholas and his family were slaughtered in the cellars of an old house in Ekaterinburg. His Parker eventually was sold in this country and hasn't, to my knowledge, surfaced since. It would be a lovely thing to see.

Almost any high-grade Parker, especially one built in the more leisurely days of the 1910s, is a particularly handsome piece. Judging from the guns that remain with us today, Parker seems on the whole to have employed the best engravers in the American industry. Typical Parker engraving is extremely delicate, quite graceful, and usually very shallowly cut, so shallow, in fact, that you'll see some old, well-used guns with engraving simply worn off.

But if E.C. Crossman was an accurate reporter, it's a wonder, in a way, that Parkers ever got engraved at all, much less well engraved. In a 1919 article on the Parker factory, Crossman describes "a bower of feminine and unclothed pulchritude that hasn't an equal. From floor to ceiling and from one wall to the other the engraving room of the Parker plant is papered with a collection of pictures of the female form divine, most of them artistic, and all of them startling." A pin-up calendar or *Playboy* centerfold tacked over a workbench apparently isn't anything new.

Though A-1 Special was the highest of the production grades, as tastefully ornate and meticulously finished as any shotgun needs to be, at least two other Parkers were even more lavishly treated. As the story goes, Parker sought to commemorate its 200,000th shotgun by building what the factory described as "the finest example of the gun makers' art ever produced by an American gun maker." It was to be called Invincible, and it would sell for $1500 – twice the price of an A-1 Special.

The first Invincible Grade was built early in the 1920s, a 12-gauge fitted with a straight-hand, Circassian walnut stock. Except for the barrels, every inch of steel was engraved in fine English scroll; game birds sculpted in gold were inlaid on the frame. The serial number, 200000, was inlaid in gold on the trigger-guard tang.

Apparently, the gun was put on display at various places around the country. After a well-publicized appearance at Kennedy Brothers Sporting Goods in Minneapolis, it was shipped west, possibly bound for Omaha or Kansas City, and was never seen again. How it disappeared and where it is now have become almost the stuff of legends. All that remains is a photograph that appeared in the 1926 and 1930 Parker catalogues.

Legend has it that a second Invincible was built at the same time as No. 200000, a companion gun with serial number 200001. There is no solid evidence that it ever existed.

So much myth and rumor and accrued to the Invincible that it's difficult to winnow out the few, sketchy grains of truth. There was, however, at least one other besides No. 200000, and the truth of it is stranger than all the fictions.

Mr. A.C. Middleton of Moorestown, New Jersey, was founder of the Victor Talking Machine Company. He liked fine guns and was a man of means sufficient to indulge his tastes. In April 1929, he contacted Parker, expressed a

DH Grade 12-gauge, built in 1913.

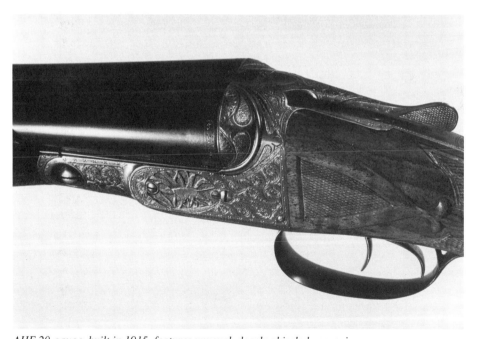

AHE 20-gauge, built in 1915, features unusual, deeply chiseled engraving.

desire for an ultra-high-grade gun, and asked if Parker Brothers would build one to his specifications.

There was something weirdly prophetic about it all. On Friday, the thirteenth of September, 1929, A.C. Middleton took possession of an Invincible Grade Parker, No. 230329 – a lovely 16-gauge ejector gun with 26-inch barrels, improved-cylinder and modified chokes, and $2\frac{9}{16}$-inch chambers. It was fitted with a half-hand stock, splinter fore-end, and two triggers. The front trigger is hinged in the European style.

A.C. Middleton never fired his Invincible. Just over six weeks after he got it, America's economy came crashing down and forced his attention to matters more pressing than a first shooting trip with a new gun. He stored the Invincible in its leather case, factory hang-tag still attached, in a closet and waited for better days.

Better days were a long time coming. Years passed. A.C. Middleton died. The Invincible waited.

When Middleton's widow died, the house sat empty for a couple of years and eventually was sold. The new owner found the Invincible still sitting in an upstairs closet. It must have been something of a shock to discover that, in addition to a fine old twenty-five room house, he'd also bought one of the world's most fabulous shotguns.

The gun, still unfired, found its way into a private collection and remained there for a few years. In 1969, Gary Herman, owner of Safari Outfitters of Ridgefield, Connecticut, bought it. It stayed in Ridgefield, about sixty miles from the factory where it was built, until 1972. No doubt some Parker collector owns it now, and I hope he appreciates it.

The 1920s were fairly prosperous years for the American gun trade, and nearly all of the important makers offered high-grade guns that approached the $1000 price tag. Not all that many actually were built, but there were enough. At Parker, the '20s were largely given to refinement. Both the Parker single trigger and the trap-style beavertail fore-end for double guns came available in 1922. Damascus barrels, the beautiful, treacherous holdovers from black-powder days, finally were discontinued in 1925. Vent ribs for doubles appeared in 1926.

The January 1, 1930, catalogue shows the doubles available in ten grades (including the Invincible and minus the PH Grade, which was discontinued sometime after 1922) and the single trap guns in five. Prices range from $55 for the Trojan to $1500 for the Invincible.

Tied as it was to an enormous hardware business, Parker also sold a wide range of shooting accessories and miscellaneous truck that goes with guns – cases, cleaning rods, jags, brushes, loop tips, chamber brushes, powder and

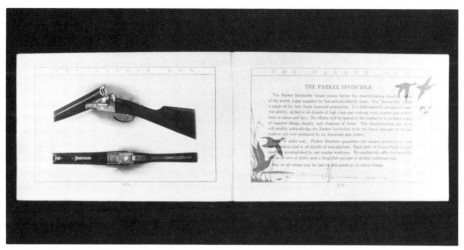

The first Invincible Grade Parker, No. 200000, shown in the 1930 catalogue. The gun subsequently disappeared.

shot dippers, ring-type case extractors, loading tools, screwdrivers, rifle targets, and more. There even were brass shell cases, reportedly made by Union Metallic Cartridge Company, with the Parker Brothers headstamp.

The stock-market crash and subsequent Depression proved to be as tough on the Parker company as it was on those who owned the guns. The hardware business certainly helped support the gun works, but the arms market didn't show much hope. In March 1931, Parker began marketing Hawes fly rods under the name Parker-Hawes. H.W. Hawes, who for many years worked with H.L. Leonard, was a first-class rod-maker, but the American economy was no better able to support a thriving trade in $50 fly rods than it was in expensive shotguns. The little plant that had turned out as many as 6000 guns per year during the 1920s, produced only about 500 in 1932 and 1933 combined. Old Reliable had become a liability. The options were grim: either close down the gun works or sell it.

Remington Arms bought Parker on June 1, 1934. America's oldest surviving gunmaker was hurting from the Depression like everyone else, but its financial base was broad enough, its products inexpensive enough to survive. Remington made no major changes in the Parker operation during the first few years. By 1936, production was up to about 2000 guns annually, but the future was by no means secure. In 1937, Remington moved the Parker machinery and a good many of the employees to the Remington plant at Ilion, New York. The International Silver Company bought the old Parker buildings in Meriden.

In the almost seventy years that Parker existed as an independent maker, it produced about 235,000 guns. When Remington took control in 1934, the inventory showed 104 completed guns on hand and a number in various stages of production. From that time until the business moved to Ilion, Parker turned out another 5562 guns.

By 1938, the machinery was running again, and production continued at a fair pace until 1942, when Remington converted most of its resources to wartime weaponry. From then on, it was only a matter of time. A few Parkers were built during the war, assembled from parts machined years before. Gun No. 242385, built in June 1942 and shipped in 1947, is widely thought to be the last Parker, but I've had the good fortune to hold No. 242387, a GH Grade .410 that also was shipped in 1947.

Parkers built after about 1935 are more appealing for their position in the historical scheme of things than for intrinsic quality. The levels of craftsmanship noticeably declined during the Depression, not because the craftsmen themselves were any less adept nor because Remington was indifferent to the quality of its products. The quality of workmanship in every American double suffered in those years, simply because hand-work was expensive, and every penny spent in building a gun had to be recovered in the selling price in a market that already had reached the limits of its purse.

Like the other American makers in the 1930s, Remington tried everything it

Parker Brothers brass cartridge cases.

could think of to infuse some life into its product line. Skeet was a relatively new game in the '30s, its popularity growing nationwide, and all the gunmakers courted the target-shooting market with a fine ardor. The 1934 Remington catalogue shows a VHE Grade Parker Skeet Special available for $139.15. By 1937, all grades except Trojan could be had as skeet guns, all fitted with single trigger, ejectors, and beavertail fore-end. Barrels could be 26 or 28 inches.

Parker guns always were extremely popular among trapshooters, and as something of a last-ditch effort, Remington followed up the skeet guns with a special double trap gun. It was available in 12-gauge only, in all grades except Trojan, equipped with ejectors, single trigger, beavertail fore-end, and vent-rib barrels 30, 32, or 34 inches long. Options included a Monte Carlo stock and even a cheek-piece.

Not many specimens of either target gun actually were built before the war brought Parker production to an end.

The postwar gun market, infatuated with the sheer firepower inherent to repeating guns, offered little room for such an old-fashioned luxury as a double. But even if it wasn't in production, Old Reliable was Old Reliable, and by the late '50s the sporting world began to see the Parker as an artifact. Prices for the old guns began to climb, and every year brought a new rumor that Old Reliable would soon be in production once again.

A generation passed before it finally happened, but Old Reliable did come back. Tom Skeuse, a long-time Parker fan and president of Reagent Chemical & Research, Inc. – makers of White Flyer targets, among other things – concluded early in the 1980s that a new Parker would find a place in the growing American market for high-quality doubles. After some unsuccessful attempts at finding a manufacturer, Skeuse struck a deal for guns built at Winchester's Olin-Kodensha factory in Japan. The Parker Reproduction was unveiled to the trade at the annual Shooting, Hunting and Outdoor Trade Show in January 1984.

In the first year, they were available only as DHE Grade 20-gauges, built on No. 0 frames. Barrels could be 26 or 28 inches; the short tubes were chambered at $2\frac{3}{4}$ inches and choked improved-cylinder and modified, the longer ones bored for 3-inch shells and choked modified and full. The buyer had a choice of beavertail or splinter fore-end, double or single trigger, straight-hand or pistol grip stock, and a hard-rubber or skeleton-steel buttplate. All were stocked in California-grown Claro walnut.

At the end of its original production life, a DHE Grade Parker sold for about $275. In 1984, the Parker Reproduction, with an Italian-made leather trunk case, cost $2800, and by 1980s economic standards, it wasn't overpriced.

Thanks to laser-guided machinery and the wonderful Japanese ability to replicate almost anything down to microscopic detail, the Parker Reproduction is more clone than copy. Action parts will interchange between the Reproductions and the older guns. Except for the showier figure of Claro walnut, the different stampings on the rib, barrel flats and water table, and the absence of *PARKER BROS.* engraved on the frame, it's remarkably hard to tell the Reproductions from the originals.

Twenty-eight-gauge Reproductions came on the market in 1985, available only in DHE Grade with the same options as the 20s. These, like the old Parkers, are built on No. 00 frames. The following year, John Allen, who at the time managed the gunroom at Dunn's and who now is proprietor of Game Fair Ltd. in Nashville, worked with Jack Skeuse of Parker Reproductions to create a Parker Reproduction specially designed and built as a waterfowl gun for use with steel shot. I field-tested the prototype Steel Shot Special and found it to perform beautifully with both lead and steel shot. Even, consistent patterns always were a primary goal among the barrel men at Parker Brothers, and they were nearly always successful – but they never bored a better set of barrels than you'll find on a Parker Reproduction Steel Shot Special. They're that good.

The Parker Reproductions got a good reception from the beginning, and interest remained high enough to prompt guns of higher grade. The BHE Grade came out in 1987 and the A-1 Special in 1988. And in 1988 Parker Reproductions reached an agreement with the U.S. Fish and Wildlife Service that allowed ten guns each year to be decorated with artwork from the current federal migratory bird stamp. These are engraved by Geoffrey Gournet, a French engraver who works at Parker Reproductions, in a combination of English scroll and Italian *bulino*, and they're lovely.

For 1989, Parker Reproductions had plans to offer 16-gauge barrels retrofitted to 20-gauge guns (a 16-bore built on a No. 0 frame would be a gem) and .410 barrels retrofitted to 28-gauge guns.

There also were plans for an entirely new gun – a .410 built on a No. 0000 frame. The Parker Reproductions people told me the new frame would be fully scaled both in width and depth – enough to make any .410 fancier foam at the mouth.

Nineteen eighty-eight was quite a year for Parkers. As if to prove the old saw about raining and pouring, Remington Arms announced in January that it would remanufacture original Parker guns on special order. According to Remington, the newly built Parkers would be available only as 20-gauge AHE Grades with 28-inch vent-rib barrels chambered at 2¾ inches and with redesigned single trigger and ejectors. Options include splinter or beavertail fore-end; straight-hand or pistol-grip stock; recoil pad, hard-rubber or skeleton-steel buttplate; stock dimensions; and chokes. They're to sell for about $13,000 apiece.

The first Parker Reproduction Federal Duck Stamp Classic, engraved with artwork from the 1988-89 federal migratory bird stamp.

And 1988 held one last, bitter surprise until the end. At Christmastime, the Kodensha plant informed both Parker Reproductions and Classic Doubles, the company then marketing the old Winchester 101, that it would no longer manufacture guns, that it was converting to automobile production. As this is going to press, there is no word as to the ultimate fate of either gun.

From the turn of the century through the Great Depression, Parker was the most highly regarded shotgun in America, in part because the company maintained an extremely aggressive advertising program and in part because they were excellent guns. Even now, it's the most famous of all the American doubles. In intrinsic quality, there actually is little to distinguish a Parker gun from its peers. The old Foxes and Lefevers and L.C. Smiths were built and finished with every bit as much skill and attention to detail. Yet Parker still is the magic name, the one that fetches the highest prices – figures that surpassed the limits of reason years ago.

But price and value have little to do with one another, and if old Parkers are overpriced, they certainly are not over-valued. They are artifacts of a graceful past, an achievement undiluted by time. A Parker tells us that beauty of form and function have a place in a day-to-day world where beauty is too often obscured. For that, if for no other reason, it has value beyond measure.

A.H. FOX

The Finest Gun in the World

He was born on the cusp between two worlds, at a moment when history seemed about to pause, take stock of things, and move on in some new direction. Behind lay the old feudal culture of the South, devastated by war and hammered by Reconstruction into a caricature of its conqueror. On his first birthday, the Unkpapa Sioux would meet briefly with Custer on a far-off Montana prairie. Further ahead lay the twentieth century, the new America where technology would blossom, an America peering for the first time past her own borders, an America that soon would prosper and consume and grow restless. He would be restless along with it.

Ansley Hermon Fox was born on Friday, June 25, 1875, in his father's house in Decatur, Georgia. His father was Addison C. Fox, homeopathic physician; his mother Louisa Ansley Fox.

As America faced the last quarter of the nineteenth century, the tempo of life moved at a plowhorse pace, but its heart was beginning to beat with the triphammer clank of factories and great machines. The character of America was about to change from pastoral to industrial, from patiently coaxing sustenance from the land to the fire and forge of manufacturing. Ansley Fox's generation would witness change on a scale previously unknown in human experience. His would be the first American generation to define its identity by the variety and the sheer scale of what it could produce.

Ansley Fox would be a manufacturer virtually all his life, a maker of things, an apostle of commerce. But he also clearly possessed some powerful sense of quality, some seemingly inexhaustible appreciation for beauty and craftsmanship. There is little evidence that he ever was content to turn out products solely for the sake of profit.

He was fond of describing the things he made as the finest of their kind. Whether they were is less important than the fact that Ansley Fox wanted them to be.

Addison Fox moved his family from Atlanta to Baltimore sometime between 1876 and the end of the decade. In Baltimore, Ansley Fox's liking for guns and shooting flourished. M.H. Wright, in a sketchy biography published in *Field and Stream* in 1908, says that from an early age his marksmanship "began to attract attention among his neighbors," which could mean anything from real skill to a penchant for shooting lightning rods off rooftops. Perhaps it was a combination of both, for he would soon prove himself to be a brilliant shot.

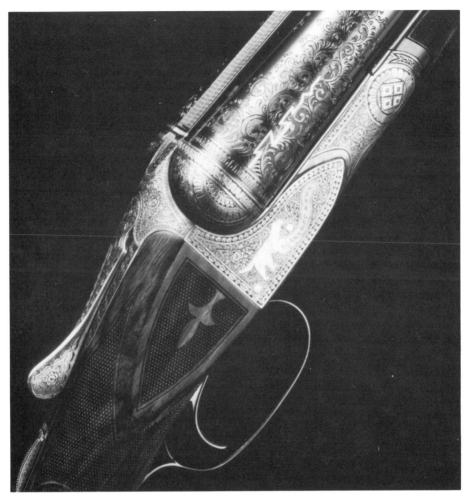

FE Grade 12-gauge, built in 1908.

Wright goes on to say that Fox's proficiency with a gun prompted him to earn a living as a market hunter for three years following the end of his public-school education. If this is true, he probably was moved more by the virtually endless shooting around Chesapeake Bay than by need for a livelihood. Market hunting was at best scarcely a subsistence, but the romance of it must have been wonderfully appealing to the adolescent son of a comfortably well-off and probably somewhat indulgent family.

However casual his market gunning may have been, Ansley Fox soon discovered a game to take seriously – trap shooting. Here, too, were worlds in transition. The great days of live-pigeon shooting were coming to a close, as the clay target was about to change the nature of the game. Like the great professional tournament and match shooters of the turn of the century – Rolla Heikes, James A.R. Elliott, William R. Crosby, and the ilk – Ansley Fox was a pigeon shooter.

By the mid-1890s, he had built some reputation around Baltimore as a pigeon shot, and on October 14, 1898, he won the Maryland Handicap, killing twenty-four of twenty-five pigeons at twenty-nine yards rise. But he'd already had a taste of fame by then – from the gun he designed.

A correspondent to *The American Field* of March 7, 1896, describes a hammerless, break-action gun invented by Ansley Fox "that bids fair to be a great success." It actually was a revised version of an earlier design. The first gun, described in a patent application filed when Ansley Fox was seventeen, never existed except on paper; the second one would change Ansley Fox's life. Joseph A. Geiji, a Baltimore gunsmith, built a prototype from Fox's plans, and the gun earned patent protection on June 30, 1896. Its design is similar to both Anson and Deeley's 1875 hammerless gun and to W.W. Greener's Facile Princeps action, invented shortly after.

The most prophetic features of this first Fox gun are its simplicity and its emphasis upon strength. The gunmaking world, too, was in the midst of change. Breechloaders had been widely manufactured for little more than a generation. Though the hammerless action was well evolved, exposed-hammer guns were still much in evidence. The new nitrocellulose powders, more efficient and more powerful than black powder, were challenging the old concepts of metallurgy and gun design.

Target-shooting is a brutal proving ground for shotguns, and Ansley Fox saw first-hand what gunmakers of the future would have to face. He must have seen a lot of guns literally fall apart under the constant pounding of tournament shooting. Merely fitting steel barrels to actions designed for black-powder shells wasn't the answer. Frames cracked, locking bolts and hinge pins wore out quickly, unshielded firing pins allowed gases to flow back into actions and wreak havoc on metal and wood. Delicate sear tolerances soon wore to the point that locks were either unpredictable or inoperable, and springs broke by the handful.

In describing Fox's 1896 patent, the *American Field* article notes that "Industrialists have been interested in the action and a stock company will probably be formed here to push its manufacture. Failing this, it is the intention of the inventor to go West, probably to Chicago, and there develop not only this, but several other equally notable inventions of which he is the author."

As it turned out, Ansley Fox didn't have to strike out for the wild West, not even as far as Chicago. The 1898 Baltimore city directory lists him as president of the Fox Gun Company, 5 West German Street. This almost certainly was an office from which Fox contracted manufacture of his gun.

And on June 29, 1898, Ansley Fox took a wife, sixteen-year-old Fentress DeVere Keleher of North Carolina. He moved out of his father's house at 313 North Carey Street and installed his bride in a home of their own a block north. Soon, but all too briefly, he had a son as well – James, born in December 1899, dead before the spring of 1902. The 1900 census, which misspells Ansley's name as "Ansel," shows them living at 421 North Carey Street.

Both the 1899 and 1900 Baltimore directories list Ansley Fox as secretary of the Fox Gun Company, now located on Stockholm Street at the corner of Leadenhall. Burr Howard Richards was president and Burr Howard Richards, Jr., treasurer – clearly principal investors in what had become a manufacturing firm.

The company seems to have found some initial success. An item in the premiere issue of *The Sporting Goods Dealer*, October 1899, says: "The Fox shot gun, invented and patented by Ansley Fox, one of the most promising young trap shots of this state, is being manufactured here now, but the trouble is that he can not manufacture the guns fast enough to supply the demand." At least a handful of these guns still exist: twist-barreled, 12-gauge doubles stamped "Fox Gun Co. Balto. Md. U.S.A." on the left side of the frames.

There was a restlessness in Ansley Fox. Within a year, in a pattern that would repeat itself again and again, he changed his livelihood, striking off on a new adventure. In the spring of 1900, he became a professional shooter, engaged by Winchester Repeating Arms to represent its shotguns and ammunition.

What prompted his departure from the Fox Gun Company is as elusive as what moved him from one business to another through most of his life. The common assumption has been that he simply was an inept businessman, but it doesn't fit the facts. That he was able again and again to secure heavy investments in his ventures is hardly a sign of incompetence.

So what moved Ansley Fox? A powerful will, for one thing, probably supported by a healthy ego. It seems clear that Ansley Fox answered only to himself. He wanted to make high-quality items that bore his name, and nothing less would do. Sometimes, not even that would do, it seems, for he set out to dominate every market he entered, no matter what the product. And he was a man often out of sync with his time, sometimes ahead, sometimes behind. His markets often either were not ready for Ansley Fox or had already left him for something else.

Nothing in his life suggests a desperate seeking for financial security; he could, if he'd chosen, have found a lifetime career on any gun-manufacturer's design staff, but that was far too tame a prospect to interest Ansley Fox.

The answer may be simpler yet. Ansley Fox may well have been one of those gifted people who can throw off brilliant ideas like sparks from a grinding wheel but who quickly grow bored with the day-to-day business of nurturing the results. Had anyone bothered to ask him what his favorite invention was – and over the course of a lifetime he invented everything from shotguns to automobile parts to machine guns – the answer might have been the same as Picasso's when asked which was his favorite painting: the next one.

In any case, with Ansley Fox gone from the scene, the Richardses regrouped in 1900 to form Baltimore Arms Company, makers of a shotgun that, while it owes something to Fox's 1896 design, was largely the invention of Frank Hollenbeck, a well-known designer of the time. By November 1904, Baltimore Arms was in receivership, its assets eventually dispersed.

Ansley Fox kept his residence in Baltimore through 1901, leaving the city frequently for trap-shooting tournaments in the East and South, representing Winchester guns and DuPont powders and ammunition. He was genial, popular among the fraternity of professional trapsmen and with the public and

Philadelphia Arms guns are fastened by a top hook and rib extension, nearly identical to that used in L.C. Smiths.

sporting press as well.

He also was a splendid shot, sometimes a brilliant one. He finished the 1900 Grand American Handicap tournament with a ninety-six-percent average – the highest of anyone who completed every event – and yet failed to win the Grand itself. A month later, on May 15, he set a world record for clay-target doubles, breaking ninety-eight targets out of fifty pair. He repeated his high-average performance at the 1901 Grand American and again failed to win the main event. In his two years of full-time shooting, Ansley Fox took part in dozens of clay-target and live-bird tournaments, but shooting never was meant to be a lasting career.

Sometime in 1901, Ansley Fox moved from Baltimore to Philadelphia, to 3534 Gratz, a quiet street that runs in fits and starts, a square or two at a time, north and south through the Germantown section of the city. His house still stands, a narrow, two-story row house with a bay window on the second floor and eaves trimmed in Victorian gingerbread woodwork. The 1902 Philadelphia directory, the first in which Ansley Fox appears, lists his occupation as "salesman."

By the end of the year, his professional shooting career was over. For some months, he'd been at work gathering financial support for a gun factory. He resigned his association with Winchester in December 1902.

In March 1904, notice appeared in trade journals that deliveries of new Fox guns would commence in July, at the rate of fifteen guns per day. These were products of the Philadelphia Arms Company of North 18th Street and Courtland, in Germantown. The company boasted a new, two-story brick building with 15,000 square feet of floor space and a slate of officers headed by Ansley H. Fox, president.

Fox knew full well what competition his new gun would face, and characteristically, he squared off to have a go at the alpha wolf. The Philadelphia Arms gun even looks like a Parker; at arm's length, if you weren't looking closely, you could easily mistake an A Grade Philadelphia Arms for a VHE Parker, with its rounded frame cheeks and dished sculpting around the hinge-pin.

But the similarities are only skin-deep. The hammerless Parker of 1904 was a hellishly complicated piece with an underlug bolt. The Philadelphia Arms gun, by any comparison, is remarkably simple. The bolting system, the central feature upon which Fox based his patent claim, comprises a rib extension and top hook. All Philadelphia Arms guns were 12-gauges with Krupp steel barrels. Mainsprings and top-latch springs are coil-type, features that would be part of all Ansley Fox designs.

The A Grade, which sold for $50, was standard. It was meant, the trade

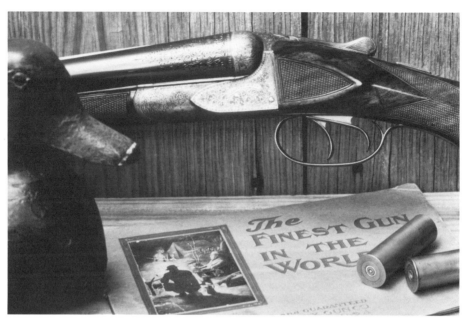

The earliest A. H. Fox Gun Company guns were built in A, B, and C grades. This C Grade was built for a member of the Fox Gun Company board of directors.

A cocking slide on the bottom of the barrel lump provides cocking leverage directly to the hammers.

journals said, as "a popular all-round weapon for the sportsman who wishes to put his money into a dependable gun on which the greatest expenditure is for quality, not ornament." But for those willing to shell out some cash for both, Philadelphia Arms would be happy to decorate its gun in any of six higher grades, the most ornate of which sold for $500.

Philadelphia Arms seems to have been a fairly successful enterprise. The guns, like all that Ansley Fox made and sold, were broadly guaranteed against defects of materials or workmanship. Specific warranties covered top-latch springs and mainsprings, and the action was guaranteed never to loosen from the effects of nitro powder.

Whatever headway Philadelphia Arms made toward finding a niche in the shotgun market, it wasn't enough to hold Ansley Fox. He soon grew restless again.

On December 28, 1904, he sent a letter to the trade magazines, announcing his resignation from Philadelphia Arms and his intention to outfit a new factory that would produce a new gun of his design. The official explanation for the split cited "business differences." There most likely were personality differences as well, for Ansley Fox was not amenable to counsel or compromise. He found another set of investors among the wealthiest Philadelphia businessmen and by April 1905 had filed articles of incorporation, citing capital of $100,000.

As promised, the news appeared in January 1906: The A.H. Fox Gun Company offered a new Ansley H. Fox hammerless shotgun, one to "compare favorably with the best of American or European makes on the market."

Ansley Fox, less modest, called it "The Finest Gun in the World."

Clearly, the new piece was the culmination of Ansley Fox's notions on what a shotgun ought to be. It is simple, strong, and beautiful. The lock itself, covered by a patent issued October 17, 1905, comprises only three parts: the hammer, with integral firing pin; the sear, carefully milled from drop-forged steel; and a piano-wire coil mainspring. The system was unconditionally guaranteed against breakage, even from dry-firing.

For the cocking system, Fox once again borrowed an idea from Greener. Instead of using push-rods, Fox lengthened the hammer toes to extend about halfway down the action bar. A cocking slide fastened to the underside of the barrel lump engages the hammers so that leverage is transferred directly from the barrels.

The bolting system, patented January 16, 1906, is a refined version of the one Fox designed for the Philadelphia Arms gun – a rotary top hook and a massive rib extension.

So few lock parts require relatively little space, and the Fox frame is the smallest of any American boxlock, gracefully filed and sculpted. It also is one of the strongest. Since there is no underbolt, the barrel lump acts only as a hinge for the action knuckle and is only large enough to provide a solid joint and to stabilize the barrels laterally; the water table slot, therefore, is relatively short, leaving extra steel forward of the standing breech. A Fox frame is as tough as they come.

The first published announcements indicate that five grades were available, priced from $50 to $500, but only A, B, and C grades show up in the early advertising. Higher grades – D and F, which probably were special-order items in the first months – appeared in advertisements by 1907.

As Dan Lefever had a few years before, Ansley Fox found himself in the curious position of competing with his own guns in the marketplace. Through 1906 and early 1907, Fox Gun Company advertising included a line that read "Not Connected With the Philadelphia Arms Company." As if to make certain that nobody missed the point, trade-journal ads in April, May, and June 1907 begin with a 70-point headline – "WARNING!" – and caution buyers that even though some guns on the market are marked "Fox," only the genuine article bears the full name "Ansley H. Fox" on the frame.

In November 1906, Fox solved several problems at once by buying Philadelphia Arms, which not only erased a competitor but also netted a virtually new, completely fitted factory. Patents and manufacturing rights naturally were part of the deal, which is why all but the earliest A.H. Fox Company Guns carry patents originally assigned to Philadelphia Arms.

Although the guns proved successful, the company had its share of problems, originating both within and without. One-sentence news items in both February and August 1908 say that Ansley Fox was considering moving his gun factory to Havre de Grace, Maryland. The move never happened, and given a firm that had only recently bought a new factory, I wonder if the whole thing wasn't some internecine tempest arising out of Ansley Fox's willful nature.

There were other willful natures in the world as well, some of them lurking at Ithaca Gun Company. In September 1908, Ithaca filed a legal brief asking the courts to restrain Burhans & Black of Syracuse from selling A.H. Fox guns. Ithaca claimed that the Fox cocking and safety systems infringed a patent issued to Emile Flues in 1895 and subsequently assigned to Ithaca Gun. The Fox Company wasn't specified in the suit, but even the most delicate-handed journalists couldn't avoid noting that the "real defendant" was the maker of the Fox gun, not the stores that sold it.

Apparently, nothing newsworthy came of the litigation. Older patents often were so broadly worded that virtually any similar item could be the target of a suit, and by 1908 the courts were inclined to take a narrower view. The U.S. Patent Office, in any case, had in 1905 accepted the Fox cocking system as patentable, so the Ithaca suit probably had little merit.

By the end of 1908, the company apparently was on a solid footing. Ansley Fox was president and general manager, F.J. Barthmaier, secretary and treasurer. Louis H. Eisenlohr, G. Brinton Roberts, H.A. Poth, Walter E. Hunt, Frank Reily, F.J. Barthmaier, J.H. Eyster, and Ansley Fox were directors. Subscribed capital totaled $400,000.

Catalogues of this period show five grades of gun, A through F, all 12-gauges with Krupp steel barrels. All were treated with some scroll engraving and handsome wood. The D and F grades, especially F, were as artful as any guns ever built in America – Circassian walnut stocks, lavish, beautifully executed engraving, and, in F Grade, the owner's signature inlaid in gold on the trigger-guard bow.

A May 1909 news item said the firm was considering an expansion to accommodate a sixty-percent increase in production. At the same time, A.W. Connor hired on as vice-president, sales manager, and member of the board. One of the best-known and most successful gun salesmen in the industry, Connor had for the previous six years served as sales manager at Savage Arms – the company, ironically, that would be the last maker of the Fox gun.

The Fox Gun Company never used testimonial advertising to the extent that Parker did, but Connor's instinct for opportunity picked up a gem. Former president Theodore Roosevelt, describing his recent African trip in the October 1909 issue of *Scribner's Magazine*, wrote: "I had a Fox No. 12 shotgun; no better gun was ever made."

Actually, Teddy's wife had ordered the gun as a gift to TR's African arsenal. When she sent payment, the Fox company returned the check, saying that it was pleased to build a gun for the great man free of charge.

Teddy wrote back:

> My dear Mr. Fox:
> The double-barreled shotgun has come, and I really think it is the most beautiful gun I have ever seen. I am exceedingly proud of it. I am almost ashamed to take it to Africa and expose it to the rough usage it will receive. But now that I have it, I could not possibly make up my mind to leave it behind. I am extremely proud that I am to have such a beautiful bit of American workmanship with me.
>
> Sincerely yours,
> Theodore Roosevelt

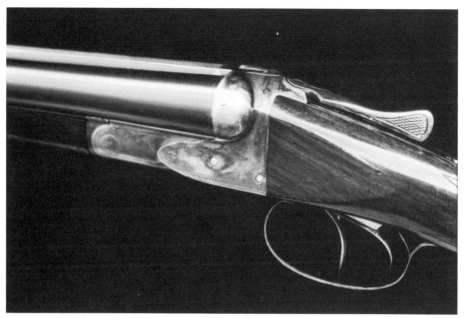

Fox Sterlingworth, introduced in 1910.

The gun, which still exists, is an F Grade made without ejectors. It is somewhat less extensively engraved than some other F Grades of the period. Notably, the barrels do not have the typical F Grade scrollwork and inlaid-gold lightning bolts. Roosevelt presumably wasn't fond of ejectors (they were a $15 option in F Grade at the time); why he didn't want the barrels engraved is anyone's guess.

At any rate, after TR's comment appeared in *Scribner's Magazine*, A.W. Connor lost no time in seeing that both the trade and the public were informed of the old Bull Moose's opinion of the Fox gun. "No better gun was ever made" appeared with Roosevelt's name in Fox advertising for several years afterward. Even a year later, gun dealers in cities where Roosevelt made public appearances set up special displays of Fox guns so that customers and passersby could browse and buy a gun like Teddy shot. The 1915 Fox catalogue uses Roosevelt's letter and an FE Grade gun (which is not the one built for Teddy) as a centerspread.

Still, there's only so much mileage in a one-sentence endorsement, even from Teddy Roosevelt, and the market for $500 shotguns was less than brisk. Competition in the gun trade was fierce, and even at $50 the A Grade Fox was a relatively pricey item. In March 1910, Fox began courting the other end of the market with a new model, the Sterlingworth.

At first, the guns were stamped simply "The Sterlingworth Gun Company, Wayne Junction, Pa., U.S.A." obviously a trade name, since it was manufactured under patents owned by the Fox Company. The trade-journal illustrations of the first Sterlingworths show a hybrid design, a gun built on a frame almost identical to that of the Philadelphia Arms gun but with a bolting system clearly that of the current Fox. In view of that, it's possible that the earliest Sterlingworths were built on leftover Philadelphia Arms frames. Many, if not all, of these early guns, including some built on the A.H. Fox frame, also featured Parkerlike sculpting around the hinge pins.

Within a few months, the name was changed to Fox-Sterlingworth, and the gun appears in Fox advertising as the Model 1911. By then, the Sterlingworths were mechanically identical to the other Foxes, except that the Sterlingworth carried a snap-on fore-end and not the Deeley-type fore-end latch that the others have.

It sold for only \$35 – which made it the best shotgun value of the time (and perhaps the best value ever offered in an American gun) – and the Sterlingworth no doubt helped vitalize the company's sales. Connor ordered advertising efforts stepped up for the entire line. A new ejector system, designed and patented by Frederick T. Russell, went into production in May 1911.

Despite it all, the Fox Gun Company was in trouble. Its advertising grew steadily more elaborate during 1910 and 1911, but there is a hint of desperation, a boy whistling his way past a nighttime graveyard, under the brave claims of flourishing sales. Finally, in April 1912, the trade was informed that Spencer K. Lewis had been appointed receiver for the A.H. Fox Gun Company. Reorganization, Lewis said, would be under way immediately. And Ansley Fox was gone again.

This time, at age thirty-six, he was out of the gun business for good. By then, America was in the grips of a manufacturing frenzy, and though he clearly was disenchanted with the gun industry, Ansley Fox wasn't ready to abandon industry itself.

But change followed change. At some point, William Gerou, who worked as a machinist in the gun factory, had introduced his employer to his sister Ellen, and Ansley Fox discovered the great love of his life.

He was married; she was not. One of the essential, and regrettable, differences between history and art is that history seldom records emotion. We'll never know what chemical spark was struck between Ellen Gerou and Ansley Fox, nor will we ever know what agonies passed between Ansley and Fentress Fox, but it ended in the Philadelphia Court of Common Pleas in the March term of 1913, when Fentress petitioned for divorce on grounds of adultery.

Following the court hearing, Ansley Fox dropped from sight for an entire year. It's possible – and my romantic bent would have it so – that he and Ellen lived together, forging the closeness that would endure for nearly thirty years, but that is scarcely more than wishful thinking, for I have no solid evidence to support it.

Still, their intentions were clear enough. On March 23, 1914, Judge J.M. Patterson issued a decree of divorce in the case of Fentress and Ansley Fox. Two days later, Ansley Fox and Ellen Gerou applied to the Clerk of the Orphans' Court of Philadelphia County for a licence to marry. The following day, March 26, 1914, they were married at All Saints' Lutheran Church by Pastor F.A. Bowers.

They lived in what had been Ellen's house, at 244 Berkley Street. From 1916 through 1919, Ansley Fox was president of the Fox Pneumatic Shock-Absorber Company. And over the next few years, he was a busy man.

In 1917, as America entered World War I, he organized the Ansley H. Fox Company, Inc., whose business is listed in the 1918 Philadelphia directory as "machine guns." Ansley Fox secured two patents for gas-operated machine guns in February 1919, one in March 1920 for a cartridge-feeding mechanism, and one for yet another machine gun in August 1921. The Ansley H. Fox Company doesn't appear in any Philadelphia directory except that of 1918; since the war to end all wars came to a close in November that year, it's doubtful that many – if any – Fox machine guns actually were built.

Machine guns clearly weren't his main interest anyway, for Ansley Fox was preparing to manufacture an automobile. The Fox Motor Car Company, Ansley H. Fox, president, first appears in the 1919 Philadelphia directory. The automobile itself was unveiled in January 1922 at the Hotel Commodore in New York City. True to form, it was beautiful, imaginative, and expensive – a two-seater coupe as trim and racy as a 20-gauge double gun. Its air-cooled engine housed six cylinders with aluminum pistons, overhead cams and valves, and developed fifty horsepower. Ansley Fox called it The Finest Car in the World.

Manufacturing trends at the time clearly favored water-cooled engines of simple design. Only sporting and luxury cars such as Duesenburg, Wills – St. Claire, Stutz, Mercer, and Marmon used overhead cams and valves, and only a handful of car-makers, notably Franklin, used the more mechanically complex air-cooling system. Only the ultrasophisticated used both. It was just the sort of market that appealed to Ansley Fox.

The Fox automobile made a good showing while it lasted. The 1923 model was a handsome sedan with a larger engine. Its impressive power and resistance to overheating made it a particular favorite among bootleggers. Unfortunately, not even they could buy enough $3900 Foxes to keep the company solvent, and the firm went into receivership in 1923.

In April 1924, Ansley Fox organized the Fox Holding Company, which bought all of the Motor Car Company patents at the receivers' sale. At about the same time, he changed his residence as well, to 5044 Erringer Place, a block-long street between Fernhill Park and the lawns of the Germantown Cricket Club. Whatever plans he had for the automobile patents apparently didn't materialize, and he allowed the holding company charter to lapse in April 1930. By then, Ansley Fox had left Philadelphia.

As it turned out, he didn't go far. In 1926, he and Ellen moved to 214 Palmer Avenue in West Atlantic City, New Jersey, where Ansley Fox organized the Seaboard Development Corporation and set about buying land around the community of Pleasantville. His plan was to create a suburban residential area called Ansley Park (in which Ansley Boulevard naturally was a principal thoroughfare). In 1927, he started the Ansley Park Construction Company and appointed his old friend and brother-in-law William Gerou as superintendent. In 1930, he built a fine home at 214 Palermo Avenue, where he would live for the remainder of his life.

In May 1931 he made the local newspapers in the midst of national controversy over the power-trust issue, with a statement supporting the notion of publicly owned utilities. The following day, May 14, the Atlantic City Press published a letter on the subject of government's relationship to private business and the public weal, signed by Ansley Fox. For a man who had spent a lifetime in private enterprise, his rhetoric in behalf of the people's welfare is as fiery as any Depression-era Democrat's.

In July 1936 he was one of several local citizens to protest when Roy Walsh, owner of a clam stand on Pleasantville Boulevard, announced that he would petition the Egg Harbor Township Committee for a license to sell liquor. Ansley Fox is quoted as saying that he had no personal objection to drinking but he felt the community should remain a place for "men, their wives and children – not saloons." Saloons, he said, would mar the quality of living in West Atlantic City and would violate its zoning ordinances besides.

He was sixty-one then, still active in businesses both in New Jersey and in Philadelphia, where he kept an office. Fox Munitions Company of 21st Street and Arch, Philadelphia, one of the last ventures to bear Ansley Fox's name, supplied ordnance equipment during World War II and in September 1945 was cited by the War Department for its contribution to victory.

And he still was an inventor of things, things less romantic than fine double guns perhaps, but things that clearly intrigued an active mind and a penchant for tinkering. He patented a cigarette lighter in 1931. But what he really had in mind was a self-lighting cigarette. As I was told by someone who knew the

Foxes during those years, Ansley Fox developed a container for self-lighting cigarettes (which he patented in 1935), an ignition device (patented in 1936), and a machine (patented in 1940) for attaching the devices to cigarettes. William Gerou was Ansley Fox's chief guinea pig for testing them; family recollection has it that his idea was successful in the self-lighting phase but that the bloody things wouldn't stay lit. Had it gone into production, he no doubt would have called it The Finest Cigarette in the World. It's a pity we missed out on that one.

Back in Philadelphia, the A.H. Fox Gun Company was not setting the shotgun world afire, but it was burning brightly enough. Within months after the 1912 receivership, new investors bought in, principally Edward H. Godshalk and his son, Clarence. The Godshalks were able executives who had made their fortune in textiles. Their first decision for the Fox gun was to expand.

To this time, Fox had built no guns in gauges other than 12. But ammunition was efficient enough that smaller bores were becoming popular, and Fox introduced its first 16- and 20-gauge guns in 1912. For advertising interest, they were called the 1912 Models, though they were identical mechanically to all other Foxes. The factory put out a small descriptive brochure to commemorate the event; it is subtitled "The Most Perfectly Proportioned Small-Gauge Guns Ever Built."

As with many of Fox's claims, there is some truth in it. Actually, 16- and 20-gauge Foxes are built on the same frame, scaled a bit closer to 16-gauge than to 20. But the small-gauge frame shows exceptional harmony in the proportions between frame and barrels. To keep the weight down, the company commissioned its own formula for steel, wonderfully stout stuff high in chromium alloy, trade-named Chromox.

Till Chromox appeared, Fox barrels were bored from Krupp steel blanks. Twelve-gauge guns were barreled with Krupp steel until World War I shut off the supply. Some small-gauge guns built between 1912 and 1918 have them as well, but at least as many were made, both barrels and frame, of Chromox. A few sets of Krupp tubes remained in inventory and were used on later guns, but the vast majority of Foxes built after 1918 were made of Chromox.

The Fox Company made minor changes in its engraving patterns over the years, but about 1910, the same time William H. Gough took charge of the engraving section, the style itself began to change. High-grade Foxes show a slowly but steadily diminishing amount of time spent in decoration and finish work. This is not to say that quality is necessarily poorer. The quality of workmanship generally doesn't change, but the amount of actual hand-work put into the guns, grade for grade, clearly is less. The reason is obvious: Fox never raised its prices much, but the cost of labor and materials escalated steadily, and the only way to survive in those circumstances is to reduce the amount of time spent on each gun.

So, by 1914, the delicate scroll that earlier graced all the high-grade Foxes had, except in CE Grade, given way to a bolder, Germanic style of deep-relief chiseling that could be done well in much less time. But because there's an exception to everything, the CE Grade, for some reason, always was engraved in graceful scroll.

A single trigger, designed by Iowa gunsmith Joseph Kautzky, had been available from Fox on special order for a few years. In 1914, the company bought exclusive manufacturing rights, and the Fox-Kautzky single trigger appeared as a catalogue item. A patent issued to Clarence Godshalk in April 1915 describes a vent rib; this most likely was meant to be part of the single-barrel trap gun that would appear after World War I. I haven't seen any Philadelphia Fox catalogue that mentions vent ribs available for double guns during this period, although that isn't to say that none were built, since catalogues during the mid-1910s begin mentioning guns built to order, and Fox always was willing to satisfy any reasonable request.

One of the made-to-order guns appears in the 1914 catalogue as the Special Trap Gun. It was built, according to the catalogue copy, "for one of Philadelphia's well known trap shots...in accordance with his own ideas in regard to engraving, checkering, finish and shape of stock, etc..." In the 1915 catalogue, the same gun is used to illustrate what now was called the X Grade, a $100 ejector gun described as "primarily a trap gun" but available in all three gauges and with the standard Fox barrel lengths of 26, 28, 30, or 32 inches. It would remain the XE Grade for as long as Fox guns were built. The XE falls between C and DE in the extent of its decoration. The engraving is bold as floral wallpaper. The XE always would be different from all other Fox grades in having an extra-long fore-end (about two inches longer than the standard splinter) with a slightly schnabel-shaped ebony inlay in the tip.

By 1915, the war in Europe was beginning to shake the American economy, and the Fox Company entered a period of turmoil. The firm struck a deal with the British in 1915 to produce Serbian Mauser rifle barrels at a rate of 2500 per day. Unfortunately, Austria overran Serbia before any barrels could be shipped. About the same time, New England Westinghouse offered Fox a subcontract to produce barrels and magazines for Russian Moisin-Nagant rifles, but history dealt another nasty turn with the collapse of the Russian Czarist government. When the United States entered the war, Fox secured contracts to build Very flare guns and parts for Colt .45 pistols. Things had a way of ending a bit too soon where Fox was concerned, and the 1918

Armistice left the company holding large quantities of barrel blanks, milling machines, experience and, once again, the short end of the stick.

Shotgun production, which had slowed to a trickle during the Great War, soon picked up again. During 1919, Fox turned out about 1300 guns, a figure roughly equal to its entire production in the war years.

And there were some changes. The B Grade, now rarest of the lower-grade Foxes, was discontinued in 1918. The following year, the single-barrel trap gun was introduced. The new single was the product of more than a year's design work and nearly two years of rigorous testing. With its tall frame and slab-sided profile, it isn't the most fetching specimen ever built, but the effort Fox put into boring and honing barrels made it a tough gun to beat. And like all Foxes, the single is hell for stout. The bolting system is a Greener-type crossbolt engaging heavy lugs on the barrel. The lockwork is typically Fox – a good, crisp sear and a one-piece hammer/firing pin forged of nickel steel, driven by coil springs wound from piano wire.

Its birthing, though, was not without complication. As the prototypes were tested, the barrel changed point of impact as it heated. The difficulty finally was traced to the rib, which was milled with posts and top strip all of a piece. The rib didn't expand as the barrel did and consequently pulled the muzzle upward far enough to send the shot swarm astray; in extreme cases, rib and barrel parted company altogether. A floating rib solved the problem. There also is evidence that some aspect of the original design led to audible vibrations when the gun was fired, a noisy bug that was eliminated only by considerable revision in the frame.

The earliest advertising for the Fox single, published during the fall of 1919, shows three grades: J, K, and L. Their decoration corresponds roughly to that of C, X, and D grade doubles. The Fox price list issued January 1, 1920, however, includes the M Grade, the single-barrel equivalent of the lovely FE Grade double.

Because it was the last of the classic American single trap guns to appear on the market, the Fox never achieved quite the popularity it deserved. Low numbers also played a part; during the sixteen years it remained in production, the Fox single was built at an average rate of only thirty-three guns per year, with a total production of only 568 in all four grades.

It won its share of tournaments, nonetheless. William C. Letterman used a Fox single to win the Pennsylvania amateur trap championship on June 20, 1923, and in the process established a new record for the tournament, 198 x 200 with 168 straight. Dr. J.D. Griffith won the Class B honors at the same tournament with 193 x 200; he, too, shot a Fox single. And Bunny Sanders won the 1934 Ladies' Clay Target Championship of North America with her

The Super-Fox was designed as a long-range wildfowl gun. The Super-Fox (right) was built on a large frame and fitted with thick-walled, specially overbored barrels. At left is a standard 12-gauge.

Fox single and a final score of 191 x 200.

In 1922 yet another new gun appeared, the Super-Fox. Though the factory identified it as the HE Grade, the Super-Fox actually amounts to a separate model. In appearance and mechanics, it is identical to all other Foxes, but the Super was built on an oversized frame and fitted with thick-walled barrels carefully bored and regulated for dense patterns at long range.

The new gun was the product of collaboration among Fox designers; Capt. Charles Askins, the best-known gun writer in America at the time; E.M. Sweeley, an Idaho lawyer whose avocation was finding ways to improve the shotgun's long-range performance; and Burt Becker, a superb Philadelphia gunsmith and probably the best barrel man in the country. John Olin, owner of Western Cartridge Company, had just brought his revolutionary new Super-X shotshells onto the market, and these cartridges combined with the Super-Fox gun brought long-range shotgunning truly of age.

The Super-Fox was made in both 12 and 20 gauges. The 20s weighed as much as 8¼ pounds, and the 12s, built on what amount to 10-gauge frames, as much as 9¾ pounds. Neither exist in great numbers; total production amounted to about 300 guns, only 59 of which were 20-gauges.

Standard chambering in the Super-Fox is 2¾ inches. Three-inch chambers, which had been available in 20-gauge Foxes since 1912, could be special-ordered in both gauges. Curiously, the standard chambering in most other Philadelphia-built Fox guns is 2⅝ inches. Some were bored with longer chambers, but not many. That's something to check out if you shoot a Fox.

The company put out a special brochure in 1922, recounting in elaborate detail all of the Super-Fox's virtues – from a discussion of its specially overbored barrels (the bores actually are 11-gauge) to endless tables showing pellet counts from a multitude of loads. In a momentary excess of enthusiasm, the maker guaranteed full-choke patterns of eighty to eighty-five percent. The advertising section apparently didn't know that a shotgun is as fickle with its favors as a teenage beauty's heart, depending upon the cartridges you feed it. Before long, they stopped making promises the guns couldn't keep, which is why most Super-Foxes are stamped "Barrels Not Guaranteed" on the barrel flats. It refers to pattern density, not barrel quality. Super-Fox barrels are as strong as any ever built, and given a load it likes, the Super-Fox is super indeed.

Riding the wave of prosperity in the early 1920s, Fox advertised guns even more highly decorated than the lavish FE Grade. From 1922 until 1930, the catalogues mention the GE Grade as available on special order. The price declined a bit in later years, but early on the GE was offered at $1100. In the American market, only the $1500 Parker Invincible cost more.

Whether Fox ever actually built any GE Grade guns is problematic. None ever appeared as a catalogue illustration, and no factory record of one has come to light. In the early 1950s, Savage Arms vice president Herbert Stewart had two guns built that have since been advertised as GE Grades – a double and a single trap gun. But the Fox gun was no longer in factory production, and both of Stewart's guns were engraved in Germany, so it's arguable that neither is an authentic GE Grade Fox.

As the serial-number information in the Appendix shows, Fox guns were numbered in blocks according to grade and gauge. The existence of some guns in a number series apart from the usual blocks naturally has prompted speculation of a special group of extremely ornate guns. It also has been suggested that the GE Grades were numbered in this block, which begins with serial number 450000.

Actually, the only thing intrinsically unusual about these guns are their numbers. Factory work-order cards exist for eight guns in the 450000 range. All were built between 1931 and 1940, apparently as office samples or as experiments in cost-effectiveness. Six of the eight are A Grades, the other two listed as having HE engraving. No GE Grades appear, and the assumption that the 450000-series guns are unusually fine has no basis in fact. I've never seen one of them, but I'm told by reliable people who have that the workmanship is well below typical Fox standards, even those of the Savage years.

The January 1, 1923, Fox price list shows the Sterlingworth available at $48 with extractors and as an ejector gun at $60.50. A Grade cost $62, $74.50 with ejectors. The HE Grade is listed at $100, CE Grade at $115, XE at $185, DE at $275, FE at $500, GE at $1100. A Fox-Kautzky single trigger cost $31 extra. The J Grade single trap sold for $139, the K Grade for $180, the L Grade at $250, and M Grade at $500.

The Godshalks clearly were astute enough to realize that shotguns alone were not likely to offer much financial stability and about 1923 organized the Fox Automotive Products Corporation as a subsidiary of the gun company. Between December 1924 and November 1929, Clarence Godshalk and other Fox employees secured a total of twenty patents for a multitude of items: automobile accessories from steering locks, a tilting steering wheel, spare-tire locks, auto lamps, and signaling devices to such other goodies as electrical switches, circuit-breakers, and toy guns with spring-loaded cartridges. The Fox Play Gun, a cute little break-action double made of stampings and sheet metal, remained a popular item for years; it was advertised, naturally, as "The Finest Toy Gun in the World."

The Godshalks' foresight stood them well. Even before the stock market collapsed, the finest gun in the world was an economic albatross. In November 1929, Savage Arms bought all manufacturing rights, machinery, and inventory and announced that production of the A.H. Fox Gun would be moved to the Savage factory at Utica, New York.

The Godshalks refitted the building with new machinery and set out to face the Great Depression as the Fox Products Company. For nearly fifty years, it turned out myriad light-industry items, from battery chargers and aircraft parts to locks, electrical outlets, and fishing reels. Fox Products remained in business until 1980.

Neither of the two great American shotguns that became foster children of the 1930s fared very well. Both Fox and Parker, taken over in 1934 by Remington Arms, were relics of a passing age, expensive to build and difficult to sell. Savage's marketing plans obviously aimed to broaden the field of potential customers. It backed the Fox as a competitor in the target-shooting market with various trap and skeet guns – the Skeeter in 1931, Trap Grade double in 1932, and various target-style Sterlingworths off and on for years. Yet another series of low-priced doubles, called the Fox Special or SP Grade, appeared in 1932.

From 1931 on, Savage catalogues list vent ribs available on double gun of A Grade or higher. Vent ribs never were catalogue items for Sterlingworth or SP Grade guns.

The Super-Fox appears in every Savage Fox catalogue, but not many actually were built during the Depression. Except for its 1934 catalogue – an anomalous document in several respects – Savage didn't advertise the 20-gauge Super after 1931. In 1934, however, Savage announced the Sterlingworth Wildfowl Grade, which simply was a 12-gauge Super-Fox without the standard HE Grade engraving, stocked in plain American walnut. The Sterlingworth Wildfowl never sold well and does not appear in the catalogues after 1940.

By 1935, K and L grade single trap guns were no longer catalogue items; by 1937 only the J Grade remained. FE Grade was discontinued in 1940. The Fox Model B, which remained in production until 1987, was introduced in 1940. It shares nothing with the original Foxes except the name. The DE Grade double is not listed in the 1941 wholesaler's catalogue, although the last Fox retail catalogue, issued in 1942, shows the various models of Sterlingworth and SP guns, graded doubles from A to D, and no single traps at all.

To its credit, Savage managed to keep the Fox gun in production until World War II, but quality began noticeably to suffer early on. Until 1933 or '34, Savage Foxes aren't much different from the Philadelphia guns of the late '20s, but then the supplies of Philadelphia-made parts, notably the Chromox steel barrel blanks, ran out. The Savage-built Foxes aren't junk, by any means, but they don't compare well with those of the 1910s and early '20s, to say nothing of the guns from Fox's golden age.

The most obvious differences are in the stock work. Really fine European walnut had been hard to come by since World War I, and in the devastated economy of the 1930s, no one could afford it, anyway. But even using lesser wood, Savage simply couldn't afford to maintain the splendid fitting, shaping, and checkering that had always characterized the Fox. Other features show a similar lack of attention. Savage-made barrels aren't as finely struck, frames are less carefully filed, lock and action parts less polished. In short, whatever had to be done by hand was done less thoroughly.

In the post-war world, the repeating gun was king, the double an antique. Savage assembled a few Foxes after the war, from parts machined long before. The last 12-gauge gun left the factory in 1945; the last of all the standard Foxes evidently was a 20-gauge SP Grade completed in December 1946.

Ansley Fox was past seventy then, retired and growing old. Ellen had died of cancer at Temple University Hospital in Philadelphia on Christmas Day, 1942. Within a couple of years, Ansley Fox had married Velma Shank, who was twenty-eight years younger than he.

On August 9, 1948, less than two months after his seventy-third birthday, Ansley Fox suffered a stroke that left him partially paralyzed. The paralysis impeded the flow of his blood, and he developed pneumonia within the week. At 5:42 in the afternoon on Sunday, August 15, his heart finally stopped. He was buried four days later, next to Ellen at Harleigh Cemetery in Camden, New Jersey. Though he had no direct connection to the sporting-arms industry during the last half of his long lifetime, his obituary in *The New York Times* on August 17 identifies him simply as inventor of the A.H. Fox shotgun.

Time inevitably has enhanced the reputations of all the great American double guns, sometimes more from romance than reality. Happily, the debate over which is "best" can never be resolved. Each has its shortcomings, and each has much to appreciate. Still, to my mind, the Fox is the best synthesis of mechanics and aesthetics, form and function. I'm as fond of Parker's mystique as anyone, but the Fox seems to me a more efficient design and certainly a more attractive gun. Small-bore Parkers have a clumsy look about them, and nearly every Parker is heavier than it needs to be. Not so the Fox, with its small frame and elegant lines. If light weight is a virtue, Fox could trim ounces better than any other maker. At just over five pounds, a lot of 20-gauge Foxes are considerably lighter than most Parker .410s.

And to my notion, Fox used better-quality wood, grade for grade, than Parker did, and the Fox stockmakers strike me as the best of any in America.

In many ways, Fox was at the leading edge of innovation in the American shotgun trade, both during Ansley Fox's tenure and in the Godshalk years as well. Three-inch chambers were available in 20-gauge guns from the very beginning of the Fox small-bores. There never has been a tougher, more durable gun steel than Chromox. The Super-Fox was the only American double designed from scratch as a long-range gun.

Both versions of the Fox ejector – the first patented in 1904, and the second in 1911 – are as reliable as any ever designed. Joseph Kautzky's single trigger is a gem. Dan Lefever's later single triggers might be as good, but none of the others even comes close. (Remington didn't choose to redesign both the ejectors and the single trigger for its remanufactured Parker just for the hell of it.)

Though the engraving that Fox used after 1914 is sometimes as gaudy as a psychedelic light show, there's more to the aesthetic impact of a shotgun than ornamentation alone. Even as Fox abandoned the time-consuming, expensive scroll, the frame-filers began adding subtle, elegant details to the high-grade guns. In XE, DE, and FE grades from about 1914 on, the frame is treated to a lovely little scallop, or rebate, at top and bottom, where the tangs fair into the frame itself. In the same grades, the tops of the fences are filed to match the arc of the barrels where they curve to meet the rib. In point of sheer artistry, only the old-style L.C. Smith frame is as gracefully sculpted as the Fox's – and

Hunter Arms gave that up in 1912 as too expensive.

The most objective criterion for comparing quality among guns is durability – not a capacity for absorbing a trainload of proof cartridges, necessarily, but rather an ability to function as it was meant to function year after year, showing consistently reliable trigger pulls, ejectors, lock parts, stocks that don't split, bolts that don't wear out before their time.

Any gun is liable to a breakdown of some sort, sooner or later, but it seems to me that quality of design and construction correlates closely with how often or how seldom a given make shows up for sick-call – assuming, of course, that we're comparing guns that exist in comparable numbers and that their ailments aren't the result of gross abuse or being run over by a truck. Among the most plentiful of the great American doubles – Parker, Fox, Smith, and Ithaca – I'd bet my favorite bird gun against last week's kennel sweepings that gunsmiths *repair* fewer Foxes in a given year than any other. Moreover, I'd bet that at least eight of every ten Foxes that do spend time in the shop are there for alteration or refinishing, not because of some mechanical ill.

The old standard gunsmithing books have little to say about Foxes, because Foxes just don't break down very often. Even now, when the most recently built Foxes are well into middle age, it's hard to find a gunsmith who's had much experience at repairing them.

But is it the "best?" If you expand the question to include shotguns worldwide and define the ideal according to how far a gun can be refined in the smallest detail, then the answer naturally is no. But if you change the question and ask if Fox is *a* best, the answer is simple: absolutely. American guns generally are not so highly refined as are the European best, but then neither is American shooting. American guns do what they do as well as any built anywhere, and a Fox does it better than most.

And there's Ansley Fox himself, quintessentially American, endlessly fascinating. Seen through the scrim of history, the picture of the man is dim. He was a risk-taker, volatile, brilliant, demanding, perhaps even arrogant. Whatever internal tides moved Ansley Fox, he clearly sought to leave behind him something of quality, something that would endure. The search must have been painful at times, both for himself and for those whose lives touched his.

The world he knew changed and changed again; its currents often seemed to run against him. He must have felt some bittersweet satisfaction in seeing the company he founded continue to produce the gun he had created and named. But by the end of his life, even the gun was gone. How he felt about that, we can only guess. It's a pity that he never knew what remembrance history would hold for Ansley Fox.

L.C. SMITH

Sweet Elsie

William Baker founded the original company, Alexander Brown designed the gun, and for almost sixty years the Hunter brothers manufactured it.

So who the hell was L.C. Smith?

He was neither a gun designer nor even an enthusiastic shooter. His career touched the gunmaking world for only eleven years. But he left his name on one of America's greatest shotguns.

Lyman Cornelius Smith was born at Torrington, Connecticut, in 1850, one of five sons born to a wealthy sawmill owner. For all the business acumen he demonstrated in later years, his early ventures were anything but auspicious. At the age of twenty-two, subsidized by his family, Smith invested in a livestock operation in New York City and was bankrupt within two years. By 1875, he was back in Lisle, New York, then the family home, with assets that included the clothing he wore, a Bible that had been a gift from his parents, and very little else.

Determined to have another go at free enterprise, Lyman Smith remained in Lisle only a few months before moving to Syracuse. There he worked for a while as a clerk but in 1876 persuaded his father to lend him the necessary capital to buy a sawmill. Lumber, as it turned out, was no more his forte than livestock had been. There is some evidence that these business loans ultimately forced the elder Smith himself into bankruptcy. But Lyman Smith was a young man whose star was rising – fitfully perhaps and dimmed by false starts, but rising nonetheless.

In February 1877, he married the daughter of former Syracuse mayor Peter Burns. It was a fortuitous match, for Burns not only moved in the best of the city's social circles but also was one its wealthiest citizens. In September that year, Smith sold off the ailing sawmill and formed a partnership with his brother Leroy and a gifted gunmaker named William Baker. Together they founded W.H. Baker and Company, 20 Walton Street, Syracuse, manufacturer of the Baker three-barrel gun. There is evidence that Peter Burns contributed substantially to financing what would become one of America's most famous guns.

William Baker was forty-one years old when he and the Smiths went into business together. Since the mid-1860s, Baker had built muzzle- and breechloading rifles in both Marathon and Lisle, New York. While in Lisle, he

L. C. Smith Number 2E Grade.

became acquainted with Leroy Smith and George Livermore, both of whom would play significant roles in his career, first at Syracuse and later in Ithaca.

Baker had a gift for firearms design. His reputation, founded on the superior quality of his rifles, was further bolstered by the three-barrel combination gun for which he earned a patent on August 31, 1875. Built first at Lisle and then at Syracuse, the Baker drilling was responsible for Lyman Smith's first financial success.

For the most part, Baker's drilling looks much like any other gun of its time, with its sidelocks and tall hammers. Not even the rifle barrel underneath the shotgun tubes was much remarkable, for European-built combination guns were not uncommon in America during the latter nineteenth century. But the gun is no more ordinary than Baker himself. The bolting system, for one thing, is typical of Baker's bent for innovation; the action is fastened by an underlug that is retracted by pushing the front trigger forward. Given the relatively mild stresses generated by black-powder ammunition, the arrangement was perfectly durable.

Contemporary advertising called the Baker drilling "hammerless and triggerless" – quite a neat trick if you take it literally. And it's quite a neat design. The sidelocks and ear hammers fire only the shotgun barrels; the rifle lock is fitted with its own hammer concealed inside the frame and cocked by a short, rocker-type lever that extends through the trigger plate. The sear is designed so that the rifle barrel may be fired by either of the two triggers.

Besides the Baker drilling, Smith and his partners offered a trigger-action shotgun of virtually identical design. Both the drilling and the shotgun were available in either 10- or 12-gauge.

By 1879, W.H. Baker and Company was doing business at the rate of $160,000 in annual sales, and the future seemed secure. But late that year or early in 1880, both Baker and Leroy Smith sold their interests to Lyman Smith. Baker stayed in Syracuse for a while, and Smith went off to Ithaca, where the two would be together again a couple of years later.

Lyman Smith continued producing Baker-designed guns. The 1881 Syracuse city directory lists "Lyman C. Smith. Manufacturer of Baker's breech-loading guns." Advertising of the period mentions "The Baker Gun, L.C. Smith, Maker." The guns themselves are stamped L.C. SMITH AND CO., MAKER OF THE BAKER GUN, SYRACUSE, N.Y. and, on the frame, BAKER PAT. Baker's name continued to appear on Smith's guns until 1883, when Baker, Leroy Smith, and others set up a new W.H. Baker & Company, Gun Works, in Ithaca. Although production of the Baker-patent guns continued in Syracuse for another three years – and the drilling until 1888 – they were stamped only L.C. SMITH.

Baker's departure left Lyman Smith without the vital resource of a designer. Certainly, Smith himself was no engineer, and without Baker or someone like him, the company was at a disadvantage for competing in a flourishing trade. Even before the 1880s reached the midpoint, it was clear that Smith's company would not long survive without a new gun to sell.

It came from twenty-four-year-old Alexander T. Brown, who had joined Smith in 1878 as a machinist. A farm boy from Scott, New York, young Brown had an affinity for mechanical design that was in every way a match for Baker's. He already held patents for a gun lock, issued November 23, 1880, and a breechloading gun, issued July 25, 1882. His third patent, issued March 20, 1883, covered a design that would be the new L.C. Smith.

Lyman Smith described it as the "Smith top-action, double cross-bolted breech-loading gun." Hiding in that thicket of hyphens was the beginning of an American legend.

The gun came on the market May 1, 1884, stamped simply L.C. SMITH. The small, tapered lockplates, low-profile hammers and top latch gave it a slimmer, more modern look than Baker's gun, but its appeal was more than cosmetic. One of the greatest challenges in double-gun design lies in finding a fastening system that will endure through long-term use. In America especially, a gun's reputation often rests heavily on the quality of its bolting. Brown's approach was brilliant.

His theory, published in *The Field* magazine in 1885, was: "A top-fastener constructed strictly on mechanical principles is the most reliable and durable fastening that can be made, as it admits of leaving the metal in the angle of the breech, or frame, where it is most needed. The function of the fastening should be to hold the standing breech against the breech end of the barrels, as well as to resist the upward motion of the barrels at the instant of firing." Plenty of others eventually agreed, William Baker, Dan Lefever, and Ansley Fox among them.

Brown's system is one of the world's best and probably the most famous feature of the L.C. Smith gun. As others had done, Brown chose a rib extension and top hook, but instead of a vertically pivoting fastener, the Smith's top hook is a steel cylinder that turns on a horizontal axis. A slot cut into the cylinder forms the actual hook, which locks into a slot in the rib extension. The cylinder also engages a lip at the rear of the extension and forms the "double cross-bolt" – a system almost identical to that of the early hammerless Ithacas, to the D.M. Lefever boxlock guns, and to the Philadelphia Arms guns manufactured by Ansley Fox.

It wasn't long before the Smith became a darling of hunters and trapshooters alike. Available in either 10- or 12-gauge, it was offered in seven grades:

Quality F at $55, E at $70, D at $95, C at $125, B at $150, A at $200, and AA at $300. All were fitted with twist barrels, from what the company called "best English stub twist" in Quality F to "fine Damascus steel" in the others.

Popular as they were, the Smith guns had one enemy, at least – an anonymous writer whose by-line was "Gun Crank." The November 14, 1885, issue of *The Field* carried a Gun Crank article titled "American and English Machine-Made Guns," in which the writer thoroughly scourges nearly every gun made on this side of the Atlantic and singles out the L.C. Smith for some particularly vitriolic abuse. On the basis of three F Quality guns he claims to have tested, Gun Crank attacks Smith on three points: poorly fitted top hook, oversized hinge-pin, and pattern percentages somewhat lower than those the company claimed. Perhaps most damning of all, he insists that contact between the barrel lump and frame is so sloppily machined that the barrels rattle when the fore-end is removed.

We'll never know whether the attack was altogether warranted, but Gun

Alexander Brown's unique cocking system uses torque rather than leverage to cock the locks.

Crank's bias so clearly favored English guns that it's questionable whether any American piece could have satisfied him. But the damage was done, and to an astonishing degree. *The Field* was highly influential, and the blot on the Smith's reputation – grown out of that one article – remained to plague the gun well into the twentieth century. History, however, has demonstrated beyond much question that Gun Crank's carping was for the most part utter nonsense.

As the hammerless gun began sweeping onto the shooting scene like a great, scouring wind, Lyman Smith began looking toward the future. Even though the hammer gun would remain in production until 1932, a hammerless action clearly was called for, and once again, Alexander Brown went to work. Two more patents issued in 1886 – one on July 13, covering a hammerless lock, and the other on October 5, covering a safety device – created yet another L.C. Smith gun and yet another legend. The first hammerless Smiths left the factory in 1886 – 281 guns that year, of which wholesalers shipped back fifteen for one reason or another. A small start, perhaps, but this was a gun destined for greatness.

Alexander Brown's hammer gun adapted easily to a hammerless version, but the Smith was more than an old design cobbled into a different shape. What was good about the hammer gun – the fastening system, especially – remained; what was new was brand-new. Push-rods or lifters fitted through the action bar are the usual means of cocking a sidelock hammerless gun, a system patterned after the splendid Holland & Holland action and now used almost universally. Brown's cocking system, different from any other, uses torque.

Smith cocking rods are in the usual place – along the sides of the action bar – but their ends are cranklike levers that engage a milled recess in the fore-end iron. When the barrels pivot down, the rods rotate and cams at the other ends lift the hammers into their sear notches. The rods, made of extremely hard steel, take an enormous amount of stress in the process, but the whole thing works and is durable besides. I never have seen an L.C. Smith with a broken cocking rod.

They also are a trap for the unwary, though. The gun cannot be reassembled if the hammers are released while the fore-end is removed. I learned this the hard way.

My first L.C. Smith was a lovely little 20-gauge Field Grade, a late-1940s gun that somehow got factory-stocked with an extremely fine piece of fiddleback walnut. I'd drooled over the thing for months before I could finally afford to buy it, and during its first evening at home it was scarcely out of my hands. I'd broken it down for cleaning and accidentally tripped both hammers. I thought little of it until I discovered that the fore-end wouldn't snap back into place.

Our ignorances sometimes have an innocent charm about them, but this wasn't funny at the time. Frantic with the fear that I had somehow destroyed my prized possession, I would happily have shot myself if only I could've put the damn gun back together long enough to do it. Fortunately, the local gunsmith was a friend – best of all, a patient one – and he let me bring the gun over at midnight for recocking and a short lecture on Smith mechanics.

Recocking actually is simple and takes only a moment with a stout screwdriver or pliers, but if you've never done it, ask someone for a demonstration before you try. Smith cocking rods are tough, but they aren't indestructible.

While we're on the subject of care, something else about the Smith deserves special mention. Few sidelock guns have been manufactured in this country. One reason is that Americans traditionally have demanded more inherent durability in our guns and generally have refused to adopt the English practice of sending guns back to the makers every year for cleaning and reconditioning. We insist that our guns stand up to all sorts of hard knocks and to the heavy loads we've always favored. Boxlocks generally accommodate all that better than sidelocks, especially in the stocks. A great deal of wood has to be removed in fitting sidelocks, which reduces bearing surface at the stock head. Any sidelock warrants some extra protection from hard blows to the stock.

Smith stocks are particularly prone to split at the rear of the sideplates. Two things contribute to this. One is that Smith plates are milled square at the edges, not beveled slightly toward the inside, as best English lockplates are. Couple this with Smith's typically tight inletting and problems start to loom. Everything is fine in dry weather, but as soon as the wood absorbs some moisture and swells even tighter against the sideplates, even light loads can turn the plates into wedges and split the stock. You can prevent it from happening – or, in most cases, from happening again – by having the inlet slightly undercut around the rear of the plates and then applying a good coat of wood-sealer. A little prevention here is worth a lot of cure, because Smiths are damnably difficult to restock, and good work isn't cheap.

When the hammerless Smith was introduced, the grade designations were changed from letters to numbers. The guns were available in six grades, from Quality 2 to Quality 7. Like the hammer guns, they were all barreled in twist and stocked in good European walnut. Also like the hammer guns, they came in both 10- and 12-gauge. Quality 2 sold for about $80 and Quality 7 for $450. There is evidence that a few Quality 8 guns were built on special order.

Though Lyman Smith had no particular talent for design, he was extremely sensitive to the potential of mechanical things. Even as the hammerless gun was making a niche for itself in the marketplace, Smith himself was looking toward a new field, one with technological implications far more complex, and ultimately far more lucrative, than gunmaking. Brown, too, was intrigued by the gadget; he'd seen one displayed at the Philadelphia Exposition in 1876. It was a typewriter.

The machine Brown saw in Philadelphia was capable of printing only upper-case letters, and Brown was certain he could do better. While the rest of the Smith factory was at work turning out shotguns, Brown tinkered in the machine shop and by 1888 had designed and built a typewriter capable of both upper- and lower-case print – the world's first such machine. He was awarded a patent for it that same year.

Lyman Smith knew a gold mine when he saw it, and even before Brown's patent came through, he put the gun works up for sale. Both Smith and Brown had long, successful careers yet before them. Had the typewriter not proven so fascinating, Brown probably would have influenced the firearms world even more. Among his patents that never went into production were an electric shotgun developed in 1884 and an air gun in 1888. The bicycle, too, was an exciting new contraption, and Brown invented a driveshaft-power bike in 1903 and two-speed bicycle gearing in 1906. Inevitably, the automobile also caught his fancy. He designed a tire that eventually became the famous Dunlop and helped design the air-cooled Franklin motorcar – Ansley Fox's arch-rival in the automobile market. Alexander Brown died in 1929.

Lyman Smith turned typewriters into a vast fortune, first manufacturing them in 1886. In 1890, having sold the gun company, he organized the Smith Premier Typewriter Company. In 1903, he sold out to the Union Typewriter Company and along with Leroy Smith and George Livermore, who still owned Ithaca Gun Company, formed L.C. Smith & Brothers Typewriter Company. This firm, in turn, merged with the Corona Typewriter Company in 1925 to become Smith-Corona and, later still, Smith-Corona-Marchant.

When he died in November 1910, Lyman Smith was president of a Syracuse bank, owned a shipyard and three shipping companies, and was an officer of a steel mill and four railroads. He had come far in the thirty-five years since going bankrupt in New York City, selling livestock.

When word that the L.C. Smith gun works was for sale reached the Sterling Valley, a few miles northwest of Syracuse, John Hunter found what he was looking for. Hunter and his brother Tom were railroad builders, Sterling Valley farmers, and businessmen who owned interests in a buckle factory and a sprinkler company in Syracuse. John Hunter had six sons whom he believed needed something to do, and he was looking to set them up as gunmakers.

In 1888, Hunter had his eye on a breechloading gun that Harry Comstock, a former Remington Arms salesman then living in Fulton, had designed

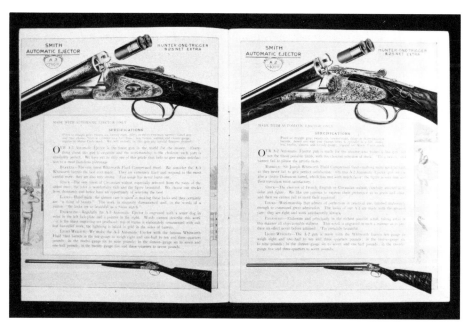

High-grade L. C. Smiths built before 1913 are among the most beautifully sculpted of all American guns.

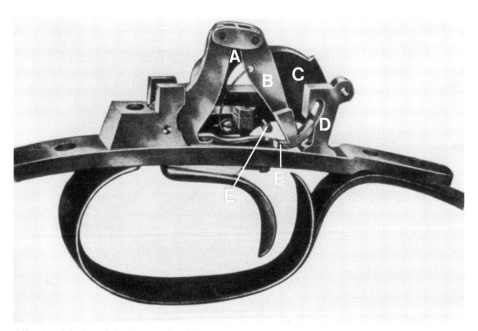

Allen Lard designed the Hunter One-Trigger.

and submitted for patent. When the already-established L.C. Smith became available, however, Hunter abandoned the Comstock gun and soon cut a deal with Lyman Smith. The Hunter Arms Company of Fulton, New York, incorporated on February 12, 1890, with John Hunter as president, his brother Tom as vice-president. five of the six sons – Will, Jim, Rob, S.C., and John, Jr. – took part immediately; Sam came on board in 1915, in charge of the repair shop.

A new factory building in Fulton was completed in 1890, and the Hunters had all of the L.C. Smith machinery, materials, and parts shipped up from Syracuse. Most of the employees came as well.

Such was the L.C. Smith's reputation that the Hunters rejected any thought they might have had about changing its name. Guns built after the transfer of ownership have HUNTER ARMS CO. FULTON, N.Y. stamped or engraved on the ribs.

Nor were the Hunters inclined to revise Alexander Brown's design. Except for the stampings, the early Hunter Arms guns are virtually identical to those built in Syracuse, including the graceful, complex planes to which the frames were filed.

Which isn't to say that the Hunters weren't up to trying something new. From 1895 to 1898, they took a brief fling at building 8-gauge hammer guns, presumably on special order. About thirty were produced in all, most of them in Quality No. 2.

At the turn of the century, Hunter Arms offered the L.C. Smith in eleven grades, beginning with No. 00, a sturdy 12-gauge field gun barreled in fluid steel. It sold for $37, $50 with ejectors. The No. 0 gun came with twist barrels, in 10, 12, and, 16 gauges and sold for $47; ejectors cost an additional $13. The No. 1 was essentially the same gun as No. 0 with a bit of engraving on the sideplates. It sold for $60 with extractors, $75 with ejectors.

Next in line came the No. 2 at $80, No. 3 at $100, Pigeon at $125, No. 4 at $150, and No. 5 at $200. All were available in 10, 12, and 16 gauges with twist barrels and in 12- and 16-gauges with steel tubes. Ejectors were a $15 option.

In the $350 Monogram gun and the $392 A-2 Grade, the customer could choose between high-grade twist or Whitworth steel barrels (or Krupp barrels for the lightweight 12- and 16-gauge versions) and among English, French or Circassian walnut stocks. The A-3 Grade, truly one of the handsomest of all American guns, sold for $740, barreled in Whitworth steel and stocked with Circassian walnut. It, too, came as a lightweight 12- or 16-gauge, with Krupp barrels.

Hammer guns were available in 10- and 12-gauges and in six grades: F, E, D,

C, B, A, and AA. All had twist barrels. Prices ranged from $55 for a Quality F to $300 for a Quality AA.

The 1904 catalogue announces the Hunter One-Trigger available as a $25 option. Three catalogue pages are devoted to its virtues, including one page titled "Handicaps Removed." According to the copywriters, the Hunter One-Trigger is a sovereign remedy for Misfits, Numbness, Fiddling, What You Think, and Lacerations.

The mechanism was the brainchild of Allen E. Lard of St. Joseph, Missouri, one of America's most prolific designers of single triggers for double guns. Lard ultimately won six patents for his work, two in 1899, two more in 1901, one in 1903, and the last in 1915. The latter two cover the first Smith trigger and a later, improved version.

There was room for improvement. Lard's selective single triggers are notable for being among the very first manufactured in the United States, but they suffered from having far too many parts, several of them much too delicate to function reliably for very long. Unfortunately, the more they were used, the more crotchety they got, and now a Hunter One-Trigger can be a gunsmith's nightmare. Small wonder that Elmer Miller used an L.C. Smith gun for his own experiments with single-trigger designs in the early 1920s.

On October 17, 1907, Hunter Arms informed the trade that, after eighteen months of tooling up, it was ready to deliver the first L.C. Smith guns ever built in 20-gauge. These would be available in all grades, built on frames milled to true 20-gauge scale, and would weigh from $5\frac{1}{4}$ to 6 pounds. Chambers were bored at $2\frac{1}{2}$ inches. A notice from John Hunter, published in the December 1907 issue of *The Sporting Goods Dealer*, says that 20-gauge barrels could be 24, 26, 28, 30, or 32 inches long, bored to any choke. Catalogues do not mention 24-inch barrels in any gauge, but a few may actually have been so built.

Stiff competition from other gunmakers in the 1900s, followed by the economic recession of the early 1910s, cut deeply into the Hunter Arms ledger books. After a hard look at their guns and their manufacturing techniques with an eye toward cutting production cost, the Hunters ordered substantial changes in both and brought the results onto the market in 1913.

The new-style L.C. Smiths are mechanically no different from the older guns but certainly are different cosmetically. Frames are blockier, less gracefully filed, and fences less intricately sculpted. Sideplates, too, are filed in curves less complex. Engraving, especially on the lower grades, is coarser, bolder; so is the checkering. Like some other makers of the same period, the Hunters clearly were bent on saving money by reducing the time spent on cosmetic hand-work.

They revised the grading system, too, adding new grades, dropping others, renaming virtually all of them and reducing the number of different grades from eleven to nine. In the earlier guns, grade marks were stamped on the water table and barrel flats. After 1913, grade names are stamped or engraved on the right barrel at the breech and THE HUNTER ARMS CO. M'F'R'S. FULTON, N.Y., U.S.A. on the left.

The new Smith line offered hammer guns in two grades. Grade F was available in 12 and 16 gauge with steel barrels 28, 30, or 32 inches long, at a price of $32.50. Grade FF came in 10-gauge only, with twist barrels of the same lengths. It sold for $35. The Hunters had revised Alexander Brown's hammer-gun design around the turn of the century, simplifying the locks and changing the shape of the hammers.

There also were two boxlock utility guns of Hunter design called the Fulton and the Fulton Special. Both were built in 12, 16, and 20 gauges with steel barrels from 26 to 32 inches long. The Fulton sold for $32.50 and the Fulton Special, with more checkering and some engraving, for $35.

In 1913, the Field Grade Smith, which ultimately would account for eighty percent of Hunter Arms production, was available in 12, 16, and 20 gauges, fitted with steel barrels and stocks of American walnut. With extractors and two triggers, it sold for $40.

The other eight grades all were chambered in 10, 12, 16, and 20 gauges and offered barrels 26, 28, 30, or 32 inches long. Extractors and double triggers were standard in all but the three highest grades; ejectors and the Hunter One-Trigger were optional in the rest.

The $50 Ideal Grade was treated with bold, shallowly cut floral engraving. The Trap Grade, at $68.75, featured trapshooting scenes engraved on the sideplates.

The middle-grade Smiths – Specialty ($82.50), Eagle ($148.50), and Crown ($200) – were barreled in steel and stocked in European walnut. They carried progressively more elaborate engraving, embellished with game birds and pointing dogs.

The highest grades – Monogram at $325, Premier at $575, and Deluxe at $1000 – are extremely ornate. Barrels could be high-quality twist or fine Whitworth steel. Stocks are of highly figured Circassian walnut. The frames, sideplates, tangs, trigger guards, and even the barrels are covered with scroll and, in Deluxe Grade, gold inlay.

The cost-saving measures apparently did little to rejuvenate Hunter Arms, and as the United States prepared to enter World War I, the company slid into deeper and deeper financial straits. The Hunters were involved in all sorts of other business interests as well, often financing them at the expense of the gun works. It ended in bankruptcy court in 1917, where a consortium of Fulton businessmen bought Hunter Arms in an effort to preserve an important facet of the local economy.

At the same time, a new L.C. Smith gun appeared. The 1917 catalogue announced the Smith One Barrel Trap Gun, available in Monogram, Crown, Eagle, and Specialty grades.

The Smith single, unlike the double, is a boxlock gun, but the design incorporates two of the double's best features: Alexander Brown's rotary-bolt fastener and crank-type cocking system.

Strong as it is, a rib extension is a difficult concept to apply in a single-barrel gun. There is plenty of room to fit it between the barrels of a double and still maintain a shallow frame; in a single, the extension must either be slimmed down considerably or moved to one side of the breech. In either case, the barrel walls must be left quite thick at the breech end. The Hunter designers reduced the depth of Brown's rib extension by about half and left it at the top of the barrel, along with enough steel to accommodate it. Brown's cocking system adapts quite well to the single.

In the first couple of years, the rib was a free-floating type. Though company advertising made much of it, the design was changed in 1919 to a rib milled, posts and all, from a single strip of steel. It was not an improvement.

Still, like the others of its kind, the Smith single proved popular, and company advertising presently began counting coups of tournaments won. In 1926, Miss Belisa Gleaves won the Virginia State Amateur Trap Shoot with a Smith single and a score of 192 x 200. She was the first woman ever to win a state trapshooting title.

The trap gun was built only in 12-gauge. The barrel could be 30, 32, or 34 inches long. Choke boring and stock dimensions were customer's choice, and he also could specify whether the trigger was placed in the center or rear position. In 1917, the Specialty Grade cost $100, the Monogram $310.

In his book on L.C. Smith guns, William Brophy notes that several single traps were built in Whippet Grade. Factory records show a dozen Whippets built between October 1927 and May 1928, each with a 32-inch barrel. Aside from serial numbers, barrel length, and shipping dates, the records offer no indication of how these guns were decorated or how they fit into the line in relation to the other grades. Brophy says he's never seen a Whippet Grade, and neither have I.

The plain Olympic Grade single was added to the line in 1928, the Eagle Grade single discontinued in 1931.

In 1920, Gifford Simonds, president of Simonds Saw and Steel Company of Fitchburg, Massachusetts, bought Hunter Arms Company. As Brophy reports, the Simonds family took little or no interest in managing the firm.

The guns themselves endured. The price list issued March 1, 1926, introduces Smith doubles in .410-bore. I'm not much of a .410 fan, but the Smiths are something to behold, sleek little guns that weigh in at 5 to 5½ pounds. Brophy indicates a total production of Smith .410s at 2665 guns, all but 290 of them Field Grade.

The Hunters apparently took a notion early on to offer the Smith in 28-gauge and built at least one – a No. 00 Grade with serial number 100. No doubt they chose to forego the expense of tooling up for yet another gun. The idea came up again in the mid-'30s but never progressed beyond a set of engineer's specifications. It's a pity. The Smith would have made a dandy 28-gauge.

But Hunter Arms was suffering badly by then, both from the Depression and from lack of attention. The physical plant, which was falling into obsolescence and disrepair even when the Hunters sold out, had continued to deteriorate. The Simonds family sold the company to Stephen J. Gilles, a former Simonds employee who had been running the firm almost single-handedly for years. Illness forced Gilles into semi-retirement in 1937, and by 1939 Hunter Arms was once again for sale.

The same year, both Trap and Eagle Grade doubles were discontinued and a Skeet Special added. The skeet gun came with a vent rib, beavertail fore-end, ejectors, and a single trigger, which could be selective or nonselective at the customer's choice.

Both Harrington & Richardson and Marlin looked it over in 1941. H&R backed off entirely; Marlin held out for a more reasonable price. Premier Grade guns, both single and double, were discontinued.

World War II put the matter on hold while Hunter Arms made parts for the Navy's 20mm Oerlikon gun and continued producing sporting guns as well. On April 25, 1945, smothered by government demands to refund $167,000 in monies advanced for wartime contracts, Hunter Arms filed bankruptcy.

In October, Marlin Firearms Company of New Haven, Connecticut, bought the company for $80,000, renamed it L.C. Smith Gun Company, and set about putting things in order. By January 1, 1946, the L.C. Smith double was available only in Field and Ideal grades, the single only in Olympic Grade. Specialty and Crown Grade doubles were reinstated the following year, the Specialty Grade single in 1948.

At one o'clock in the morning on January 16, 1949, a thirty-foot-square section of the factory's main floor collapsed, plunging fourteen milling machines and other equipment into an eighteen-foot raceway under the building. The only casualty, as it turned out, was the L.C. Smith gun. The

Marlin people considered moving everything to New Haven but in the end decided to finish work on the guns already in production at Fulton, put the machinery, parts and other fixtures in storage at New Haven, and call it quits. The last catalogue, issued in 1950, listed the inventory remains.

Some things refuse to die without a struggle. Through the '50s and most of the '60s, the Smith was only a memory growing fonder every year. Then, in 1967, Marlin surprised just about everybody by bringing the L.C. Smith back again. The new gun was built in two grades, Field and Deluxe Field, at prices of $350 and $400. Neither carried any engraving. Frames and sideplates were brightly color-cased, and the Deluxe was stocked in fancy American walnut.

They were available only in 12-gauge with 28-inch barrels, two triggers, and extractors. Both grades came fitted with a blacked-aluminum vent rib.

The new Smiths were good guns, and not overly expensive by 1960s standards. Their limitations, though, did them in. The shotgun market was once again falling in love with double guns but not with 12-bores; shooters wanted 20s and they wanted single triggers, ejectors, steel ribs, and engraving – all of which looked like too great an investment for Marlin's peace of mind. With 2539 guns built, the new Smith left the scene in 1972.

At one time, Smiths were the among the most easily and cheaply obtainable of the great American doubles, and I owned a pile of them in younger years. That first 20-gauge was the best dove gun I ever owned, and it bagged a lot of pheasants when I was a graduate student in Iowa. I still keep an old No. 2 ejector 16-gauge, mostly for sentimental reasons. It doesn't fit worth a damn, and I've never bothered to have the stock bent. But some days, when the October air is clear and the world smells of bright leaves and chilly mornings, it's enough just to carry it through some woodcock coverts I know, through the world that both of us were made for.

LEFEVER

Uncle Dan's Doubles

For the first twenty-five years of his long career, Daniel Myron Lefever built rifles. He learned the skills from one of the great American gunsmiths of his time and learned it well. Even in what probably was the most creative era in American arms-making, Lefever stands out as an authentic genius, and he helped launch a revolution that changed the face of New World gunmaking forever – not as a builder of rifles, but as a shotgun man. And as a legend known everywhere as Uncle Dan.

The Lefevers arrived in America in 1690, an ancient Huguenot family driven out of France by the religious persecution of the seventeenth century. One of the emigrants' sons, Philip Lefever, born at Esopus, New York in 1710, established himself in 1731 as a gunmaker and general gunsmith in Lancaster County, Pennsylvania, and successfully pursued the trade for more than thirty years. His son George later was an officer of the Continental Army in the American War of Independence.

By the early nineteenth century, a branch of the family lived in Ontario County, New York, where Dan Lefever was born on August 27, 1835. His genius for mechanical things blossomed early, and in April 1848, his mother bound him out for five years' apprenticeship to the great riflesmith William Billinghurst at Canandaigua. The notion of becoming a gunsmith apparently was well to the young lad's liking; almost sixty years later, he wrote, "I walked eleven miles through the snow…to learn to make guns."

In 1853, his indenture completed, Lefever spent a few years in Auburn, New York, and moved to Rochester about 1860, where he struck up a partnership with another riflesmith, J.A. Ellis. The little shop was by then famous for the beautiful, superbly accurate rifles that dominated the local shooting matches. It seems obvious that Dan Lefever saw the future with remarkable clarity. When the breechloading gun was, even in Europe, still in its infancy, Lefever was one of the first men in America to make it a reality. The excellence of his work in converting muzzle loaders to breechloaders not only bolstered a growing reputation but also placed him squarely in the forefront of the coming age. He was, even then, a man ahead of his time.

Although his primary work during these years was rifle-making, Lefever began experimenting with shotguns almost immediately. Between 1854 and 1870, he built a number of two- and three-barrel combination guns, but the experiments went slowly in the early years, interrupted by the cannons of war.

The New York State Company of Sharpshooters left Rochester in 1862, bound for Virginia and the bloodbath of the Civil War. Each man carried a fine 'scope-sighted Lefever rifle – perhaps the greatest tribute to his skill, since each man also paid for his own weapon.

In 1870, Lefever went back to Auburn and formed a partnership with Francis S. Dangerfield. It appears that Dan Lefever suffered some inability to get along with business partners. He was involved in several such relationships, none lasting longer than a few years and not all of them with other gunmakers. He may have taken on some partners for their financial skills.

In any event, he and Dangerfield worked together for three years. In September 1872, Dangerfield was awarded a patent, assigned to Lefever, for a thumb-operated bolting system for a break-action gun. Lefever had been experimenting with break-action breechloaders at least since 1867. Whatever else was going on at the time, a shotgun was taking shape in some corner of Dan Lefever's busy mind.

Lefever and Dangerfield called it quits in 1873. Lefever moved to Syracuse and in October 1874 entered a partnership agreement with a man named Barber, previously an agent with the Mutual Benefit Life Insurance Company. In 1875, L. Barber and Company of 51 Clinton Street put out a forty-page catalogue advertising "Barber and Lefever Patented Breech Loading Double Barrel and Single Barrel Sporting Shotguns and Rifles."

The following year, Barber was out of the picture, and it was Nichols and Lefever of 109 Gilbert Street, Syracuse. John A. Nichols was a gunmaker in his own right, and even though the partnership wasn't much longer-lived than the rest, it was wonderfully productive.

In the 1870s, the arms-making world was poised on the brink of change. The hammerless breechloading gun was about to come into its own, and in doing so, it would sweep away all that had come before. In England, W.W. Greener, working from Theophilus Murcott's 1871 patent, built a hammerless breechloader that won a prize in the Centennial Exposition at Philadelphia in 1876. At the same exposition, William Anson and John Deeley, representing Westley Richards of England, showed their invention – the world's first hammerless gun cocked by leverage from the barrels. And Dan Lefever, who apparently was the only important American gunmaker at the time to take the hammerless action seriously, was at work.

In dealing with the problem of how best to fasten the action of a break-open gun, Lefever brought the rib-extension principle though several stages of evolution. He later wrote: "In 1867 I commenced experimenting on breech loaders with breakdown action, my first idea being to bolt as far as possible back of the hinge joint, and used a round head top fastener. After several years' use, I found the round head acted as a wedge and spread the slought [sic] in the standing breech and the action became loose, I then used and patented the square head top fastener." The improved rib extension, protected by a patent issued June 25, 1878, was the final evolutionary phase of the first successful Lefever shotgun.

It wasn't the first hammerless breech-loading gun built in America. That distinction goes to Charles Sneider of Baltimore, but Sneider's few guns would never have the impact on the American trade that Dan Lefever did. Even though he was still refining the design and would not receive patent protection until June 29, 1880, Lefever exhibited a prototype at a Sportsmans Association show in St. Louis in 1878, competing for the judges' favor against twenty-one of the world's finest shotguns. There were two gold medals at stake, one for the best American gun and another for the best gun in the world. Dan Lefever won them both.

It was, for the most part, a conventional-looking sidelock gun. Like Greener's, it had a cocking lever on the left side of the frame; like the guns that followed, it bore the unmistakable mark of Lefever's brilliance. A rocker-type thumb piece on the top tang operated two bolts – one fitted to a bite in the barrel lump and another that engaged a slot in the rib extension. It was graceful and wonderfully strong.

There is a fairly widespread belief that Lefever developed his hammerless action from Murcott's English patent. I'm not sure how this got started, but it isn't true. Greener used the Murcott design as a point of departure, but Dan Lefever didn't, and the Lefever action is quite different from Murcott's.

Lefever and Nichols dissolved their partnership in 1878. The following year, Nichols advertised himself as the sole maker of the Nichols & Lefever gun; by then, Dan Lefever had set up shop at 78 East Water Street, Syracuse, and informed the trade that he was sole manufacturer of "The Celebrated Lefever Hammerless Guns."

The trade apparently responded well. Over the next four years, Lefever produced about 3000 of his lever-cocking guns. They were available in 8, 10, and 12 gauges (possibly in 14, 16, and 20 gauges as well) and in six grades – E, D, C, B, A, and AA.

Other makers responded well, too. H.A. Linder of Germany built a number of side-lever guns on Lefever's patents and exported them to the United States under the Charles Daly name.

Still, Dan Lefever saw his side-cocker, celebrated or not, as a transitional design. By 1883, he had improved the gun to the point that he could see a great potential for mass-production and in June 1884 signed papers of incorporation that made Lefever Arms Company a reality. The following year,

The Lefever action hinges on a ball-and-socket joint.

Lefever's multipurpose cocking hook.

a new gun replaced the side-lever. It was called the Automatic Hammerless, and it was a masterpiece.

The new design did away with the side lever and replaced it with a system that uses leverage from the barrels to cock the locks – from which came the "automatic" part of the name. The thumb-piece latch remained, but the underbolt was gone, and the fastening system relied solely upon the rib extension and top hook. Within a few years, the thumb-piece, too, was discarded in favor of a top lever adapted from Dangerfield's patent.

All told, the Automatic Hammerless is the most innovative – and unquestionably the most completely adjustable – double gun ever built. Lefever called it the "compensated action," a gun so thoughtfully designed and cleverly executed that virtually every part of the action can be adjusted and every type of wear corrected with nothing more sophisticated than a screwdriver.

Instead of a conventional hinge pin, Lefever barrels pivot on a ball-and-socket joint. A heavy, tempered screw, rounded at one end, is fitted into the end of the action bar. The rounded end protrudes into the water-table slot and matches a socket milled into the barrel lump. Should either ball or socket wear to the point that the knuckle loosens, the joint can be tightened merely by seating the screw slightly deeper.

To compensate for any looseness that might develop through wear on the sides of the barrel lump, the lump itself is split and fitted with a tapered setscrew. This, when seated more deeply, spreads the lump enough to refine the fit. The fore-end iron, too, has a patented feature for further eliminating wear in the action joint.

The cocking system is typical of Dan Lefever's particular genius. At the heart of it is a cocking hook in the water-table slot; this engages a pin in the barrel lump. The hook and the hammers are joined at a central pivot point, so that cocking leverage of an extremely high mechanical advantage is directly assisted by the weight of the barrels. The fore-end iron plays no part in cocking, which makes the gun easy to open and relieves a certain amount of stress from the hinge joint.

As if all that weren't useful enough, Lefever's cocking hook serves two further functions. The top of the hook is rounded, camlike, and acts as a primary extractor to nudge fired cartridge cases a quarter-inch or so out of the chambers. The ejectors therefore served only to kick already-loosened cases free, which takes considerable stress off the ejector mechanism. The cocking hook also serves as a check to dampen stress on the hinge should the action be opened with unusual force.

The cocking levers can be synchronized to ensure that both locks reach full-

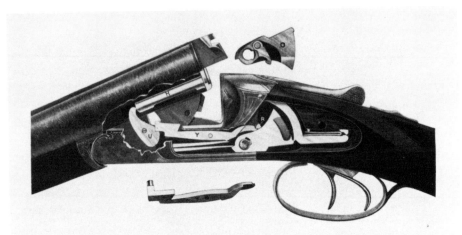

The cut at the top of this page shows the entire lock and ejector mechanism of a Lefever Ejector gun.

No extra main spring is used to operate the ejector on the ejector gun. The main spring in lock operates both the lock and ejector.

In the lower cut F shows ball joint screw between lug on barrels and frame.

A turn of this screw will make the gun as tight after years of shooting as when it passed the rigid inspection at the factory.

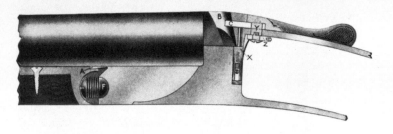

The Automatic Hammerless is nearly as simple in design as the A. H. Fox.

cock at precisely the same instant; trigger-pulls are adjustable to as light as two pounds; and the safety is convertible from automatic to manual – all by the turn of a screw.

The top fastener, milled as part of the top latch, engages a slot in the rib extension, and it, too, is adjustable. As Lefever says in an early catalogue: "This bolt is so arranged that it can be moved down by a slight turn of the compensating screw resting on top of it; consequently the barrels can always be held down tight against the frame, and the action can never get shaky or rattle."

Although the Automatic Hammerless is fitted with sideplates, it is not a true sidelock gun. In early guns, in the serial-number range of about 12000 to about 25000, some lock parts are fastened to the plates and some to the frames. In guns numbered higher than 25000, all lock parts are mounted to the frames, and the plates simply allow allow ready access to the lockwork.

By 1889, the Automatic Hammerless was available in eight grades. Lowest were F, which sold at $75, and E, at $100 – plain, sturdy guns decorated with only line engraving and stocked with straight-grain walnut. Grades D ($125), C ($150), and B ($200) were treated with progressively more elaborate engraving and stocked in fine European walnut. The top grades, A at $250, AA at $300, and the splendid Optimus at $400, were beautifully engraved and finished. Barrels were of best-quality twist or Whitworth steel and stocks of lovely French walnut. Buffalo-horn and skeleton-steel buttplates were available options for all grades.

Dan Lefever did a great deal of conversion work during the early Lefever Arms years, turning old, worn-out muzzleloaders into virtually new breechloading guns. He charged $75 to $100 for the job and guaranteed that the conversion would be undetectable. No one, the catalogues declared, could tell one of Lefever's conversions from a breechloader built from scratch.

At the same time, Lefever Arms would, on special request, build double rifles and combination guns in grades similar to those of the Automatic Hammerless. Prices for double rifles began at $125 and for double combination guns at $115, both in E Grade.

Lefever's drillings are wonderfully clever. Because the rifle barrel is mounted on top of the shotgun barrels, the top fastener from the Automatic Hammerless wouldn't work. Instead, there are twin bolts, one over each shotgun barrel, operated by the then-standard rocker-type thumb-piece latch. The rifle barrel had its own separate lock, cocked by the thumb piece. The front trigger fired the rifle barrel, and the weight of pull could be adjusted for the rifle mode without affecting its weight adjustment in shotgun mode. The drillings sold for $200 to $300.

Dan Lefever may have put up the original Lefever Arms capital himself, but by 1889 he once again had some partners. The catalogue that year lists A. Ames Howlett as president, J.F. Durston treasurer, and Lefever himself as superintendent. Subsequent events suggest that Howlett and Durston even then owned majority interest. Considering his track-record in partnerships, Uncle Dan must have known from the beginning that it couldn't last.

Nonetheless, the Gay 'Nineties were good years at Lefever Arms. A new grade appeared in 1892; at $75, the Ideal or G Grade clearly was meant to be a utility piece, and for several years it was the workhorse of the line. It would be the biggest seller of all Lefever grades.

In 1893, an Optimus Grade gun, which served as Lefever's exhibit at the World's Columbian Exposition in Chicago, won First Premium and Diploma from the exposition judges.

Two more grades were added to the Lefever line in 1899. The I and DS (or Durston Special) grades are identical except for the grade stampings. Both sold for $25 retail. Neither was made with cocking indicators or with the rounded doll's-head rib extension typical of higher-grade Lefevers. Instead, both used flat, easily machined extensions slotted at the end. There is some evidence that the I Grade was made on contract for Schoverling, Daly & Gales in New York and not marketed through the usual Lefever jobbers. In any event, it never appeared in Lefever catalogues and later earned the dubious distinction of being the only grade that Lefever Arms ever discontinued.

The predictable friction between Dan Lefever and his partners reached a peak at the turn of the century. It was, no doubt, the familiar story: businessmen on the one hand, insisting upon trimming every possible penny from the manufacturing process, and the old gunmaker on the other, refusing to give an inch where quality was the question.

In any case, Uncle Dan left Lefever Arms for good in 1901. Ironically, he would spend the remaining years of his life building guns that competed in the marketplace with other guns that bore his name. And he retained ownership of his Lefever Arms stock as well, which shortly would create a situation bordering on the bizarre.

Lefever had five sons, all of them skillful tool- and gunmakers, and by December 1901 they were all in business together under the style of D.M. Lefever & Sons, Syracuse. On the cover of their first catalogue, a line of type reads: "Not Connected With Lefever Arms Co."

While Lefever Arms continued producing guns according to the original Automatic Hammerless design, Uncle Dan launched the New Lefever, a gun the catalogue describes as "purely an American invention of our own, with no foreign ideas attached." It was pure Dan Lefever, in any case.

The New Lefever is a boxlock action conceived on principles established by Anson and Deeley. The bolting system comprises a massive, flat-sided rib extension engaged by a Greener-type cross-pin and a secondary lug. So much for the absence of "foreign ideas."

Still, the New Lefever is a splendid gun. Nitro powders were coming onto the scene at the time, and Lefever clearly designed his new gun with optimum durability in mind. The rib extension is three-quarters of an inch long and deep and a quarter-inch thick; it's brazed to the barrels and was guaranteed against damage by the heaviest loads of either nitro or black powder. The cross-pin, of tempered cast steel, is tapered to compensate for wear and is backed up by an eighth-inch-thick lug that engages a notch at the end of the rib extension. In the earliest version, the cross-bolt is square; guns built in 1902 and later use a cylindrical bolt.

Like the Automatic Hammerless, the New Lefever used the ball-and-socket hinge and the old cocking hook, which performs five separate functions. Besides cocking the locks, it also cocks the ejectors, serves as a primary extractor and extractor stop, and acts as a check hook.

The sears are adjustable for weight of pull down to two pounds. Ejectors may be converted to extractors by turning an adjusting screw. The safety is a roller instead of the usual sliding button, offering, the catalogues insist, a more positive action and greater protection against its "coming into contact with the hand by the recoil of the first barrel, being thrown to safe, thus preventing the discharge of the second barrel as is often the case with the old style safety."

As to the matter of the boxlock action itself, the 1905 catalogue has this to say:

> Many of the old Lefever customers will undoubtedly wonder why we changed our old style lock plate action to the box or solid frame. The following will explain:
>
> 1st – We found by using it we could get a stronger action and do away with several ounces of surplus metal, and every sportsman who shoots in the field and brush knows that ounces get to be pounds at the finish of an all-day's hunt.
>
> 2nd – It does away with a great many joints and small parts of wood around the lock plates which are constantly checking and springing away from the metal parts, allowing the dampness to get in the locks and action and rust the same.
>
> 3rd – It gives much quicker and cleaner working locks with a trigger pull absolutely perfect; no lost motion or play to either trigger.
>
> 4th – It admits of a change of trigger pull without interfering with the working of the locks or action. In all these changes we keep the same shape and symmetrical bearings as in the old Lefever guns.

The 1901 catalogue shows the New Lefever in seven grades, each designated by both a number and letter. All were ejector guns, offered in 10, 12, 16, and 20 gauges, barreled either in Damascus or Krupp fluid steel, and available with straight-hand, half-hand, or pistol-grip stocks. The line began with Grade 8E at $75 and continued through grades 7D at $100, 6C at $120, 5B at $150, 4AA at $220, 3 Optimus at $300, and the lavish Uncle Dan Grade, highly engraved and inlaid with gold, at $400.

By 1902, the company was operating under a new style, D.M. Lefever, Sons & Company, and one Samuel S. Hale is pictured on the catalogue cover along with Uncle Dan and three of his sons – Charles, Frank, and

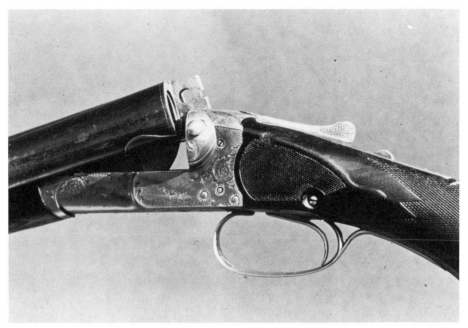

Uncle Dan's New Lefever, an extremely well-built boxlock; 8-E Grade.

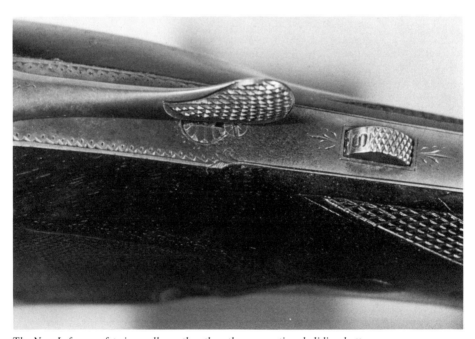

The New Lefever safety is a roller rather than the conventional sliding button.

George. They still were "Not Connected With Lefever Arms Co."

Uncle Dan invented a number of gun-related implements and accessories over the years, and one of them brought him into federal court in January 1902. Lefever Arms filed the suit, alleging that a bore-cleaning brush sold by D.M. Lefever Company infringed a patent for a similar item manufactured and sold by Lefever Arms. The suit asked the court for a restraining order against further manufacture and sale and for damages. In reporting the news, the Syracuse correspondent to *The Sporting Goods Dealer* rightly noted that "Mr. Lefever retains his stock in the old company and is, in a way, fighting himself."

In its next issue, February 1902, the *Dealer* reported that information from the U.S. Patent Office showed a patent for a "gun cleaner having a yielding wire brush" issued to Dan Lefever on May 22, 1900, and that Joseph Rosenburg of the Lefever Arms Company received a patent for a similar device on April 9, 1901. How it all ended is not recorded, but the cleaning tool continued to appear in D.M. Lefever catalogues and in Lefever Arms catalogues as well.

Like a river building dry land where little or none existed before, the westward migration that settled North America had by the turn of the century created a well-tamed and well-peopled Midwest. Less crowded than the East and less demanding of day-to-day survival than the still-wild country farther west, middle America was a pastiche of farmland laced together with habitat where small game flourished, and the Eastern gunmakers found there a greater and greater market for their wares. In the last twenty years of the nineteenth century, small gun factories had sprung up all across the Midwest, from Ohio to Missouri. All would prove relatively short-lived, but the demand for sporting guns remained.

By 1902, Uncle Dan and his sons were looking west, looking for someplace where a manufacturer might conveniently keep in touch with both a growing number of Midwestern customers and the older, more established trade along the Atlantic coast. Within a year, they found a two-story factory building in Defiance, Ohio. It was already fitted with steam power and shafting, so gun-making machinery could be installed and run as soon as it arrived. The Lefevers reorganized, raising enough capital to finance both a change of location and expanded production, and on October 3, 1904, the last of the machinery arrived in Defiance. A month later, still operating as D.M. Lefever, Sons & Company, they were building guns once again.

Less than a year later, in August 1905, the Lefevers moved again, this time to Bowling Green, Ohio, some forty miles east of Defiance. They apparently reorganized again at the same time, for the firm now became D.M. Lefever

D. M. Lefever advertising and guns all carried the phrase "Not Connected With Lefever Arms Co."

Company. The reasons for the move aren't clear but probably centered on a need to reduce production cost. The total number of Lefever boxlocks actually built was surprisingly low, probably no more than about 1200 guns from 1901 through the middle of 1906, and the Lefevers may have discovered that the shotgun market simply would not support the increased production they had anticipated with the move to Defiance.

Though Bowling Green would be the end of the line, the old creative energy still burned.

Although Lefever Arms didn't show it as a catalogue item until 1913, Dan Lefever had designed a single trigger mechanism for double guns as early as

1898. Over the next few years, he and his son Charles designed other single triggers, one of which is listed in the 1902 D.M. Lefever catalogue. One of them, designed by Charles Lefever in 1903 and patented in August 1905, appears in the 1905 catalogue issued from Bowling Green. Uncle Dan and Charles collaborated on yet another design, for which patent protection was issued January 23, 1906.

All Lefever single triggers are good ones, certainly better than any of the others available at the time. They operate with little friction – consequently with little wear – and seldom double. The barrel selector in the Lefever Arms guns is linked to the safety button; push it forward from the *SAFE* position and the right barrel fires first; pulling it backward reverses the sequence. The selector for the D.M. Lefever guns is a cross-bolt through the stock cheeks, just above the trigger.

The 1905 catalogue shows some changes in the D.M. Lefever line. Grades 7D and 3 Optimus are gone; two new grades and an entirely new model appear for the first time. The two new grades are at the bottom of the line – the $60 0 Excelsior and the $90 9F. The 8E Grade now sold for $100, the 6C for $150, 5B for $200, 4AA for $300, and the Uncle Dan for $400. Ejectors were standard in all grades except 0 Excelsior and were a $10 option in that grade. The single trigger was standard in Uncle Dan Grade, a $15 option in the rest. All grades were available in 12, 16, and 20 gauges only.

The new gun was a single-barrel break-action piece meant for clay-target trap shooting, and it was the first high-quality single trap gun built in America. In fact, considering that the sport of trap shooting was in 1905 still in transition from live pigeons to clay targets (and therefore still evolving from a two-shot to a one-shot game), Lefever's may well have been the first American single trap gun of any quality. I know of none manufactured here any earlier.

According to the 1905 catalogue, the single trap gun came in 12-gauge only with a 26-, 28-, 30-, or 32-inch barrel. There is no description of the mechanics except a note that it, too, features the ball-and-socket hinge. The price is quoted as "$38 and up," so it may have been available in high grades. In any case, there were precious few built in any grade; my old friend Bob Elliott, who has written a good book on Lefever guns, estimates total production of single traps at perhaps two dozen, certainly no more than fifty.

As a footnote to the Lefever singles, it's possible that another maker eventually built more of them than Uncle Dan did. In researching his excellent monograph on American single trap guns, my friend Frank Conley turned up evidence of 181 singles built by the Three Barrel

Gun Company of Moundsville, West Virginia, between 1908 and 1910. The guns, Frank tells me, are virtually identical to the D.M. Lefevers, down to the ball-and-socket hinge. Uncle Dan's son Frank Lefever worked at Three Barrel Gun Company for a while during those years, and it's likely that the singles were built under Lefever's patent.

In mid-1906, Uncle Dan, seventy years old and suffering stomach ulcers, retired from his lifetime's work and moved back to Syracuse. His sons left with him, and Lefever's erstwhile partners – M.B. Chidester, Frank W. Thurstin, and James G. Hickox – hired L.N. Walker from New York to serve as general manager of the D.M. Lefever Company.

Uncle Dan died in Syracuse on October 29. An obituary in the December 1906 issue of *The Sporting Goods Dealer* called him "one of the most noted gunmakers of this country." True enough.

The factory in Bowling Green soon closed down for good, despite brave claims in the sporting press about the demand for D.M. Lefever guns. The fact is, they never were in great demand, although the genius of Uncle Dan made them among America's best.

Meanwhile, back in Syracuse...

The Lefever Arms shotgun underwent no substantial design changes in the years following Uncle Dan's departure. There were some minor revisions, but the gun still was the Automatic Hammerless, and it enjoyed a substantial following among American sportsmen. The Durston family controlled the company; J.F. Durston was president and treasurer, his two sons, A.H. and M.H., serving as vice-president and secretary.

The 1913 catalogue, the last that Lefever Arms issued as an independent company, is a delightful piece of literature, thirty-four pages describing Lefever guns in general and particular, replete with earnest italics and the florid prose in vogue at the time. The introductory page begins with the admonition that "the man who makes a mistake when buying a high-grade shotgun, is the man who tries to judge between many *hair-splitting* claims. He fails to grasp and keep in mind the *main point* in gun-action and construction. Wading through pages of catalogues which try to make a lot out of the difference between 'Tweedledum and Tweedledee' ends in the reader's confusion."

Eighteen pages later, lest anyone still harbor doubts about which is Tweedledum and which Tweedledee, we're given a nineteen-point list of "Exclusive Lefever Advantages," beginning with the modest observation that it is "the simplest, quickest and strongest action in the world." The copywriter, whoever he was, earned his pay.

It was Lefever Arms at full flower. The catalogue lists guns in twelve

94

grades, in five gauges, and at prices ranging from $37 to $1000. The DS Grade was offered in 12, 16, and 20 gauges with Dura-Nitro Steel barrels, plain walnut stocks, and no engraving at all. The H Grade, at $44, could be had with either Best London Twist or Carman Fluid Steel barrels, English walnut stocks, and a bit of scroll engraving on the sideplates. Grade G, at $57, was the lowest-grade gun available in 10-gauge. Barrels were of twist or Royal Nitro Steel. Grade F completed the lower-priced guns. At $80, it was available in 10, 12, 16, and 20 gauges with twist or Premier Nitro Steel barrels and stocked in English walnut.

The mid-range grades – E, D, and C – offered strikingly handsome guns at prices of $100, $125, and $150. In all three, the customer could choose between barrels of English twist or Krupp steel and among the gauges 10 to 20.

The high grades are works of art. The gravure cut of the $200 B Grade shows lovely English scroll on the plates around an artfully done cameo engraving of a brace of setters. The AA Grade ($300) differs from the $250 A Grade by virtue, according to the text, of "more elaborate engraving, inlaying, checkering and finishing." All three were barreled in English twist or Krupp steel; B Grade stocks were of English or French walnut, while grades A and AA offered the option of French or Circassian walnut "of rich figure."

The Optimus Grade was $400 worth of truly magnificent shotgun. Select Circassian walnut stocks were matched with barrels of highest-quality English twist or Whitworth steel, certified by Sir W.G. Armstrong of Whitworth & Co. himself. Elaborate scroll engraving covers the sideplates and frame. Dogs and birds are inlaid in gold on the plates, the top latch, the fore-end escutcheon, trigger guard, and frame, set off by thin gold bands around the breech ends of the barrels and on the safety button.

As if that weren't luxury enough, there was the Thousand Dollar Grade, of which the catalogue says: "We show no cut of the Thousand Dollar Grade, as sportsmen's requirements vary to such an extent in a gun of this grade that we prefer to build the gun exactly to their specifications." It was, at the time, the most expensive gun in America.

Ejectors were standard in the top four grades and were available in the rest for $15 above list price. For an extra $10, guns of E Grade and higher could be had in 8-gauge. The single trigger was a $25 option.

Just as the Great War in Europe was about to begin, a recession in the American economy left all of the gunmakers competing in a diminishing market for expensive guns. The outbreak of World War I in 1914 helped revitalize certain segments of the economy, notably agriculture, and eventually would create a boom in the arms industry, but not for sporting guns. Even though half of its products sold for less than $100, Lefever Arms was a small company that produced relatively pricey items in small numbers – only about 63,000 guns over its entire thirty-one-year history. The Durstons struggled along until 1915 and then sold out to Ithaca Gun Company. With that, the last of Uncle Dan's splendid guns were gone.

But not for long, in name at least. In 1921, Ithaca brought out the Lefever Nitro Special, a modest gun that sold for $29. It was a sturdy utility piece bearing the unmistakable mark of Ithaca design and had little in common with its predecessors aside from the Lefever name. Serial numbers began at 100000.

It may not have been beautiful, but the Nitro Special was tough. Factory records refer to it as the first gun Ithaca designed specifically for modern ammunition, and an advertising flyer dated February 15, 1922, says that the first lock was dry-fired more than 77,000 times and the first gun fired some 100,000 times without any malfunction. The completely redesigned action was fitted with stout coil springs and the stock attached by a drawbolt that added considerable strength at the wrist. It was a gun to be used.

The earliest Nitro Specials were available in 12, 16, and 20 gauges. In 12-gauge there was a choice of 28- or 30-inch barrels; the others were 28 inches only. The right barrel could be bored modified or cylinder and the left modified or full. The black walnut stocks were of industry-standard dimensions with no special factory alterations available. By 1928, it was also available as a .410 with 26-inch barrels.

The Nitro Special's reception apparently was encouraging, for Ithaca brought out the Lefever single-barrel in 1927, an unassuming hammerless gun that sold for $16. Officially, it was called the Lefever Long Range Single Barrel Field Gun; it also was available as a vent-ribbed trap gun.

The single was made to virtually the same specifications as the double: 12, 16, and 20 gauges and .410-bore, all with plain walnut stocks and no embellishment aside from a flying goose stamped on either side of the frame. Ithaca records indicate that roughly eighty percent of the Lefever singles built were plain-barrel field guns.

An A Grade double, only slightly more ornate than the basic Nitro Special, was added to the line in 1934. Workhorse guns, all of them.

As Ithaca geared up for wartime production, the Lefever single was first to go, discontinued in 1942. The Nitro Special hung on a bit longer and went out of production along with all of Ithaca's doubles in 1948.

Because they were built in such small numbers, the old Lefevers are hard to come by these days. A fair number of Nitro Specials still turn up on the market and fetch modest prices. The real gems, the Automatic Hammerless and the D.M. Lefevers, don't come cheap, but the hardest part is finding one. Those who own one or two seem to hang onto them – and with good reason. To understand why, just listen to the old-timers talk about the guns that Uncle Dan built.

THE CELEBRATED

ITHACA GUN

—:o:—

STRONGEST, SIMPLEST AND BEST AMERICAN GUN MANUFACTURED.

—:o:—

BAKER'S

LATEST AND BEST INVENTION.

—:o:—

MANUFACTURED BY THE

ITHACA GUN CO.

ITHACA, NEW YORK, U. S. A.

Ithaca Gun Company catalogue, 1885.

ITHACA

The Guns from Fall Creek

W hen William Baker parted company with L.C. Smith about 1880, he was at something of a loose end. He'd been a working gunmaker for more than ten years, successful both technically and financially, but always lacking the ability or the desire to put down roots.

Exactly what he did in the following months is a mystery. The 1880 Syracuse city directory lists W.H. Baker as a "segar maker," and he was still in Syracuse by 1881. But his mind teemed with ideas that had nothing to do with "segars," for whatever else he may have been, William Henry Baker was a shotgun man.

His old friend Leroy Smith, who had left his brother Lyman's company in Syracuse at the same time Baker did, was in Ithaca, and by the end of 1882, William Baker was there, too. A new partnership was forming, comprising Baker and Smith, Smith's brother-in-law George Livermore, Smith's son Lou, J.E. VanNatta, and Dwight McIntire. On February 7, 1883, they created W.H. Baker & Company, Gun Works. Their plant was a little wood-frame building on the outskirts of Ithaca, on the steep banks of Fall Creek.

By the time the first catalogue appeared, dated 1885, the operation was called Ithaca Gun Company. Baker apparently wanted his new design clearly distinguished from previous guns, for the 1886 catalogue carries the following by way of introduction:

> Having many inquiries as to what distinguishes the "Ithaca Gun" from the original "Baker Gun," of which I was the inventor, and for a time the manufacturer, I will say: The "Ithaca Gun" has the top lever, instead of the trigger action, an entirely new arrangement of locks, and construction, making it more desirable in every respect; for which reason it was thought best not to have it conflict in name with the old gun.

> Sincerely thanking my numerous friends for their liberal appreciation of my efforts to produce such work as our progressive shooting demands, and trusting that the "Ithaca Gun" will continue to merit their patronage and that the pleasant business relations formerly existing, may be continued with the Ithaca Gun Co. I am

> Very Truly,
W.H. Baker

Ithaca, N.Y., May, 1885

The covers of the the 1885 and 1886 catalogues show an engraving of a handsome top-lever gun labeled "the strongest, simplest and best American gun manufactured."

The first Ithaca, like the others of its time, was a hammer gun, but an unusual one. Instead of using sidelocks as he had earlier, Baker designed a sturdy boxlock action with the hammers mounted at the rear of the frame. This not only gave the sear and tumbler assemblies the greatest possible protection from damage and the elements, but it also made advantage of the boxlock's durability at the head of the stock.

In other respects, the gun was conventional: twist barrels with a doll's-head rib extension and an underbolt fastener. "Baker's latest and best invention," the catalogues say. They probably were right.

The Baker Model, as it came to be called, was made in 10- and 12-gauges only, with barrels 30 or 32 inches long. There were six grades altogether, from Quality A with English stub-twist barrels and American walnut stocks, through B, C, D, E, and F. The five higher grades were barreled in good twist and stocked with English walnut. Prices ranged from $35 for Quality A up to $200 for the elaborately engraved Quality F.

Ithaca's success apparently did no more to curb Baker's restlessness than had his earlier achievements with L.C. Smith. His brother, Dr. Ellis Baker, founded the Syracuse Forging Company in July 1885, and William wasn't long in joining the new venture. He left Ithaca in 1887 and was made plant superintendent in Syracuse. The name subsequently was changed to Syracuse Forging and Gun Company, predictably enough, and two new models of Baker gun were produced there. Following a fire that destroyed the plant early in 1889, the operation was moved a hundred miles west to Batavia. Production there was just getting under way when William Baker died on October 10.

William Baker left sportsmen and gunmakers a great legacy. His genius is unquestioned, his stature among American designers undiminished. The guns produced under his own name never have achieved the reputation they deserve, but without him there probably never would have been an L.C. Smith or an Ithaca.

Ithaca continued producing the Baker Model for a few years after Baker left the company, but the future clearly demanded a new design. Hammer guns were passing. The Baker Model went out of production in August 1889, with a total of 10,534 guns built.

By then, a new Ithaca gun was in production, a hammerless boxlock designed by toolmaker Fred Crass. The locks, although simple by some standards, were fairly complex systems involving cocking levers, mainsprings, sear springs, sears, and hammers, all as separate parts. Bolting was by means of an underlug and doll's-head extension. Catalogues made much of the self-compensating fore-end, pointing out that the "act of cocking the Gun draws the barrels more closely to the frame, and the levers for the most perfect check, taking all strain from the hinge joint." Baker had made similar claims for his fore-end design, and the two actually were not greatly different.

The Crass Ithaca was available in six grades, identified by numbers 1 through 6. Materials and decoration were virtually identical to the various Baker Model grades. The No. 1 sold for $50, No. 2 for $60, No. 3 for $80, No. 4 for $100, No. 5 for $150, and the lovely No. 6 for $200. All grades were chambered in 10, 12, and 16 gauges.

This first hammerless Ithaca was a popular gun. Over the eleven years it was in production, a total 76,847 were built.

If the Crass Model had any serious flaw, it was in the complexity of the locks. A few minor design changes made around the turn of the century by an engineer named Lewis created the Lewis Model, which appeared in 1904. (Before 1926, all Ithaca guns were named for their designers; Ithaca Gun Company was able to supply no information, not even first names, concerning Lewis or the man named Manier whose design followed Lewis'.)

Lewis altered the shape of the cocking levers and repositioned the leaf-type mainspring. Otherwise, there is little difference between the Lewis and Crass models. The Lewis Model was the first Ithaca chambered in 20-gauge, introduced, like the gun itself, in 1904. By 1906, when it was superseded, 29,569 Lewis Model guns were built.

Design work, however, was drawing closer to a breakthrough. With the appearance of the Manier Model in 1906, the Ithaca truly was a new gun. The locks were completely revised, the flat V-springs discarded in favor of coil springs, and the cocking system comprised a small pushrod instead of the cumbersome levers of previous models. The bolting system, too, was changed, with the doll's-head redesigned as a slotted rib extension, and a top hook was added to augment the underlug.

In all, 21,771 Manier Model Ithacas were built before production was discontinued in 1908.

Both the Lewis and Manier guns could well be considered transitional models, as their brief lifespans would seem to indicate continuous experimentation and design revision. It remained for Emile Flues to bring the old-style Ithacas to perfection.

Flues was a free-lance gun designer who lived in Bay City, Michigan, around the turn of the century, and he was a good one. The Flues Ithacas are wonderfully simple, extremely strong, and as thoughtfully designed as any American guns.

Emile Flues designed the greatest of the old-style Ithaca guns; No. 2 Grade.

The Flues Model Ithacas are fastened by both an underbolt and a rib extension and top hook.

By loosening a setscrew, the Flues Model underbolt can be adjusted to compensate for wear.

Flues reduced all of the various lock parts to three: hammer, sear, and mainspring. He elongated the hammer toes to form integral cocking levers that engage a sliding cocking piece fastened to the barrel lump – much the same principle that Ansley Fox had used just a couple of years earlier. Such direct leverage between barrels and locks makes the gun easy to cock and allows the use of a stiffer mainspring that, in turn, speeds lock time proportionately. The mainspring exerts its force downward on the hammer toe, well forward of the pivot point, an arrangement that allows a very short hammer fall – less, in fact, than half an inch.

Just after the Flues Model went into production, Ithaca employed Cornell University's engineering school to measure lock speed. The results showed a lock time of 1/625 second, a fact that Ithaca proudly reported in catalogues and advertising from 1910 until it took all double guns out of production after World War II. Today, some finely tuned guns can make an Ithaca seem glacially slow – but not many. Few factory guns, old-time or current, can match the old Ithaca triggers.

The Flues Model's bolting system is virtually the same as Manier's design. The top-hook bears against the rib extension at two points, and the underlug fits a deep bite in the barrel lump, a system the factory called "three-point bolting." Both the sliding bolt and the bite are deeply tapered to take up wear. As an additional means of keeping the action tight, the underbolt rides in a collar that's fitted with a heavy setscrew. When the screw is loosened, the bolt can be repositioned to seat more deeply into the bite. Regardless of factory claims, there is no such thing as a break-action gun that won't loosen, but the Ithaca will shrug off a lot of wear before it needs a trip to the gunsmith's.

The early hammerless Ithacas were offered in a multitude of grades. Lowest was the Field Gun, a plain, workmanlike shotgun devoid of decoration except for a bird dog stamped on either side of the frame. Other grades were numbered, 1 through 7. In addition to the standard numbers, there was a No. 1 Special that had fluid-steel barrels instead of the customary twist; a No. 1½ with slightly more engraving than a No. 1 and slightly less than a No. 2; and a special pigeon gun with Krupp steel barrels, called the No. 2 Krupp. All three were discontinued sometime before 1926. The No. 6, too, was dropped, first as a single trap gun in 1919 and then as a double in 1921.

Ithaca was unique among American makers in fashioning at least some of its own twist barrels. While others imported twist tubes from England or Belgium, Ithaca barrel-maker Bob Edwards was the only American to successfully forge his own, marketed under the trade name American Flag Damascus. Like Dan Lefever, Edwards was something of a legend in the American trade, widely known as Uncle Bob. He began his career in 1861 at a barrel shop in Brookton, New York, making both steel and twist barrels for the trade and for the U.S. government; according to old payroll records, he worked at Ithaca as early as 1882, which means that he was one of the original staff of the W.H. Baker works.

Nonetheless, the day of twist barrels was coming to a close. Some Ithaca guns were barreled in fluid steel as early as 1902, but the change came slowly. Just as the earliest breechloading guns met with mistrust and disapproval from the more conservative element among shooters, so steel barrels were spurned by some. There were some outrageous claims made about the old twist tubes, including sonorous pronouncements that they were in fact stronger than solid steel, but nitro-powder ammunition eventually proved its own point. Having seen some old barrels unwound and laid open by smokeless cartridges, I can only hope the old boys changed their minds with minimal loss of fingers and eyesight.

As the new century rolled into its second decade, Ithaca continued to flourish, turning out an average of 20,000 guns per year. Twenty-eight-gauge guns first appeared in the line in 1911. The company was financially healthy enough to absorb some smaller, less-stable gunmakers. About 1913, Ithaca bought Union Firearms Company of Toledo, Ohio, and about 1923 purchased the Wilkes-Barre Gun Company, founded by former Ithaca barrel-brazier George Parry. A great many sources claim that Ithaca also bought Syracuse Arms Company about 1915, but Ithaca Gun Company historian John McMorrow told me that company records contained no evidence of that purchase.

But Ithaca did buy Lefever Arms Company in 1915, a purchase that would further bolster Ithaca's standing in a market already thinning as small makers found the competition more than they could bear.

Ithaca's guns were earning a reputation for strength and reliability that extended beyond the upland fields and duck marshes. In 1908, Wells Fargo & Company contracted for a number of shotguns to be used by company guards. The first were delivered in February 1909: 12-gauge guns with 26-inch, cylinder-bore, fluid-steel barrels. Through June of that year, a total of 231 Wells Fargo guns were built, including thirty 10-gauge hammer guns built in May. These were of A Quality with 24-inch twist barrels.

In 1911, barrels were shortened to 24 inches and remained so as long as Ithaca built guns for Wells Fargo. With the exception of the 1909 10-gauges, all were barreled in solid steel. Production continued through June 1917, averaging about 100 guns per year. In addition to the factory serial numbers, taken from the Flues Model series, each gun carries a Wells Fargo number and the legend "W. F. & CO. EX." stamped on the frame.

Year-by-year production figures and serial numbers are listed in the Appendix.

One of the greatest – and certainly the most enduring – Ithacas appeared almost as the first shots of the European war were being fired. In 1914, Ithaca introduced its famous single-barrel trap gun.

Relatively little information on the early guns remains. There were four prototypes built in 1914, numbered 246892, -3, -4, and -5. The factory refers to the early singles as Flues Models, and Emile Flues probably was the principal designer. The serial numbers were taken from the same series as the Flues doubles, and the trap gun's bolting system was a cross-pin and underlug combination, much on the order of the Flues double.

Originally, it was available in the standard Ithaca grades, but about 1916, John Philip Sousa ordered a gun decorated to his own taste and thereby created the highest-grade Ithaca of all. At the time, the great bandmaster and composer was president of the Amateur Trap Shooters Association and one of the most famous men in America. The gun was exquisitely ornate, its frame, breech, fore-end iron, and furniture covered in small scroll and highlighted by dogs and ducks inlaid in gold. At Sousa's request, Ithaca master engraver Bill McGraw decorated the trigger guard with a bare-breasted mermaid worked in gold.

There's no way of knowing now whether it was the overall appeal of the gun itself or just the mermaid, but Ithaca decided to make it a standard grade, available on special order and named Sousa Grade, naturally. Most were single trap guns, but a few Sousa Grade doubles were built as well – three Flues Models and nine New Ithaca Double guns, although one of these was mistakenly designated "$1000 Grade." At first, the Sousa Grade sold for $500; in three years, it was up to $700 and continued to climb.

At the other end of the scale, the plain Victory Grade, priced at $75, was added to the line in 1919. As with the Ithaca doubles, the grades differed only in decoration and wood quality; otherwise, all Ithacas were identical.

By 1921, Frank Knickerbocker completed a design that made the Flues single obsolete, and the older gun was taken out of production. The first Knickerbocker gun – or simply Knick, as it came to be known – was No. 4000000, sent from the factory on May 31, 1922, to Mr. Bob Smith of Boston.

Even until very recently, the Knick was the ultimate trap gun, a paragon of ruggedness, simplicity, and handling quality. Hammer and sear are located in the center of the frame and powered by a vertically placed coil mainspring that bears against the hammer's toe. Cocking is accomplished by a rod and cam system, and the action is fastened by a double-wedge bolt near the top of the standing breech. This bears against twin extension lugs on the breech face;

when the Knick is locked, it's *locked*. Trap guns take more punishment than any other shotgun, and the Knick proved more than equal to the task.

The Knick drew trapshooters like ducks to sweet water. By 1935, six men had won the Grand American Handicap using the Ithaca single, a feat celebrated in catalogues and on company letterheads: A.E. Sheffield, Charles Young, Mose Newman, Elmer Starner, Charles Larson, and John Henry.

There were other fans, too. Annie Oakley shot an Ithaca, both in competition and in exhibitions. General Dwight Eisenhower and General George Marshall were given highly engraved presentation guns. Jack Dempsey and Al Capone owned special-order Ithaca guns, engraved by Bill McGraw.

The years brought changes to the Knick, at least cosmetically. The No. 6 Grade was discontinued in 1919, the Victory Grade about 1937 and the No. 7 in the early 1960s. In 1937, the Sousa Grade was renamed $1000 Grade; by the end of World War II, it was the $1500 Grade. After that, the name changed at intervals of a few years and in increments of $500. It was the $5000 Grade by 1975 and, to those who loved the Knick, worth every penny.

Even in its glory days, the Ithaca single wasn't built in great numbers. Total production probably was no more than 6000. Most are still in use.

Although certainly not a company to shy away from experiments, Ithaca never was much given to producing oddities. The doubles and the single trap and, after 1937, the Model 37 pump gun were the mainstays. But for a few years, Ithaca made one piece that is almost unique. They called it the Auto & Burglar Gun – a double shotgun with 10-inch barrels and a pistol stock. The Auto & Burglar was announced to the trade on June 5, 1922, a wicked-looking four-pound 20-gauge that sold for $37.50.

A shotgun-pistol isn't all that unusual. Before federal regulations placed minimum limits on barrel length and overall length, a number of makers produced one-hand shotguns. They usually were 28-gauges and .410s, and virtually all were single-shot. So far as I know, Ithaca is the only company that ever made a double.

From the trigger guard to the fore-end, the Auto & Burglar looks like any 20-bore Ithaca. It has double triggers, a tang safety, and the conventional snap-on splinter fore-end. The pistol grip has a sharp drop and a tall spur at the top to keep the gun from slipping back through the hand under recoil. The barrels have no choke.

The earliest of them were Flues Models, and about 2500 were built. When the New Ithaca Double replaced the Flues in 1926, the Auto & Burglar changed, too, and 1240 standard versions were built in NID design. No records exist to indicate special-order Auto & Burglar Guns made in

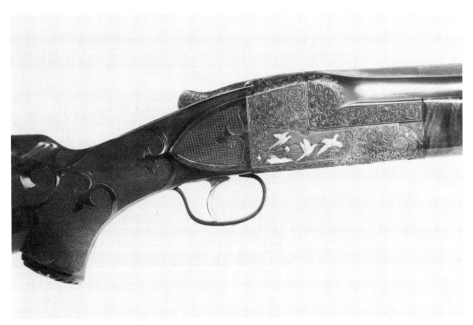

$5000 Grade Ithaca Knick.

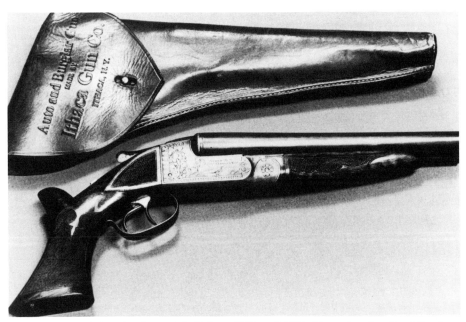

The Ithaca Auto & Burglar Gun was built from 1922 until 1933. Shown here is a No. 4 Grade, the only high-grade Auto & Burglar ever built.

Flues Model, although there was at least one – a little No. 4 Grade, probably the only high-grade Auto & Burglar ever made. There also is evidence that at least one 28-gauge Flues was made; so far as the records indicate, it was the only one.

In the NID series, records show eight Auto & Burglars built on special order: five .410s (including one made in 1928 for Emile Flues), two 20-gauges, and one 16-bore. I hope whoever bought the 16 was a big man, because even in 20-gauge, the Auto & Burglar is a fearsome gun to shoot.

Years ago, when I worked as an officer of the Mt. Pleasant, Iowa, police department, I found an Auto & Burglar Gun in the arms locker. Nobody could remember exactly how it came to be there, and it hadn't been fired in years. Being at the time still heavily into the I'll-try-anything-once scene, I took it out to the police range one afternoon. After about half a box of shells, I couldn't decide which end of the damn thing did the most damage. Grip-to-bore angle was at least eighty degrees, making the recoil purely savage. There was no way to keep a straight wrist, thanks to that plow-handle grip, and it did its best to crease my head every time I pulled the trigger. It doesn't take much of that to enjoy all you can stand. I was glad to stow it back in the locker and shoot my .44 Magnum for fun.

The Auto & Burglar was discontinued in 1933, and for years federal regulations made it something of an outlaw. But about ten years ago, it was reclassified as a curio, so anyone holding a valid collector's license can buy one legally. But neither easily nor cheaply. A great many undoubtedly have been destroyed and, given a total production that probably didn't exceed 4500, Auto & Burglar Guns are scarce these days. Even one in semi-decent condition is likely to cost $800 or more. Believe me, you can live without it.

As good as the Flues Model was, Ithaca designers continued their quest for improvement. Cartridge design was rapidly changing to make best advantage of the new nitro powders, and gunmakers continually sought means of adapting guns to more powerful ammunition. Cartridge-makers also were in the midst of a great housecleaning, ridding themselves of literally thousands of redundant loads and standardizing shell cases. Consequently, Ithaca and the others began standardizing their chamber boring. In 1924, Ithaca established $2\frac{3}{4}$ inches as standard boring in 12 and 20 gauges, $2\frac{9}{16}$ inches in 16-gauge, and $2\frac{7}{8}$ inches in 10-gauge.

New ammunition ultimately demanded a new gun. Since it was developed during black-powder days, the Flues Model's capacity for withstanding stress was limited, and by the early '20s it was clear that simply modifying Flues' design wasn't the answer. The new gun wasn't long in coming. When it appeared late in 1925, it marked the beginning of a new era – the Ithaca

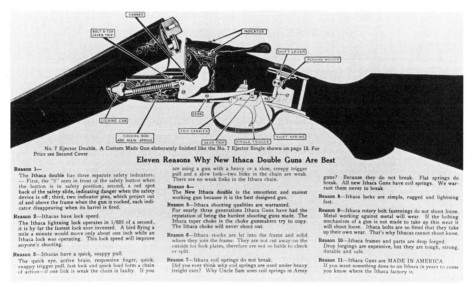

No. 7 Ejector Double. A Custom Made Gun elaborately finished like the No. 7 Ejector Single shown on page 15. For Price see Second Cover

Eleven Reasons Why New Ithaca Double Guns Are Best

Reason 1—
The Ithaca double has three separate safety indicators: — First, the "S" seen in front of the safety button when the button is in safety position; second, a red spot back of the safety slide, indicating danger when the safety device is off; third, two indicator pins, which project out of and above the frame when the gun is cocked, each indicator disappearing when its barrel is fired.

Reason 2—Ithacas have lock speed.
The Ithaca lightning lock operates in 1/625 of a second, it is by far the fastest lock ever invented. A bird flying a mile a minute would move only about one inch while an Ithaca lock was operating. This lock speed will improve anyone's shooting.

Reason 3—Ithacas have a quick, snappy pull.
The quick eye, active brain, responsive finger, quick, snappy trigger pull, fast lock and quick load form a chain of action—if one link is weak the chain is faulty. If you

are using a gun with a heavy or a slow, creepy trigger pull and a slow lock—two links in the chain are weak. There are no weak links in the Ithaca chain.

Reason 4—
The New Ithaca double is the smoothest and easiest working gun because it is the best designed gun.

Reason 5—Ithaca shooting qualities are warranted.
For nearly three generations Ithaca Guns have had the reputation of being the hardest shooting guns made. The Ithaca taper choke is the choke gunmakers try to copy. The Ithaca choke will never shoot out.

Reason 6—Ithaca stocks are let into the frame and solid where they join the frame. They are not cut away on the outside for lock plates, therefore are not so liable to check or split.

Reason 7—Ithaca coil springs do not break.
Did you ever think why coil springs are used under heavy freight cars? Why Uncle Sam uses coil springs in Army

guns? Because they do not break. Flat springs do break. All new Ithaca Guns have coil springs. We warrant them never to break.

Reason 8—Ithaca locks are simple, rugged and lightning fast.

Reason 9—Ithaca rotary bolt fastenings do not shoot loose. Metal working against metal will wear. If the bolting mechanism of a gun is not made to take up this wear it will shoot loose. Ithaca bolts are so fitted that they take up their own wear. That's why Ithacas cannot shoot loose.

Reason 10—Ithaca frames and parts are drop forged. Drop forgings are expensive, but they are tough, strong, durable and safe.

Reason 11—Ithaca Guns are MADE IN AMERICA. If you want something done to an Ithaca in years to come you know where the Ithaca factory is.

The New Ithaca Double is radically different from the Flues Model and is the greatest Ithaca double of all.

shotgun come of age. They called it the New Ithaca Double, a simple enough name for what unquestionably is the finest Ithaca of them all.

Its outward appearance isn't much different from the Flues guns, but the NID was a radically new gun inside. The Flues cocking system, with its sliding cocking piece and long hammer toes, was replaced by a push-rod pinned to the hammer and operated by a cocking cam in the fore-end iron. The heavy coil mainspring is wound around the cocking rod so that hammer movement, in both cocking and firing, is always actuated from precisely the same angle. Lock time still was the famous 1/625 second.

Ithaca also did away with Emile Flues' sliding underbolt, so that the NID relies solely on the rotary top hook for fastening. This allowed more steel to remain in the frame for strength, and the top hook certainly is sufficient for solid bolting. In the earliest guns, however, the slightest deviation in the radius of the top hook would cause the action to pop open when the first barrel went off. An unnerving little quirk, no doubt.

But that particular bug was soon evicted, and the NID set about proving itself one of the best American guns of all. It was offered in eight grades altogether: Field, No. 1, No. 2, No. 3, No. 4, No. 5, No. 7, and the fabulous Sousa Special. All were stocked in good American walnut and barreled in solid steel. Early NID's had snail-ear cocking indicators at the top of the frame; these were discontinued in 1936.

Ithaca's first .410-bore gun was added to the NID line in 1926 and was available in all grades. Both .410-bore and 28-gauge guns were bored for 2½-inch shells until 1931, when chambers were lengthened to 2⅞ inches. The .410 was lengthened again, to three inches, in 1935.

Barrels could be 26, 28, 30, or 32 inches long. Weight ranged from 5¾ pounds in .410-bore to nine pounds in Super 10-gauge. Available options included a ventilated rib, beavertail fore-end, ejectors, and single trigger.

In 1921, Ithaca introduced the Lefever Nitro Special, details of which are in the Lefever chapter. A second economy gun, the Western Long Range Double, appeared in 1929. Both guns were built on essentially the same action; most parts, in fact, are interchangeable. The Western was available in 12-gauge with 26-, 28-, 30-, or 32-inch barrels; in 16-gauge with barrels 26, 28, or 30 inches; in 20-gauge with 26- or 28-inch barrels in .410-bore with 26-inch barrels only.

In 1945, three years before it and all other Ithaca-made doubles were taken out of production, the Western Long Range gun sold for $27.25. A rubber recoil pad cost an additional $3, a single trigger $3.53, and ivory beads could be had for $1.51.

When the Western Cartridge Company developed the 3½-inch Magnum 10-gauge cartridge in 1932, no factory gun was chambered for it. Spencer Olin of Western struck a deal with Ithaca vice-president Lou Smith to create one of the most famous wildfowl guns ever built. The Ithaca Magnum 10 is a heavy-frame version of the NID, scaled up in proportion to the big cartridge. To help accommodate the stresses of the heavy 10-gauge load, Ithaca redesigned the barrel lump to extend through the bottom of the frame and act as a recoil lug. Thirty-two-inch barrels were standard, 34-inch tubes optional.

Captain Charles Askins, one of the most influential gun writers of the time, owned the first Magnum 10, a No. 5E with serial number 500000, and did much to bring the big gun to the attention of American gunners. He said: "It is a magnificent arm...I take the Ithaca 10 when I really need range."

The Magnum 10 was built on special order only and took about six months to complete. It was available in all grades. Although the serial numbers range from 500000 to 501010, only about 850 guns actually were made. After 1937, about fifty of the Magnum frames were fitted with 12-gauge barrels bored for the three-inch cartridge. Production of the Magnum 10 was discontinued in 1942.

Tough as the mid-1930s were for all the gunmakers, the NID was in its heyday, popular the world over. Major Harry P. White wrote in *Sportsman's Digest*: "How much grief will a good gun stand? I have an ancient Ithaca that lay in the bottom of the Yangtze River in China for over 48 hours, went through two Sahara Desert sand storms, was laid on by a camel, has had thousands of the heaviest possible loads fired through it and it's still on the job."

By 1935, the Field Grade sold for $39.75, the No. 1 for $51.35, and the No. 2 for $62.15. In these grades, the Magnum 10 cost $10.80 extra. The higher grades, which now came with ejectors as standard equipment, began with No. 3E at $100.10; the No. 4E was $130, the No. 5E $189.60, the No. 7E $379.20, and the Sousa Special sold for $812.50. Any of these could be had in Magnum 10-gauge at no additional charge.

The line of doubles also included a skeet gun, introduced in 1935, a Field Grade with a beavertail fore-end. It sold for the same price as the Field Grade game gun, but for an additional $46, it could be fully set up with ejectors, vent rib, single trigger, and ivory beads.

The Victory Grade single trap gun cost $108.40 and the No. 4 $146.25. Prices for the No. 5, No. 7, and Sousa Special singles were the same as those for the doubles of the same grades.

No. 4 Grade Flues Model, a faithful old friend.

111

The Ithaca doubles, like the others, were casualties of World War II. During the war, the factory produced .45 Colts and some Model 37 pump guns for aircraft gunners' training. Afterwards, attempts to resuscitate the old doubles soon faltered and failed. The age of technology and firepower had arrived, demand clearly ran in favor of repeaters, and the cost of building good doubles had gone well past what the average shooter was willing to pay. So Ithaca let the old ones go in 1948. Only the single trap remained. The last No. 4E singles were shipped in 1977. It was still available on special order when Ithaca closed down in December 1978 and later reappeared during the Ithaca renascence. The last Dollar Grade was finished in May 1981 and the last Knick of all, a No. 5E, in June 1982. Ithaca Gun Company declared bankruptcy in 1986 and probably will build no more guns, certainly no more single traps.

All told, Ithaca's craftsmanship never was as meticulous as Parker's, nor did the guns even approach the graceful beauty of the Foxes or the old-style Smiths. But for excellent guns at good prices, they were hard to beat, and the Knick probably is the best of all the American singles. For many years, my favorite bird gun was a No. 4 Flues. When I found it, the poor old thing was a cosmetic wreck, and the wood looked as if it had been attacked by beavers. With a new stock, a thorough scrubbing, a choke job, and fresh blacking on the barrels, it and I went through a lot of miles and a lot of birds – ducks, geese, pheasant, quail, turkey, woodcock, grouse, prairie chickens, sharptails, barnyard pigeons, and more. It was the only gun that ever got me a limit of ruffed grouse – five birds – with six shots, and the only gun that's ever taken a true double of woodcock in my hands. I may yet do both those things again with some other gun, but I don't think I'll feel the same way I did then. Other guns impress me more, for various reasons; none ever has been a more faithful friend.

REMINGTON MODEL 32

The Hard-Times Wonder

When the Great War was over, America reveled like an amusement park gone out of control. She glittered and danced in the arms of jazz and bathtub gin, lavished herself with baubles, flirted with decadence and scandal. Shoeless Joe Jackson and seven other Chicago White Sox players were indicted for conspiring with gamblers to fix the 1919 World Series. A craze for marathon dancing stirred controversy across the country. Thousands of women mourned the death of Rudolph Valentino; one even shot herself in a fit of grief. Mae West paid a $500 fine and spent ten days in jail, convicted of indecency for her role in a Broadway production titled *Sex.* Charles Lindbergh flew the Atlantic alone in the cockpit of "The Spirit of St. Louis," and Babe Ruth hit sixty home runs.

For a while, they were golden years. Wealthy sportsmen demanded more and more elaborately finished guns and were willing to pay prices till then unheard of. The Sousa Grade Ithaca sold for $700, the Deluxe Grade L.C. Smith for $1000. In 1923, A.H. Fox offered its GE Grade gun on special order for $1100. Parker topped them all with the fabulous, $1500 Invincible.

The party lasted just over ten years, until October 1929, and then the gilded palace fell in ruins, the atmosphere turned from gay to grim.

The effects of the economic crash rippled outward in both space and time like a great lurch of geologic plates. At the epicenter, the paper markets – stocks, bonds, and the like – crumbled first. By Thanksgiving 1929, the stock market was a shambles, its fortunes rendered as insubstantial as the paper and ink that sustained it. Hard goods, more resilient, kept their balance longer, but the aftershocks eventually caught up. Within a few years, virtually no commercial endeavor remained unshaken.

The firearms industry reacted like all the rest. The weak fell first, particularly those whose products were most closely tied to a buying power grown fat on a diet of paper. The yeoman guns, like those who bought them, held out longer. Between 1931 and 1933, the total value of all products in the firearms industry decreased by about $1.4 million, a thirteen-percent decline. Not surprisingly, the market for double guns collapsed almost altogether; the number of guns produced fell from nearly 40,000 in 1931 to fewer than 8,000 by 1933. The resale market suffered just as badly. High-grade guns for sale at a pittance gathered dust in pawnshops and gun-club racks.

But while the demand for highly decorated shotguns hit rock bottom in the

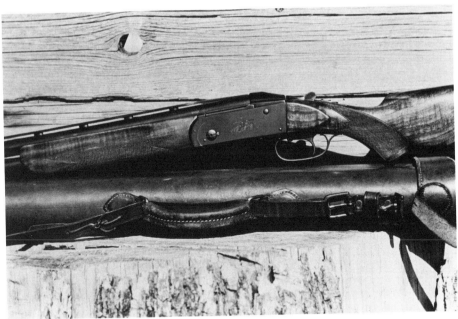

The Remington Model 32 was the first factory over-under made in America.

early 1930s, the gun market itself was far from dead. Hunting and shooting were no less popular than before, and well-built guns that could be offered at reasonable prices continued to sell. Repeaters, both pumps and autoloaders, had been selling steadily stronger since the turn of the century. But even in hard times, there was still a place for the double.

Target shooters, especially, preferred the double's superb handling qualities, which no repeater could match. The new game of skeet, invented just after World War I, became extremely popular during the late 1920s, attracting legions of gunners. Shotguns tailored to the games opened a whole new market, and the gunmakers were quick to seize it.

As he had often done during his long career, John Browning showed others the way. His Belgian-built Superposed, the last gun John Browning designed, appeared on the American market in 1931 and immediately caught the fancy of target shooters who recognized features of the over-under as superior, for their purposes, to even the classic side-by-side.

Among American makers, Remington Arms was the first to recognize the over-under as the coming thing. Remington had built double guns before – a series of excellent side-by-sides, both hammer guns and hammerless, from 1874 to 1910 – but the over-under offered something completely new, something for the future. In May 1930, Remington began design work on what was to become the first machine-made over-under shotgun ever built in America. It would be named the Model 32.

The new gun was the brainchild of Crawford C. Loomis, who had begun his career at Remington in 1912, revising the Browning-designed Model 11 autoloader to fit Remington's production techniques. In the years that followed, he became one of Remington's most prolific designers, creating, among others, the Model 31, the only pump gun in the world that was as good as Winchester's Model 12. For the Model 32, Loomis ultimately earned a total of six patents, dating from March 3, 1931, to July 14, 1936.

When it first appeared on the market in March 1932, the new Remington was greeted as the herald of a new age. F.C. Ness, writing in the May 1932 issue of *The American Rifleman*, had this to say: "Its advent marks the beginning of a new era for shotgun enthusiasts because the low price achieved at last places the over-and-under type of gun within the reach of the average gunner." As it turned out, he was right. The Standard Grade Browning Superposed sold for $107.50 at the time; the standard Model 32 cost $75.

It was more than just a well-made gun at a good price. Crawford Loomis' rich imagination and technical brilliance had come up with features never seen before on a factory shotgun of any kind.

First, the bolting system. The over-under gun poses some unique problems in designing a way to fasten the action. In order to accommodate the vertically stacked barrels, the over-under's frame has to be deep to begin with; add an action joint that pivots on the typical barrel lump and fastens with an underbolt, and it's deeper still. The rib extension and top hook that serve so splendidly on a side-by-side gun are hopeless for an over-under.

Browning chose a shallow barrel lump and underbolt for the Superposed. That he had to split the lump to make room for the cocking lever suggests that the approach is a compromise. Crawford Loomis saw a better way.

His solution is ingeniously simple. Instead of using hooks or pins or bolts, Loomis designed a sliding cover that holds the barrels in place from the top. Operated by a conventional top latch, the cover rides in slots milled into the top of the frame and engages stout rails on the sides of the upper barrel. Bearing surfaces are tapered to compensate for wear. Because it is linked eccentrically to the top latch, the cover travels slightly less than a quarter-inch forward and back and not only bolts the action but also shrouds the junction of barrels and breech, protecting the shooter from gas blowback in the event of a pierced primer or ruptured case head.

Instead of a barrel lump and full-width hinge pin, the Model 32 action pivots on trunnions mounted in each side of the frame. These match with semicircular notches on the sides of the lower barrel. This arrangement, which

115

now is the virtual world standard design, allows for a shallower frame, for one thing, and, for another, takes optimum advantage of the over-under's inherent superiority in recoil dynamics.

Unlike the bores of a side-by-side double, which lie in a plane well above the shooter's shoulder, an over-under's barrels – the lower one, especially – align virtually straight with the heel of the buttstock. Moreover, because the barrels must shoot to the same point of impact at a given distance, bore centers of all double guns are farther apart at the breech than at the muzzle. Recoil force, therefore, tends to drive a side-by-side's buttstock upward while at the same time torquing right or left. An over-under, on the other hand, tends to recoil nearly straight back against the shoulder. The slight downward torque of the lower barrel – customarily the first fired – directs recoil toward the shoulder and away from the cheek.

These phenomena usually aren't of much consequence in the game fields, where shots are fewer, but cumulative recoil certainly is something to be reckoned with on the firing line at trap or skeet. Which goes a long way toward explaining why the over-under is the choice of so many serious target shooters.

If there's an equivalent in game shooting, it's driven birds. The over-under never has been very popular in England, and the British never have been fond of heavy loads, but even so, shooting incoming pheasants at high angles all day can leave you feeling as if you've gone all fifteen with Muhammad Ali. Any day I feel compelled to cork off two cases of shells, they will either be extremely light loads or I'll shoot them from an over-under.

(One day in 1888, Lord Walsingham, the great English game shot, killed 1000 grouse, played cards until five o'clock the next morning, and remarked that he'd never felt better in his life. Among my shooting chums, it's common knowledge that Lord Walsingham was a lot tougher than I am.)

Another of the Model 32's novel features – or at least novel at the time – is the absence of fillets between the barrels. Where Browning and others soldered thin strips of steel from muzzles to breech, Crawford Loomis, evidently thinking of target shooters, left open space. Heat dissipation is the main reason. Gun barrels heat rapidly in target shooting, which produces both visible heat waves and physical changes in the barrel itself. You can lose sight of a target in the shimmering mirage of heat waves, and a hot, expanding barrel that's firmly fastened to a cooler one can cause a noticeable change in the shot swarm's point of impact.

The Model 32's separated barrels expose more surface to the air, promoting optimum heat loss by convection. Leaving off the fillets also reduces the weight of the barrels by an ounce or two, which permits slightly thicker-walled

The Model 32's barrels are not rigidly joined at the muzzles, allowing them to expand independently.

tubes for the same balance and overall weight. In the prototypes and perhaps in a few of the first production guns, the barrels were rigidly joined at the muzzles, which did nothing to solve the heat-expansion problem. This was remedied early on with a slip-ring barrel hanger, a principle the factory called the Remington Floating Barrel. The hanger is soldered to the upper barrels and simply forms a loop around the lower one, so that either barrel can expand and contract without affecting the other.

In the grips of an enthusiasm for selling guns – certainly forgivable considering the state of things in the 1930s – Remington even claimed that the separated barrels reduced air resistance to one's gun swing. Maybe so. I've owned a dozen or more over-unders of every type and have shot them many thousands of times at both targets and game, and I've never noticed the difference. If it does help, that's fine with me; my swing needs all the help it can get.

The earliest 32s had double triggers, but by 1937 all of the target guns were made with an excellent single selective trigger, factory-adjusted to a weight of pull between 3½ and 5 pounds. In 1938, the single trigger became standard for all models. Unlike Browning's recoil-set single trigger, the Remington trigger is mechanical and shifts instantly from one sear to the other, even if the first hammer falls on a dud shell or an empty chamber. The selector is a button in the forward end of the trigger itself. Lock time is extremely fast, and both the sears of my old 32TC trap gun break at about four pounds with a crisp, clean release that makes a lot of newer guns seem pretty shabby by comparison. I've never had them honed; so far as I know, they're just they way they were when the gun left the factory fifty-five years ago.

For an inexpensive gun, the Remington 32 has some thoughtful features about it. The ejectors, though complex by current standards, work as well as any; all Model 32s had them. The safety, a conventional thumb-button on the top tang, is adjustable. There are three tapped screw-holes in the side of the top tang, accessible when the buttstock is removed. By moving a setscrew from one hole to another, the safety can be made automatic or manual or it can be locked out altogether. If you fail to shoot at a trap or skeet target because you forgot to take the safety off, it's counted as a miss, and some trap guns are made with no safety at all. That's fine on the trap field, but trap guns are dandy tools for high-flying doves or ducks, and a field gun without a safety is a disaster looking for a good place to happen. Some shooters prefer a safety that automatically clicks on each time the top is opened; others don't. With the Model 32, you can have it any way you want.

The Model 32 was intended to be a high-quality gun at a modest price, and most of the factory's attention went toward performance and reliable

F Grade engraving by Carl Ennis, c. 1938. (Photo courtesy Remington Arms Company.)

mechanics. To keep production cost at a minimum, Remington never built the 32 in any gauge but 12. Still, there were high grades available, some of them wonderfully ornate.

The lowest grade was the 32A Standard – a plain gun with skillfully checkered, straight-grained American walnut stocks, decorated only with a bird dog roll-stamped on each side of the frame. The 32 Skeet, 32S Trap Special, and 32TC Target grades were similar in appearance to the Standard Grade, although they were stocked with progressively fancier wood. The high grades – 32D Tournament, 32E Expert, and 32F Premier – were treated with excellent hand engraving, fancy checkering, and highly figured walnut.

A, D, E, and F grades were available with 26-, 28-, or 30-inch barrels, either plain or with an optional solid rib. The skeet gun could be had with 26- or 28-inch tubes; plain barrels were standard, both solid and vent ribs available at extra charge. The TC came fitted with a vent rib on 30- or 32-inch barrels. You could get extra sets of barrels for all models and grades.

Although the Model 32 never reached the point of being absurdly expensive, rising manufacturing costs inevitably hiked the prices. The Standard Grade cost $99.50 by 1936. The 1939 catalogue lists the Standard at $126, the 32D at $276.50, the 32E at $326.50, and the 32F at $411.50. Custom stock dimensions cost an additional $15 for Standard, Skeet, and TC guns and came free of charge in the high grades. Extra barrels cost $60 a set.

A year later, as war once again stalked the world, the Standard gun was up to $153.55, extra barrels $73.15. The Skeet sold for $157.50 with plain barrels, $166.90 with solid rib, and $182 with vent rib. The TC cost $188.70, the 32D $336.85, 32E $397.80, and 32F $501.35.

The 1941 catalogue showed only the TC, at $164.10, and noted that a shortage of raw materials would delay delivery of all other models until the following year. By then, though, it was a different world. In 1942, Remington converted its machinery to produce military hardware, and the Model 32 was discontinued. It appeared again in the 1947 catalogue but with an overprint that read NOT AVAILABLE.

In his excellent book, *The American Shotgun*, David Butler quotes 5053 guns as total production – a figure that Remington Arms refuses to confirm, deny, or amend. I have no reason to dispute Butler, nor have I any reason to quarrel with the Texas gun dealer who told me that he once owned a Model 32 with a serial number in the 6000 range. Suffice it to say that about 6000 of them were built over the ten-year period between 1932 and 1942. Production runs of only 600 guns or so each year gave Remington some thorny problems with only expensive solutions. Like all double guns, the 32 required a lot of hand fitting, and labor costs were going up. Faced with that and with the options of either retooling machinery to produce only a few guns each year or leaving the machines tooled up and idle most of the time, Remington cost accountants saw little likelihood that the Model 32 could compete in the post-war market.

But it was too good to die. In the late '40s, Remington sold manufacturing rights for the Model 32 to the old Austrian firm of Heinrich Krieghoff, which by then had moved from its old home in Suhl to the newly created West German Federal Republic. In its new factory at Ulm, Krieghoff revised some aspects of Crawford Loomis' original design and began producing the Krieghoff Model 32 – such a close copy of the Remington that components of the fore-end, the top latch, the ejector system, and the bolting mechanism are interchangeable.

Target shooters embraced the Krieghoff as fondly as they had the old Remington, and for nearly thirty years it was the standard by which target guns were judged worldwide. In the late '70s, responding to competition from Italy, Krieghoff redesigned the gun somewhat and renamed it K-80. It's now marketed under the style Shotguns of Ulm; in most respects, it's still the old Model 32, and it's still a great gun.

Almost from the moment the Model 32 was discontinued, American shooters besieged Remington with pleas to build the old gun again. For years, the answer was the same: too expensive. But by the late '60s computer technology opened a whole new world of possibilities in gun design and manufacture, and a team of Remington engineers began working with designer John Linde, seeking to do what Crawford Loomis had done a generation earlier – design a well-made over-under that combined high quality and a reasonable price.

Design work and factory tool-up took four years. When the Model 3200 came on the market in 1973, it wasn't a $75 gun, but considering the economic differences between 1932 and 1973, a base price of $450 was no bad deal.

It looks like the Model 32, but most of the similarities are only skin-deep. The frame has more mass to it, largely because the designers added curved lugs on either side of the barrels at the breech; these fit into recesses milled inside the frame. The trigger, too, was redesigned and lock time reduced to about 1.6 milliseconds. The safety, a clever but not very convenient mechanism, also is the barrel selector. Overall, the Model 3200 is tough and reliable. It's also heavier than it needs to be, and though not at all a bad-handling gun, it doesn't have the same good feel that the old 32 has.

Field, trap, and skeet versions were available from the beginning. Highly ornate target guns, called "One of 1000," were built in 1973 (trap) and 1974 (skeet). A magnum waterfowl gun appeared in 1975. A live-bird model, priced at $1175, came on the market in 1979, followed in 1980 by a skeet gun with four sets of barrels.

The Model 3200 never really caught on as a field gun, probably because of its weight and blossoming price tag, and the Field Grade was discontinued in 1978. The standard Trap Grade had gone out of production the year before. The more ornate Competition Grade target guns and the four-barrel skeet set held on longer, but by the early '80s sales were flagging badly. Remington discontinued all versions of the Model 3200 in 1984.

There are still plenty of 3200s on the used-gun market now, but the old Model 32s are growing harder and harder to come by. You can search for years without finding one of the high grades; not even the factory knows how many D, E, and F grades were built, but there couldn't have been more than a handful in all. Presentation or custom-built guns seem to have been equally few, although there was at least one – a Model 32 with two sets of vent-rib barrels, single trigger and fancy wood that was, according to Remington, "shipped to Kerr Sport Shop intended for Clark Gable." (Gable liked shooting and hunting almost as much as he appreciated the company of lovely women. In June 1936, Carole Lombard gave him a DHE Parker 28-gauge as a token of her affection. It should happen to you and me.)

A Model 32 in original condition can be almost as hard to find as a high grade. The wide, flat expanses of steel in the frame made it a favorite candidate for custom engraving, and a lot of Model 32s were engraved and inlaid in Germany during the 1950s, when a lot of excellent German workmanship could be had for very little money. Some of those are magnificent, but upgrades aren't the real, factory quill. The majority of 32s probably were target guns, and target shooters being what we are, most of them have by now been restocked, reribbed, reblued, or in some cases, utterly butchered. Whoever owned my old TC gun before I did was at least merciful enough not to alter the stocks (most of the original varnish was even intact), but for some reason he found it necessary to have a new rib put on. No matter. It shoots, and that's why I bought it. It's a dandy pigeon gun, and it's even won some trapshooting trophies for me. The way I shoot, that's a good track record for any gun. It'd be worth more if it were completely original, but I wouldn't like it any better.

Still, a 32 is a 32, and that's enough to fetch a handsome price. In the early '30s, a Remington advertisement showed a Model 32 and posed the question: "Would you pay $1000 for this gun?" At the time, it was an effective approach. Nowadays, though, $1000 is a bargain for just about any Model 32 you can find – if you can find one at all.

WINCHESTER MODEL 21

The Last American Classic

On November 28, 1926, U.S. Secretary of Commerce Herbert Hoover described the American standard of living as the highest in the nation's history. Both production and consumption had reached higher levels than ever before. Americans owned thirty-nine percent of the world's automobiles. At the end of 1927, General Motors paid out more than $65 million to its shareholders in the largest single stock dividend ever. Three months later, Wall Street set a new record for a day's trading, with nearly five million shares changing hands.

But for some, the flash and glitter of the Roaring Twenties was a counterfeit bauble wearing thin. Secretary Hoover's 1926 report conceded that some unemployment, primarily in the textile industry and in coal mining, blemished the otherwise rosy economic picture. By 1928, the Commerce and Labor departments were at odds over just how serious the unemployment problem really was. Commerce said that two million Americans had no jobs; Labor put the figure at four million – ten percent of the work force. In a frighteningly short time, Secretary Hoover, as President Hoover, would learn that things could get a lot worse.

In the gun trade, cracks began to show in the pleasure palace walls early on. Even by the mid-1920s, one of the giants was coming to its knees.

At the turn of the century, Winchester Repeating Arms Company had the sporting-arms market by the tail, courtesy of John Browning's particular genius. Between 1883 and 1900, Winchester bought manufacturing rights to a total of forty-four Browning guns. The ten that actually went into production – seven rifles and three shotguns – were the best repeaters in the world, and they gave Winchester a position in the market that no other manufacturer could touch.

It all began to change in 1902, when Browning refused to sell his new autoloading shotgun outright and Winchester president T.G. Bennett refused to pay Browning a royalty for manufacturing the gun. Within four years, both Fabrique Nationale and Remington Arms were producing the Automatic-5, and Winchester began losing ground in the shotgun market. In the mid-1910s, the Model 12 pump gun infused the company with some new vitality, but the war in Europe soon brought production of American sporting guns to a virtual standstill.

The demand for military hardware was at first a windfall, but Winchester's expansion proved too rapid and ultimately ill-planned. After the Armistice, the company was left with newly constructed machine shops and warehouses that could not be integrated into its peacetime operations. Labor costs began to climb, and a series of fixed-price contracts acquired during the war became a steady drain on Winchester's already overburdened resources. As the 1920s wore on, first one item and then another was added to the line of products in hopes that diversity would stop the decline. But roller skates and radiators and flashlights and diaper-washing machines weren't the answer. Winchester common stock, which had reached an absurd value of $2500 a share during the war, was almost worthless ten years later.

But even though it was caught in the maelstrom of twentieth-century economics and suffering from mismanagement at the corporate helm, Winchester's design department hummed with creative energy. Late in the '20s, chief designer Thomas Crossley Johnson, William Roehmer, and George Lewis began work on a new gun, unique under the circumstances and, to all appearances, foolhardy.

For one thing, it was a double gun, an odd choice in a market infatuated with repeaters. For another, it was a gun unlike anything that Winchester had built before.

It wasn't, though, the first double to bear the Winchester name. In 1878, responding to an unusually high demand for game guns in New York City, Winchester imported a number of guns from England and sold them through its store at 312 Broadway. The guns were built by W. & C. Scott, Christopher Bonehill, Richard Redman, and other Birmingham makers, and they sold so successfully that Winchester subsequently ordered another lot, these to be engraved with the company name. These were 10- and 12-gauge hammer guns (and at least one 16), twist-barreled and fitted with rebounding locks. The higher grades were treated to some scroll engraving. Dollar for dollar, they were as good as any American guns of the period.

Their popularity started the company thinking about manufacturing its own shotguns, something that Winchester had never done before. Factory designs were in the works by 1881, and limited production began in 1882 – doubles built on barrels purchased from English and American sources, with the rest of the parts made in New Haven. Apparently, only a handful actually were completed.

The American shotgun market at the time was minuscule to begin with, and English makers supplied the greater share of it. Colt, too, was beginning to turn out high-quality double guns, and Winchester realized that selling imported guns was one thing while investing in full-scale production to compete in an already thin market was quite another. Both companies

Early Model 21s were built with double triggers.

concluded that a couple of big slices of the economic pie were better than several small ones, and in 1882 they agreed that Winchester wouldn't manufacture doubles if Colt would get out of the ammunition business.

The following year, in response to nearly twenty years of lobbying by the arms industry, the U.S. government imposed a thirty-five-percent tariff on imported guns. It was a long-term benefit to the American trade, but in the short-term it wrecked the market for the English Winchesters. In May 1884, the New York shop sold off the inventory.

What Winchester got from the whole affair was a keen appreciation of what might be gained from the shotgun market. Repeaters, Winchester's stock in trade, naturally were especially tempting. Christopher Spencer had just brought out his slide-action gun, and even though it wasn't setting the world afire, the whole notion held promise. Winchester would choose a John Browning lever-action, the Model 1889, as its first real venture into shotgun building, but facing the grim wasteland of the Great Depression forty years later, some memory of how auspiciously the double-gun trade had begun must have rung a faint bell in the executive offices.

By 1929, the only top-lever, break-action gun ever in full production at the Winchester factory was the Model 20, an inexpensive single-barrel built from 1919 to 1924. Since the new double was the company's second attempt at that type of action, it was named the Model 21. Production began in 1929, and the first guns were delivered to warehouse inventory in March 1930.

Hardly anyone noticed. The stock market collapse was the death blow for Winchester Repeating Arms. When the account books were closed at the end of 1930, they showed more than $8 million in red ink, and the company shortly was in receivership.

With little money to spend on advertising, the first announcement of the Model 21 amounted to a simple notice in the factory price list of January 2, 1931. The Model 21 Standard Grade, it said, in 12-gauge only and with double triggers, was for sale at a price of $59.50. A single trigger and ejectors would be available April 1.

The gun might well have languished in the warehouses and died a quiet death but for the interest and efforts of a man from Illinois. On December 22, 1931, John Merrill Olin appeared at the federal courthouse in St. Louis and laid out $8,100,000 for the purchase of Winchester Repeating Arms. He was at the time just over a month past his thirty-eighth birthday, and he was taking a monumental risk.

The Olin family – John, his younger brother Spencer, and their father Franklin – already were successful manufacturers of powder and brass. Their Western Cartridge Company, largely through John Olin's invention of the Super-X shotshell, was revolutionizing the American ammunition industry. Nonetheless, the Winchester purchase cut deeply into their resources. Financing in those early Depression years was almost impossible to obtain, and the Olins had pledged their personal investments and had put together a series of ninety-day loans through the First National Bank of St. Louis. Looking ahead, they realized that owning a gun company would assure an outlet for their cartridges and powder and brass, and the Winchester bankruptcy was the just the opportunity they needed.

Among the things that John Olin found when he arrived in New Haven was a double gun that showed all the promise of greatness. As one of his first steps in putting the company back on its feet, he expanded and intensified promotion of the Model 21. By the end of 1932, Winchester-Western, now bereft of its money-losing products and primarily a gun company once again, turned a $168,000 profit. Under John Olin's brilliant management, Winchester sales amounted to more than $17 million by 1934 and almost $30 million by 1937.

The Model 21 had little to do with Winchester's comeback, but it's as good an example as any of the focus that John Olin chose. To all appearances, the Model 21 was not unlike the other good double guns of its time. It was a bit plainer than most, but what it may have lacked in cosmetic appearance, it more than made up in durability. Principally George Lewis' work, the Model 21 design brilliantly integrates classic aesthetics with the best technology available in the 1930s.

The frame and barrels are milled from excellent chrome-molybdenum steel, and Lewis chose an unusual but highly effective way of joining the barrels. It's a variation of the chopper-lump system used by the British, in which half the barrel lump is forged integrally with each tube and brazed into a single unit. For the Model 21, the half-lumps are machined to form a dovetail joint, so that barrels are interlocked, pinned, and soldered. With the dovetail holding the assembly firmly together, the solder provides an adequate bond. Since solder flows at relatively low temperature, there's no danger of altering the temper of the steel.

A lot of writers, following the lead of Winchester's own advertising, have expended a world of fuss and feathers effusing over the uniqueness of the 21's dovetailed barrels. The method is unique among American guns, but it wasn't new. Nineteenth-century Belgian gunsmith Henri Pieper used the same method for his line of Bayard guns. Pieper probably didn't invent the notion, but he apparently was the first to give it the name by which it is commonly known in Europe: *demi-bloc*.

In any case, what's important here is that Winchester was willing to take the extra milling steps necessary to produce the strongest gun it could build, a

Model 21 barrels are made on the demi-bloc principle, with chopper lumps forged as part of each tube and fastened together with a dovetail joint.

characteristic of nearly all the great Winchesters. It eventually would get the company into deep economic trouble, but there's no denying that the old-style Winchester guns are hell for stout.

Early on, John Olin recognized the Model 21's immense strength as a useful selling point. By that time, the ammunition industry had shifted almost entirely from black to smokeless-powder loads. But the change came slowly, and the question of shotgun strength was an item of high controversy. Like Damascus barrels, black powder still had its champions, even in the 1930s. Those with an eye on the future, however, realized that if full advantage was to be made of smokeless ammunition, guns would have to be stronger. Olin's own Super-X cartridge offered more power and greater killing range than any shotshell ever had before, and he saw the Model 21 as the gun to handle it.

To prove his point, Olin personally selected a 12-gauge Model 21 at random from warehouse stock and began gathering similar doubles from other gunmakers around the world. In one of the most dramatic destruction tests ever conducted, the guns were test-fired with round after round of proof loads. Designed to generate a chamber pressure of some $7\frac{1}{2}$ long tons – about 16,500 units of pressure, or half again the stress generated by the heaviest commercial loads – proof loads are used to test guns for structural flaws. The process normally involves firing one or two such loads, but Winchester continued firing until the guns broke down or blew up.

The Purdey held up through sixty shots. After a BSA double broke down at 150 rounds, only the Model 21 remained, and when it had digested 2000 proof loads, the test was stopped. The technicians then disassembled the gun and checked every part against the original gauges; it showed no discernible change or damage of any kind. Commenting on the test almost fifty years later, John Olin said, with characteristic understatement: "There was no near competitor in strength nor endurance to the Model 21."

Still, the proof-load destruction test doesn't prove the others to be inferior. The British never have shared our penchant for high-powered shotshells, and their guns, especially the London best, are tailored to a specific maximum load, usually the relatively light, one-ounce English game load. If that was the case with the English guns used in the Winchester test, then the only valid conclusion possible is that the Model 21 is extremely durable.

Not that durability has been much of a problem with the old Winchesters. Parker Ackley once rebarreled a Model 97 pump gun to .30-06, just for the hell of it. And, without any alteration of the locking system, it worked.

Correctly seeing that gun capable of digesting 2000 blue-pill proof loads had other possibilities, Olin began thinking of a double rifle built on the Model 21 action. Under the direction of Edwin Pugsley, who was then in charge of

Winchester's firearms research, two prototype rifles were made up in 1937. Model 1895 rifle barrels chambered for the .405 WCF cartridge were lathe-turned and used as liners in standard, 26-inch 20-gauge barrels. Leaf sights were fitted to the ribs and the barrel assemblies mounted on standard 20-bore frames.

While the .405 isn't the hottest round ever developed, it's only slightly less powerful than the .375 Holland & Holland, and that's plenty to ask of any shotgun action. The Model 21 apparently was well up to the task.

But there wasn't much demand for double rifles in America, and the project ultimately was shelved. The two prototypes were the only such guns built. One currently is on display at the Winchester museum; the whereabouts of the other is uncertain.

The Model 21's bolting system is beautifully simple, only a single, tapered underbolt that engages a deep bite in the barrel lump. Since double-gun bolts are more likely to wear from slamming the action shut than from firing, the depth at which the Model 21 bolt seats in the bite is adjustable by means of a setscrew.

By the end of 1931, the Model 21 was available in 12, 16, and 20 gauges. The 12-bores could be had with 26-, 28-, 30-, or 32-inch barrels, 16s and 20s with tubes 26, 28, or 30 inches long. In those early days, only matted ribs were available, but ventilated ribs eventually were added as options – first in 1932 for 32-inch barrels, in 1933 for 30-inch tubes, for 26-inch in 1938, and for 28-inch barrels in 1947.

Although its mechanics never were changed in any major way, the Model 21 stock design was refined somewhat in the mid-1930s – the result of a meeting between two of the great names in American gunmaking. One cold morning in the fall of 1934, John Olin shared a duck blind with Frank Parker, scion of the Parker gun family. Olin was shooting a Model 21, and Parker, of course, had brought along one of the doubles that bore his name. Between flights, the conversation naturally turned to guns, and Parker was impressed by the quality of the fledgling 21. It was a beautiful thing, he said, though the shape of the buttstock seemed more appropriate for a canoe paddle than a shotgun.

Olin mulled that over for several weeks and decided that Parker was right (and, in fact, he was). Not long after, the Model 21 took on a new look; stocks were slimmer, straighter, the contours more carefully sculpted, and the pistol grip more clearly defined. It was the last step in the perfection of the the 21.

During its history as a production gun, six types of Model 21 were built in a total of five different grades. In 1932, Tournament and Trap grades were added to the original Standard. Tournament Grade was available both as a field gun

129

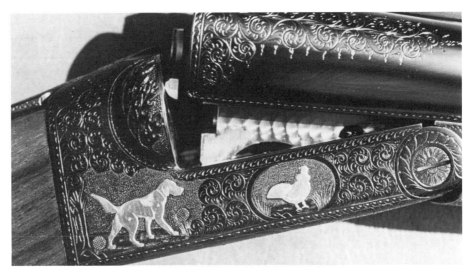

In later years, the Model 21 was available in several styles of factory engraving and gold inlay.

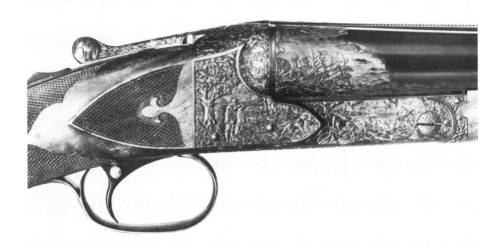

One of John Olin's personal Model 21s, engraved by Kornbrath.

and as a trap gun. The following year, the Custom Built Grade was added, and the skeet gun was made available in Standard, Trap, and Tournament grades. Tournament Grade guns were discontinued in 1936.

The Duck Gun first appeared in 1940 – a Standard Grade chambered for the 3-inch cartridge. The same year, all Trap Grade guns were discontinued, and the Standard Grade Trap Gun was added. The Custom Built Grade was dropped in 1941 and replaced in 1942 with the DeLuxe Grade.

Ejectors and an excellent single trigger were available as options through the 1930s. Authorization to discontinue extractors came November 19, 1941, and to discontinue double triggers June 8, 1944. All Model 21s built after January 1, 1950, were fitted with single trigger and ejectors as standard equipment.

Stocks in all grades were made of good, figured American walnut and were nicely checkered. European walnut could be had on special order. At little or no extra cost, the customer could order his stock made with special features – a Monte Carlo comb, a cheekpiece, or straight hand – and cut to his particular dimensions. A splinter fore-end was standard, but a beavertail – to my eye, the most attractive beavertail ever made – was also available on request.

While the majority of Model 21s were made without decoration, optional factory engraving was made available over the years. By the early '50s, there were six different standard patterns, ranging from simple line work to elaborate English scroll that covered the frame and extended over the breech-ends of the barrels. Two different patterns of custom checkering and stock carving also were available.

Fine engraving is an art mastered by few, and the factory-engraved Model 21s are the work of only a handful of artisans. George Ulrich, who died in 1949, engraved the earliest guns. John Kusmit, a student of Ulrich's, began work as a Winchester engraver in 1938, and he in turn taught the craft to his younger brother Nick, who was apprenticed in 1953. Since then, Jasper Salerno, Hank Bonham, Joe Crowley, and Pauline Muerrle also have engraved Model 21s at the factory.

Twelve-gauge Model 21s are by far the majority, though a fair number were built in 16 and 20. Twenty-eight-bores and .410s are relatively rare. The 28-gauge was first offered in 1936 as a special-order item; factory records do not indicate the exact number built, but there probably were no more than about 200 altogether.

The first .410-bore Model 21, No. 25087, was built for John Olin in December 1950. It was equipped with two sets of vent-ribbed barrels, 26 and 28 inches long, both bored skeet and skeet. In April 1955, a third set was added, 26 inches long, vent-ribbed and choked modified and full. Two sets of 28-gauge barrels were made up for the same gun in August 1955, both 26 inches long and fitted with vent ribs. One set was bored skeet and skeet, the other modified and full.

Parenthetically, all of Olin's personal guns were made with the tighter choke in the right barrel. As an enthusiastic skeet, quail, and grouse shooter, he felt that firing the left barrel first offered less recoil-torque disruption to a fast second shot.

From 1955, .410-bore Model 21s were offered on special order. Like the 28-gauges, the .410s were built on 20-gauge frames. About forty-five .410s were built altogether, with about thirty-five sets of .410 barrels made up as extras for 20-gauge guns.

Although the Model 21 started out as a relatively inexpensive piece, rising manufacturing costs soon drove the prices up. A Standard Grade Skeet Gun that sold for $111.25 in 1938 cost $396 by 1951. In the mid-'50s, Winchester's share of the American market was clearly in decline. The guns cost so much to produce that they were fast losing their competitive edge. Flinty-eyed accountants took a long look at the whole Winchester line and came up, among other things, with the revelation that no Model 21, when assigned its share of factory overhead, ever had sold for a profit.

No doubt there was some talk of dropping the gun altogether – not an unreasonable option under the circumstances. But John Olin loved the Model 21. He'd saved it once from certain demise, had made it one of the most famous shotguns in the world, and he wasn't about to let it be discontinued out of hand. Since Winchester found it difficult to make a profit on the gun through the usual marketing system of factory to jobber to retailer to customer, Olin chose the simple expedient of cutting out the middlemen. In 1959, the Model 21 was taken out of regular production and transferred to the Winchester Custom Shop. To that time, about 28,840 had been built.

In January 1960, the 21 became available on a strictly custom-made basis. The production grades, Standard and DeLuxe, were replaced by three new ones: Custom, Pigeon, and Grand American. The customer could choose from a full range of options in gauges, barrel length, chokes, ribs, bead sights, and butt pads. Stocks could be straight-hand or pistol grip, could have a cheekpiece or Monte Carlo comb, and were made to individual specifications in length of pull, drops, pitch, and cast.

Decoration ranged from classic, subdued engraving and checkering to elaborate scroll and inlays worked in gold. The Grand American Grade came with two sets of barrels. The customer's initials could be engraved on a gold stock shield or inlaid in gold on the trigger guard. His name was engraved on the rib, along with the legend "Custom Built by Winchester."

In the 1960s, the Custom Grade sold for $1000, the Pigeon Grade for $2500, and the Grand American for $3500. Predictably, prices rose steadily, by 1980 reaching $6210 for Custom Grade, $9430 for the Pigeon, and just over $14,000 for the Grand American. Nonetheless, orders averaged about thirty per year, according to Winchester.

It is no particular secret that the Model 21 remained alive, even in the Custom Shop, solely at John Olin's insistence. But when the company was put up for sale in December 1980, it looked like the end of the line for the 21. Happily, it wasn't.

By 1982, with the company reorganized as U.S. Repeating Arms Company and licensed by Olin to use the Winchester name, the Model 21 was available in 12, 16, and 20 gauges, Custom and Grand American grades, at prices of $9500 and $19,500, respectively. For $30,000, you could get a Grand American built in 28-gauge or .410-bore – or, for $35,000, one with a set of barrels in each bore.

At the same time, USRAC offered small-bore sets – a Grand American gun with three sets of barrels, 20, 28, and .410 – at the handsome sum of $50,600. Within a couple of years, the price was up to $54,648. So far as I know, only one such set ever was built.

By 1985, the 21 was once again available in three grades: the Standard Custom-Built, at $7500; the Custom, at $21,060; and Grand American, at $32,400. You could get the two lower grades in 12, 16, and 20 gauges and the Grand American in 28-gauge and .410 as well.

The 1980s represented the passing of an era for the Model 21. Born in hard times, it struggled through depressions, inflations, shooting wars, and the less bloody but no less intense corporate battles for economic survival, and it survived them all. USRAC catalogues still list it as available on special order, though I doubt that any have actually been built for several years.

But whether USRAC decides to let it drop or whether it simply withers for lack of interest, the old 21 has a secure niche among the best American guns, among the best in the world, for that matter. Had the L.C. Smith, the Lefever, the Ithaca, or the Fox had a John Olin to look after them, they, too, might still be with us. But for his efforts on its behalf, the 21 would have gone the way of its peers long ago.

Even beyond the guns that Winchester produced, the American sportsman owes John Olin a substantial debt. His Super-X cartridge, with its radically shortened shot string and improved ballistics, was a breakthrough to the modern age of shotgun ammunition. His affection for dogs led to establishment of the famous Nilo Kennels, where important advances in breeding and training have contributed to the steady improvement of gun dogs. For years, Olin helped fund veterinary research at his alma mater, Cornell University, in a wide range of canine diseases and genetic ailments – from effective prevention of parvo virus to development of artificial hip joints for the treatment of dysplasia.

Such a story deserves commemoration, and a Model 21 built in 1980 does just that.

Grant Tom is an importer by trade, by avocation an AA-class skeet shooter and a collector of Winchester Model 21 guns. In 1978, he conceived a gun to honor John Olin.

"It seemed," he says, "the logical conclusion to the Model 21 story. Without John Olin, there wouldn't be a Model 21.

"I contacted Mr. Olin, explained what I had in mind and asked permission to order a 21 built in his honor. I think he was a bit surprised at first – that someone would want to do that. Mr. Olin is a modest man."

Nonetheless, Olin lent his support to the project and assured Tom that this would be the only Model 21 of its kind authorized by the Winchester factory.

The gun was two years in the making. It is a 20-gauge Grand American Grade, No. 33131, with two sets of barrels. One set is 28 inches long, bored with 3-inch chambers, and choked modified and full. The other is 26 inches with 2¾-inch chambers, improved-cylinder and modified chokes. Both sets are fitted with vent ribs, red bead front sights and ivory middle beads. The buttstock and fore-ends are of high-grade American walnut, checkered and carved in fleur-de-lis patterns. The butt pad is leather-covered.

It was the last gun that Winchester master engraver Nick Kusmit completed before he retired. A portrait of John Olin's Grand Champion springer spaniel, Saighton's Sizzler, is inlaid in gold on the right side of the frame. On the left is a similar portrait of his Grand Champion Labrador, King Buck. A gold-inlay portrait of John Olin himself graces the trigger plate, above a facsimile of his signature, also in gold. On the frame is a gold quail and grouse, and there's a gold woodcock on the trigger guard. The rib is engraved "Custom Built by Winchester in Honor of John M. Olin."

Other Model 21s have reached high levels of collector status in the past few years. At the Las Vegas Antique Arms Show in 1978, one of the auction items, sold to benefit the Winchester Museum, was a .410-bore Grand American skeet gun, No. 32667. A Massachusetts man bought it for a price believed to be the highest to that time ever paid for a new American long gun – $31,500. The gun subsequently changed hands several times, and the price changed, too: to $42,000, to $48,000, to $60,000, to $94,000. According to Ronald Stadt, in his excellent book on Winchester shotguns and shells, the gun was offered for sale in 1982 at an asking price of $125,000.

And there is Nash Buckingham's Model 21, which like the John Olin gun, commemorates an important figure in American sporting history. Olin and Buckingham first met in Chicago, at the 1919 Grand American Handicap and for nearly fifty years maintained a friendship that, in John Olin's words, "wore well." Buckingham played a key role in demonstrating to the rest of the world the wonderful capabilities of Olin's Super-X cartridges and was a central figure in the game-restoration movement of the 1920s and '30s, including serving a stint as Director of Game Restoration for the Western Cartridge Company.

In 1962, Buckingham received Winchester-Western's Outdoorsman of the Year award, in honor of outstanding achievement in wildlife conservation. To mark the occasion, Winchester presented Mr. Nash with a Model 21 made up in the classic Buckingham mold.

The gun, No. 26792, started as a Standard Grade Duck Gun, built in 1953 and delivered to warehouse stock. Its 32-inch barrels were bored full and full, and it carried a typical pistol grip stock and recoil pad. It was still in the warehouse in January 1962, when Buckingham was chosen to receive the award. The decision to include a presentation gun in the affair no doubt was John Olin's, based on his long friendship with Buckingham; in any case, Buckingham was the only Winchester Outdoorsman of the Year to receive one, though he wasn't the first to receive the award.

For so famous a waterfowler, the Duck Gun was a natural choice, and No. 26792 was sent to the Custom Shop with orders that it be engraved to Custom Grade standards, fitted with a beavertail fore-end and straight-hand stock with checkered butt. The rib is engraved "Custom Built by Winchester for Nash Buckingham," and a gold oval set into the right-hand side of the stock is engraved "Presented to/Nash Buckingham/Winchester/Outdoorsman of the Year/1962." The trigger guard carries the initials "NB."

Originally presented in a leather leg o' mutton case gold-embossed with Buckingham's initials, the gun later was treated to one of Marvin Huey's splendid oak-and-leather trunk cases.

Buckingham probably never fired the "award gun," as he always referred to it, and it's in mint condition even today. Hal Hamilton, of Birmingham, Alabama, owns it now, and I'm grateful for his generosity in sharing the story.

There is something uniquely American about the Model 21, something that represents American gunmaking even more poignantly than the Parker or Fox or Smith or the others. Perhaps it's the gun's yeoman ruggedness combined with the grace of another age. It never was a handmade gun in the same sense that a London best is handmade; none of the great American doubles were. But guns like the Model 21 – and men like John Olin – serve to remind us that the American gun trade always has exercised a particular gift for technology and always has held firmly to a belief that the practical ideal is at least as important as the aesthetic. For any number of social and economic and even geographic reasons, the American game gun is a species apart from all the rest, definitive of the American approach to durable goods during a time when the manufacture of durable goods was definitive of America herself. And the Model 21 is the last of that particular breed, the last survivor of American best.

Part II
TODAY'S BEST

An eighteenth-century English sportsman, properly attired, with his flintlock gun and dogs. The larger dogs, presumably a setter and a pointer, were used to point and flush game; the little spaniel's job was retrieving.

BRITANNIA RULES

The sporting gun, as we know it, is essentially a British invention. Though the origins of the smooth-bored gun reach back to the ancient dynasties of China, and though the major phases of its evolution took place in Europe, the English ultimately defined both the gun and the wingshooting sport.

And in the process of doing so, the British transformed an ungainly, unreliable tool into the most complex and functional work of art the world has ever seen.

During the time when French, Italian, and German armorers were evolving the matchlock into the wheellock into the flint gun, the Englishman bent on taking game did so with a variety of nets, snares, and springes. Guns were heavy, awkward, slow to fire – all but useless for anything except a motionless target and not always reliable enough even for that. Sport, in any case, was the prerogative of the nobility, pursued with the hound and the hawk and the longbow.

The Restoration brought a new influence. When King Charles II returned to England in 1660 from exile in France, he and his retinue brought with them slender flintlock fowling pieces and a curious new sport, that of shooting birds on the wing. Given the cachet of the King's patronage, wingshooting soon caught the fancy of the English gentry.

The English countryside played its own part in shaping the nature of the sporting gun. It was a man-made landscape of small fields and tiny woodlands, ideal for small game. Its compressed size and dense human population made it equally unsuited for the rifle, and in any case, by the end of the seventeenth century, there were virtually no large animals left south of the Scottish highlands.

If the nature of the countryside and the game it supported demanded a short-range gun, the nature of the English shooter demanded a fine one. Unlike the military, so hidebound by tradition that as late as 1902, British cavalry troops launched saber charges against Boers armed with Mauser rifles (with predictable results), English sportsmen were eager for new developments in sporting guns and were willing to pay handsomely for them. Almost from the moment that Charles restored the monarchy and its corollary class of noblemen to England, English gunmakers took their place among other London bespokemen – hatters, bootmakers, tailors, and the like – and began transforming the French fowler.

The Rise of the London Gun

The process took just over a hundred years. The seminal mechanical breakthrough came in 1787, when Henry Nock of London patented a breech-plug that provided more reliable means of igniting a powder charge and also shortened the time lapse between pulling a trigger and actually firing a shot. The percussion cap loomed on the horizon, soon to be followed by self-contained cartridges, but by 1820, the sporting gun had reached nearly definitive form in the hands of such makers as William Parker, Joseph Gulley, Thomas Mortimer, Durs Egg, James Purdey, and most influential of all, two brothers named Manton.

Neither of the Mantons – John, born in 1752, and Joseph, born in 1766 – actually contributed anything of great substance to the mechanical nature of the gun. Their inventions, as Geoffrey Boothroyd comments, were more often frivolous than significant. Nonetheless, the Mantons' impact upon gunmaking was profound and remains undiminished today. Though the two brothers were of one mind on matters of how a gun should be made and went about it with essentially equal skill, Joseph was the more famous and by 1800 was regarded as the finest gunmaker in England.

The Manton influence was threefold. For one thing, they defined the style of the English gun and therefore by extension defined the nature of the game gun for all the world and for all time – the slender, lightweight side-by-side double,

A fine 20-gauge flintlock by Joseph Manton. The apparatus below the hammer is a "gravitational stop," a safety device that Manton designed and patented. When the gun is in a vertical position, the weighted lever pivots back and blocks the hammer; it helped prevent a gun from accidentally firing during loading.

trimly stocked, with a perfect harmony of form and function in its clean, simple lines.

The Mantons also established the style and taste of decoration that became the standard by which fine guns worldwide are judged: metalwork filed in graceful curves and engraved in delicate scroll; wood polished to a fine sheen and richly finished in oil; barrels deeply blacked; the whole effect subtle, restrained, elegant.

Perhaps most important of all, the Mantons established standards of craftsmanship in which perfection was the only acceptable level of performance, standards that every man who worked in the Manton shop was expected to meet. And so many of those workmen went on to establish businesses of their own, that the Mantons virtually fostered one of the greatest generation of gunmakers that the world has ever seen: James Purdey, Charles Lancaster, Thomas Boss, Joseph Lang, William Moore, William Grey, William Greener (father of W.W. Greener), and others. Purdey, who worked for Joseph Manton from 1805 to 1808, later said of his old employer, "But for him we should all have been a parcel of Blacksmiths." (The admiration was to some extent mutual. After Purdey opened his own shop on Princes Street, Manton remarked to the famous sportsman and writer Peter Hawker: "Purdey gets up the best work next to mine!")

By the mid-nineteenth century, the percussion cap had made the flintlock obsolete, and makers in both London and Birmingham had brought the muzzleloading gun to perfection. A great revolution was about to begin.

It started in 1851, at the Great Exhibition in London, where Casimir Lefaucheux of Paris displayed his breechloading pinfire gun. If you set aside the various linen and paper pouch-type cartridges that date back at least to the latter sixteenth century, Lefaucheux's cartridge, designed in the 1830s, was the first recognizably modern shotshell. B. Houillier, another Frenchman, patented an improved pinfire cartridge in 1846. Lefaucheux had been building hinge-action guns for these shells for nearly twenty years, but neither the guns nor the cartridges had sparked much attention among English makers.

That changed at the Great Exhibition, when Joseph Lang, gunmaker, of 7 Haymarket, London, saw the Lefaucheux display. The notion of a break-action gun struck Lang's fancy, and by the time the shooting season began the following year, he was ready with his own guns built in the Lefaucheux image. Sportsmen and other makers alike took notice.

Charles Lancaster took the breechloader a step further in 1852 with improvements in both the bolting mechanism and the cartridge design. Lancaster's action operated by an under-lever that, when moved to one side, cammed the barrels slightly forward before they pivoted down on

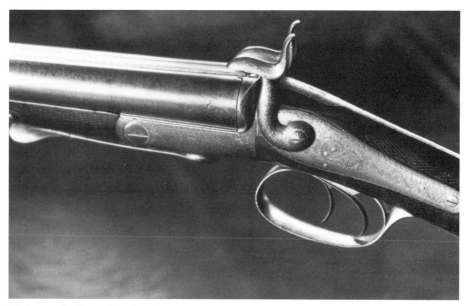

Pinfire gun by James Woodward. The lever under the fore-end opens the action, a design typical of early pinfires.

the hinge pin. James Dougall of Glasgow, who later opened a shop in London, developed his famous "Lockfast" bolting system along the same lines. Both Lancaster and Dougall were working with pinfire ammunition, although Lancaster developed a brass-headed shell that functioned much like a modern rimfire. In 1855, a Frenchman named Pottet patented a cartridge that looks remarkably like the typical shotshell of the early twentieth century; it became the first commercially produced shot cartridge to use a centerfire primer. George Daw, a London maker at 57 Threadneedle Street, altered Pottet's design of the primer and secured an English patent for the whole cartridge in 1861. Shortly afterward, the Eley brothers contrived to break Daw's patent, and centerfire shotshells were all the rage in England and on the Continent by 1866.

Both Dougall and Lancaster enjoyed considerable success with their cam-and-lever bolting systems. Henry Jones, a Birmingham maker, improved matters considerably with the double screw-grip fastener, also called the T fastener, patented in 1859. It, too, uses a side-pivoting underlever. The fastener itself works on the principle of the inclined plane, and by engaging the barrel lump with two bearing surfaces, it's immensely strong.

The lever, though, has to be manipulated both in opening and closing the action; makers of big-bore double rifles liked it because it offered plenty of strength and made no sound, but neither shotgunners nor riflemen cared much for the time it took to latch the action by hand. Westley Richards developed an early snap action – possibly, in fact, the earliest of any – in 1858; this used a rib extension that somehow hooked into the standing breech. A better system, one that ultimately became the standard not only among British guns but among guns worldwide, soon appeared, and the earliest version came from France.

In 1858, François Schneider of 13 Rue Gaillon, Paris, obtained a French patent for a bolting system that comprised an underlever, a round bolt that extended through the action bar to mate with a notch in the barrel lump, and a stout spring to drive the bolt into place. All a shooter had to do was close the action and the gun locked itself. Schneider secured an English patent on the design in June 1861. George Daw bought the patent rights almost immediately, made some improvements, and got a patent of his own in 1862. For several years, Daw's snap-action gun and his self-contained cartridge were a great success.

Creative energy flowed through the English gun trade like electric current. At almost the same time George Daw received a patent for his revised snap action, Thomas Horsley, gunmaker at 10 Coney Street, York, patented a similar system in which a single, spring-driven underbolt fastens barrels and

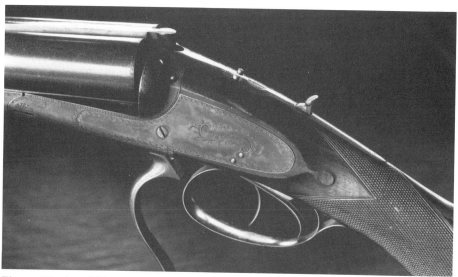

Thomas Woodward "Acme Hammerless" action. Underlever guns remained popular until the turn of the century; Woodward's version, patented in November 1876, is a snap-action design and uses a Purdey double underbolt.

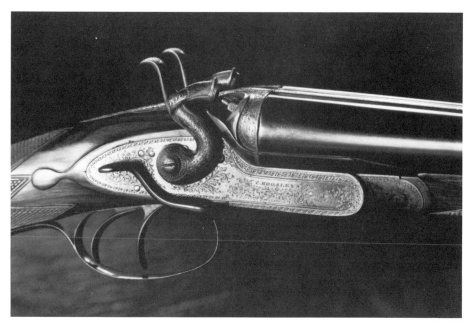

Sidelever snap-action hammer gun by Thomas Horsley.

breech. This system uses an underlever. The following year, 1863, Horsley patented a snap action with a top lever, which the shooter pulls backward to open the action. Eighteen sixty-two also saw the first appearance of Westley Richards' doll's-head fastener, a bolting system that relies on a rib extension and top hook instead of an underbolt. Dozens of makers worldwide eventually adopted the same principle in one form or another, alone or combined with an underbolt.

A third Thomas Horsley patent, issued in 1867, covers a mechanism by which the firing pins rebound into the frame after the cartridge is fired, thereby eliminating the need to pull the hammers to half-cock before opening the gun. John Stanton, a lockmaker in Wolverhampton, Staffordshire, perfected the rebounding lock in patents issued in 1867, 1869, and 1877. In Stanton's lock, the hammers themselves rebounded to half-cock after striking the pins. The principle readily applied to hammerless locks as well, and by 1880, Stanton's design was a standard in both the London and Birmingham trades.

As center-primed cartridges supplanted the pinfire system, the problem of extracting fired cases became more pressing. Paper cases often swelled and stuck to the chamber walls (they still do). The pinfire shell at least offered something that the shooter could get hold of, but a center-primed cartridge doesn't, and cases often had to be pried out with a knifeblade or rammed out with a rod down the muzzles. During the 1860s, several makers developed extractors, which not only loosened the cases but also withdrew them a quarter-inch or so, allowing the shooter to pull them out with his fingers. This inevitably led to a search for some means of ejecting cases altogether.

Joseph Needham developed the first ejector system in 1874. Literally dozens of similar systems appeared over the next few years. Most makers put their ejector mechanisms in the fore-end, though a few – notably John Dickson of Edinburgh – chose to house ejectors in the frame. All of them performed identical functions, ejecting only fired cases while extracting unfired cartridges and presenting them to the shooter's hand.

Even as the exposed-hammer breechloading gun approached the zenith of perfection, its successor appeared. With the matter of bolting the action solved in several ways, makers focused their attention upon getting the hammers off the outside of a gun and into its action body.

Actually, concealing the hammers inside the frame was relatively simple. How to cock them was something else again.

Some sort of lever was the most obvious solution. The best of the early designs were those in which one lever served the dual function of cocking the locks and operating the bolts, and the first of these to achieve commercial success was patented in 1871 by Theophilus Murcott of 68 Haymarket, London. W.W. Greener, in fact, credits Murcott as a primary influence in the popularity of hammerless guns in general. Perhaps so, but Murcott certainly wasn't alone.

George Gibbs and Thomas Pitt entered a joint patent in January 1873 for "improvements to Breech Loading firearms." Though their ideas included self-cocking guns of both exposed-hammer and hammerless types, they also had worked out a system in which the underlever simultaneously withdrew the bolts and cocked the locks. In the earliest of these, the lockwork is fastened to the trigger plate. A later design puts the locks on more conventional sideplates.

The most successful of the Gibbs & Pitt inventions adapted their original 1873 design to a top-lever system. This gun, to all outward appearance a typical modern sidelock, actually incorporates two different cocking systems. The top lever is linked to both the bolt and the locks, and the locks cock if the lever is moved fully to the right. But if the lever is moved only far enough to retract the bolt, a cam on the barrel lump pushes the bolt fully to the rear as the barrels drop down, permitting cocking leverage to be applied by either of the shooter's hands or by both hands together. John Bentley built a number of these Gibbs & Pitt guns, and George Daw marketed them.

Though lever-cocking guns remained popular for some years, the last great step in the evolution of the modern gun came in 1875, when

William Anson and John Deeley, of the old firm Westley Richards, patented their design for a hammerless gun cocked by the leverage of its barrels. Some of the actual mechanics would take on a variety of forms, but the Anson and Deeley action eventually would become a standard for break-action guns worldwide.

It is, for one thing, the soul of simplicity, comprising only three basic lock parts: a hammer or tumbler, a mainspring, and a sear. The toe of the hammer reaches forward into the action bar, where it engages one end of a cocking lever. The other end goes through the action knuckle into a notch in the fore-end iron. As the barrels pivot on the hinge pin, the fore-end iron pivots the cocking lever at the same time, lifting the hammer into the sear notch.

The Anson and Deeley design promotes an action of remarkable strength and durability, owing in part to its uncomplicated mechanics and in part to the fact that the lockwork is fully contained inside the frame. The cocking-lever concept works perfectly well with sidelock guns – and in fact virtually every cocking system in the world today is predicated on the same concept – but the boxlock design, as the Anson and Deeley system has come to be known, is one of the greatest inventions in arms-making history, as makers everywhere have proven for more than a hundred years.

By the turn of the twentieth century, fifty years after it began, the great

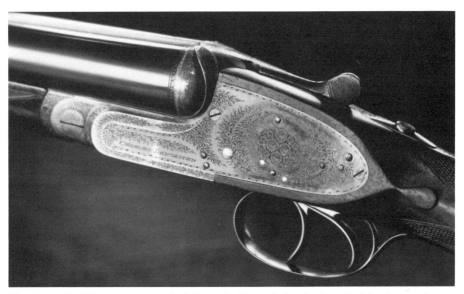

The classic English game gun reached the peak of its evolution by the end of the nineteenth century. This fine Charles Lancaster Twelve-Twenty is a good example – an elegant, beautifully finished six-pound, two-ounce 12-gauge.

revolution was all but over, and the profuse outpouring of inventive energy began to subside. The world would never again witness an era of such pervasive, widespread creativity. In the years that followed, the English gun would grow steadily more homogeneous, both in appearance and mechanics, as one and then another patent expired, making the best features from a variety of guns available to all makers. Today, the typical best-quality British gun is "British" in the broadest sense, for regardless of whose name appears on the lockplates or barrels, it truly represents the best efforts of craftsmen over three generations.

In fact, a best-quality sidelock game gun built anywhere in the world today, whether in London, Birmingham, Elgiobar, St. Etienne, Brescia, or Gardone, most likely is made on an action that ultimately was refined by Holland & Holland, the barrels and frame fastened together by a double sliding underbolt designed and patented by James Purdey the Younger in 1863. The bolt and top latch most likely are connected by the spindle that William Middleditch Scott invented in 1865. The ejectors will be either John Deeley's, patented in 1886, or Thomas Southgate's, patented in 1893. And the style of it all will show the ageless influence of Joseph and John Manton.

Decline and Fall

The foregoing, I must confess, is thin beer compared with the extraordinarily rich, remarkably diverse gunmaking trade that existed in England during the nineteenth century. One could write an entire book on the period and never finally exhaust the subject. Any number of such books, in fact, have already been written, and if our understanding of the nineteenth century English gun trade still remains incomplete, it isn't the fault of the many able researchers who've had a go at it. The numbers alone are staggering. In 1868, there were 578 firms directly active in the gun trade in Birmingham. An 1871 census shows 5391 people employed in the Birmingham trade and 1431 in the London trade. More than 2200 more worked in the provincial trade. Scotland and Ireland, too, had a share of gunworkers. Certainly, not all of these people were gunmakers, and not all of the gunmakers built sporting guns. But even among the literally hundreds who did, extant guns often are painfully few and records range from remarkably complete to all but nonexistent. The definitive history of British gunmaking probably never will be written.

Shooting was immensely popular during the latter years of Victoria's reign and through the brief Edwardian Age that followed. This was the period of elaborate shooting parties at the great country estates, much the social vogue among the upper classes. Nowhere else in time or space has such a vast social institution centered on the gun. Small wonder, then, that the game gun reached such a pinnacle of excellence and refinement.

But if the nineteenth century is a vast trove of still-untold stories, what came next, unfortunately, is all too easily manageable. The twentieth century has been brutally cruel to England and, by extension, to the English gun trade.

The 1914-1918 war devoured an entire generation of young men. Together, the combatant nations mobilized about 63 million troops; more than ten million died and 21 million more were wounded. Nine hundred thousand British soldiers died in combat, 60,000 of them in a single day at the battle of the Somme. Both sides lost 1.2 million men at Verdun. Thousands more, soldiers and civilians alike, died in the influenza epidemic of 1918-1919, a scourge that claimed more than 20 million lives worldwide.

The war was economically devastating as well. Goods destroyed through shipping losses alone totaled 15 million tons, nine million tons of which were British. Other European countries lost more men; none of the Allies lost a greater proportion of its population.

The obscene, bloody horror of World War I swept away an era. Once the greatest nation on earth, England was never the same again. Her industries flourished briefly and then all but collapsed in 1920, as British foreign trade, in which both Germany and Russia had formerly been key markets, came to a virtual standstill. The dissolution of the vast British Empire, which began in the 1930s, further eroded her already battered economy.

World War II was the final blow. British military losses actually were fewer than they had been during the previous war – about 360,000 English soldiers and civilians and almost as many colonials – but by then England had fewer lives to give. Through the summer, fall, and winter of 1940, the German Luftwaffe dumped bombs by the thousand on London and the industrial cities of Liverpool, Coventry, Bristol, and Birmingham. By the time the war in Europe dragged to its bloody end, the British economy was in shambles. The further, final collapse of the Empire in Asia and Africa over the next twenty years was anticlimactic.

As they have always done, the British people coped as best they could. The post-war welfare state, supported by an enormous rate of taxation, all but erased the upper social and economic class – the class that once had supported a healthy trade in fine sporting guns. For the past sixty years, with two generations of craftsmen decimated by war and its domestic economic base destroyed, the English gun trade has dwindled, until only a handful of makers remain. But for foreign markets, especially those in

Europe and the United States, it might have disappeared altogether.

As John Wilkes puts it, the English gun trade is a nineteenth-century industry struggling to survive in the Space Age. Steadily escalating costs, both for materials and labor, have driven prices of bespoke English guns to daunting levels, while at the same time, a diminishing pool of craftsmen leaves ever-fewer people to build them. Add in a growing competition, especially from Italy, and *struggle* clearly is the key word.

As this appears in print, only nine gunmakers remain in England: Purdey, Holland, Wilkes, Evans, Boss, and Bland in London; Scott, Powell, and Richards in Birmingham. In Scotland, Dickson's and David McKay Brown still build guns.

Not all are equally active in the trade. Thomas Bland & Sons organized in 1862 as Thomas Bland (Gunmaker) at 411 Wittall Street, Birmingham. The firm opened a London shop in 1875, though the gun and rifle works remained in Birmingham. By the 1960s, the Birmingham works was closed and much of Bland's trade was in rather roughly finished boxlock guns built by another Birmingham maker. Reportedly, Bland's shop on King William Street in London is today devoted solely to repair work, and rumor has it that Bland soon may close altogether.

Other makers, though, appear to do a healthy business, indeed. The niche may be shrinking, but you still can order best English guns of names that go back almost to the beginning.

James Purdey & Sons

Richard Beaumont has written an excellent book on the gunmaking Purdey family, which I certainly will not attempt to duplicate here. For the full story behind this brief summary, I recommend *Purdey's, the Guns and the Family*.

The first James Purdey learned the fundamentals of gunmaking from his brother-in-law, Thomas Hutchinson, to whom young Purdey was indentured in August 1798. He was fourteen. Almost from the beginning, he moved in the first rank of those responsible for the evolution of the gun.

In 1805, his apprenticeship completed, Purdey hired on at Joseph Manton's shop on Oxford Street. He apparently learned his trade well, for Manton, who suffered neither fools nor second-rate craftsmen, soon promoted him to the job of head stockmaker.

He left Manton's in 1808 to become stockmaker and lock-filer for

Alexander Forsyth. The parish minister of Belhelvie in Aberdeenshire, Scotland, Forsyth was a passionate tinkerer both with firearms and explosives. When he discovered a priming powder that could be detonated simply by a sharp blow, he instantly recognized its potential, designed a gunlock to use it, and spent a year experimenting further under the aegis of the Kings' Master General of Ordnance. The next Master General failed to see any future in the idea and withdrew government support. Forsyth, who by then had all but invented the entire percussion system, opened his own shop at 10 Piccadilly in June 1808, with James Purdey aboard.

Purdey opened a shop of his own at 4 Princes Street in 1814. To quote Richard Beaumont: "He built single and double flintlock guns, duelling pistols and flintlock rifles. He also experimented with the new detonating system, later known as 'percussion', which he had studied while working with Forsyth. He had made a reputation as an excellent craftsman during his employment with Manton and Forsyth, so his name was already known in shooting circles."

Purdey's trade continued briskly. By the early 1820s he was building guns and rifles (he was especially fond of rifles) for English and European nobility. He soon earned royal patronage as well, beginning in 1823 when His Serene Highness the Prince of Leinegen bought a 14-bore Purdey gun. Guns exported to India during this period eventually would make Purdey's the favored maker among the vastly wealthy Indian princes.

In 1826, Purdey bought Manton's old shop on Oxford Street. His son and successor, James Purdey the Younger, was born two years later. Queen Victoria became a Purdey customer in 1838, a relationship that eventually earned Purdey an appointment, which remains current today, as gun and cartridge maker to the royal family.

Though he was primarily a gunmaker, the first James Purdey dealt in any sort of quality goods or services that showed the promise of turning a pound or two. His ledgers from the 1820s and '30s show that he sold razors, cutlasses, bayonets, salmon hooks, cigars, boarded J. Sherwell's dog for nine weeks, and mended a fishing rod for Mr. Higginson.

Purdey's success rested primarily on two factors, both of which have characterized Purdey guns ever since: flawless craftsmanship and a conservatism that seldom strays from the oldest traditions of gunmaking. Like his old teacher, Joseph Manton, James Purdey wasn't one to embrace the new until he was convinced it was better than the old. Manton never did abandon the flintlock, even after the percussion system had proven itself superior. Purdey, not quite so hidebound as Manton but cautious nonetheless, clung to the muzzleloader well after many of his colleagues had switched to breechloading designs. Purdey's didn't build its first breechloading gun until

May 1858, almost six months after James the Younger succeeded his father as owner of the business.

Still, conservatism does not preclude resourcefulness, and the second James Purdey was a talented designer. The earliest Purdey breechloaders were pinfires, followed closely by guns built for various kinds of centerfire cartridges. Some were break-action type; others were designed so that the barrels could be unlatched and slid forward to expose the breeches, rather than pivoted downward on a hinge. Like most his contemporaries in the English trade, Purdey settled finally on the hinge-action gun, and in seeking the best means of fastening the action, he struck upon the simple notion of a spring-driven, sliding underbolt that bears against two notches in the barrel lump. He received a patent for the idea in May 1863.

The earliest form of the Purdey bolt used an underlever. Purdey adapted the same fastener to a top lever and earned a second patent in 1870. Eventually, the Purdey bolt in combination with the top-lever spindle that William Scott of Birmingham patented in 1865 would become the world's most widely used system for bolting the action of a side-by-side gun. It still is.

James the Younger ruled both the firm and his family with a critical eye and never hesitated to point out shortcomings in either. In 1880, replying to a letter from his son and eventual successor Athol Purdey, he took the young man,

Like his peers, James Purdey experimented with various ways of operating a break-open action and designed at least two types of "thumb-break" snap actions in the 1860s. In both, the action lever is in the bottom of the frame, and the shooter opens the gun by pressing the lever forward with his thumb.

then twenty-two, to task for poor spelling and even returned Athol's letter with spelling errors corrected. A similar intolerance for anything less than perfection would characterize every Purdey generation. Though they could at times be almost brutally insensitive toward each other and toward company employees, the same intolerant attitude and intense pride in the quality of work would do much to ensure the continued excellence of Purdey guns.

They had much, in fact, to be proud of. By 1880 Purdey's held the reputation as the finest gunmaker in England, and success would continue unabated for more than a generation, until the great war of 1914-1918 brought the entire nation almost to its knees.

One of the most important of all contributions to Purdey's success came from Frederick Beesley. Born in 1846 and apprenticed in 1861 to Moore and Grey, gunmakers, of 78 Edgewater Road, London, Beesley was a gifted designer. In December 1879, he wrote James Purdey, offering first option on a hammerless action of his own invention, designed, he said, "on a principle *entirely different* to any other in the market."

As it turned out, Beesley was right. Like other makers in the late 1870s, Purdey had adopted the Anson and Deeley concept of the hammerless gun, in which barrel leverage cocks the locks as the action is opened. It works perfectly well, as the past hundred-odd years have proven, but resistance from

The famous Purdey self-opening action was designed by Frederick Beesley in 1879. Cams at the action knuckle cock the locks as the gun is closed.

the mainsprings, which are compressed as the locks cock, makes an Anson and Deeley action somewhat stiff to open. Beesley, by placing cams at the action knuckle and cocking rods through the action bar, created a gun that cocked on closing. Since the mainsprings bear against the cocking rods after the gun is fired, the Beesley action is virtually self-opening. All the shooter has to do is work the top lever to withdraw the bolt; the mainsprings help start the barrels moving on the hinge.

Beesley obtained his patent on January 3, 1880. James Purdey liked the idea immensely and under a contract executed on August 5, 1880, bought all manufacturing rights to the Beesley action for the fourteen-year term of the patent. (Beesley obtained an American patent for his action in November 1881. It was reissued in February 1883, and Beesley assigned both to James Purdey.)

Beesley reportedly worked at Purdey's for a while and then went into business on his own account at 2 Saint James Street, London. By the time he died in January 1928, at the age of eighty-two, he was one of the most respected gunmakers in England.

The Beesley action all but gave James Purdey a corner on the upper strata of the gun market. It's unquestionably an ingenious piece of work, and Purdey's built it beautifully, but an action that cocks on closing has no particular practical advantage over one that cocks on opening. The mainsprings have to be compressed *sometime*, and if Beesley's action is easy to open, it's equally hard to close. But the people who could most readily afford to pay £66 for a best-quality Purdey gun also employed loaders, so the self-opening action had a certain prestige appeal.

(There is a famous, almost certainly apocryphal, story about an American visiting a famous London gun shop, the name of which seems to change according to who's telling the story. Upon being handed a best self-opening gun, the man examines it, works the action, and remarks that it is rather stiff to close. Drawing himself to full height in his pin-striped suit, the shop man says in a lofty tone, "My dear sir, *our* customers do not close their own guns." A fiction, no doubt, but probably true enough in spirit, at least, to explain an important part of Purdey's appeal.)

With business so brisk, Purdey's had outgrown the old Manton shops on Oxford Street, and after buying the necessary leases, James the Younger contracted with B.E. Nightingale to rebuild Nos. 57-60 South Audley Street, at the corner of Mount Street, as the Purdey shop. Purdey's remains at that address today.

Those who insist that firearms history should comprise endless lists of barrel lengths and chokes will no doubt be bored by Richard Beaumont's book

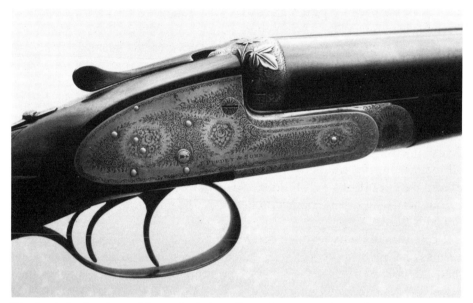

The classic Purdey, the world's standard of excellence, has remained virtually unchanged for more than a hundred years.

on Purdey; those who understand that the history of any gun is mainly the history of the people who have built it will be fascinated. Even when business prospered, as it did at the turn of the century, the Purdeys themselves were heir to all the problems that beset any family. Athol, whose spelling had so offended his father, had the further misfortune to marry Mabel Field, the sixth-generation great-granddaughter of Oliver Cromwell. She clearly had no more sense of humor than her Puritan ancestor did and in fact appears to have possessed no sense of anything other than herself. A petulant, arrogant, rude, and complaining woman, she seems to have blamed her husband for everything wrong in the world since the dinosaurs went extinct.

Since its product amounted to a luxury item, the Purdey firm nearly failed in the aftermath of World War I. A few orders trickled in after 1919 but scarcely enough to meet expenses. In 1922, Athol visited America in a low-key marketing tour, and the American market ultimately became an important source of orders. The first trip, in fact, resulted in one of the most interesting, if not the most successful, of all Purdey guns.

Both Woodward and Boss were at the time enjoying fine success in selling over-under guns in Europe and the United States, and enough Americans asked for a Purdey over-under that Athol decided to give it a try. Purdey's had built a number of over-under rifles before the turn of the century, but Athol was deeply mistrustful of over-under actions. The classic Purdey bolt doesn't adapt well, and Athol was reluctant to put the Purdey name on any gun that might have the slightest weakness in its fasteners.

Years before, Edwinson Green of Cheltenham and later of Birmingham had patented an over-under action that contained six fasteners and a rib extension. When he saw one of Green's guns, Athol finally was convinced that an over-under could be made sufficiently strong, and in 1924 he instructed Purdey works manager Ernest Lawrence to make up a prototype using Green's ideas. Lawrence's son Harry, who later would become a director of Purdey's, built the prototype (and, in fact, actioned all of the Purdey over-unders built before World War II).

The result weighed eight pounds, two ounces. Harry Lawrence immediately saw that he could improve the handling quality by getting rid of a few bolts, but Athol wouldn't hear of it, and over the next three years, Purdey's built eight of these guns. I've handled one of them, a monstrous club of a thing that's as heavy as a bridge timber. Only Purdey's skill in achieving some decent measure of balance saves it from being a complete though extremely well-built disaster.

After Athol retired, his son Tom agreed that the over-under would be a better gun if it were lighter, and Harry Lawrence redesigned the action to eliminate two bolts and the rib extension. Even reduced by half a pound, it still was heavier than a game gun ought to be, but the revised Purdey over-under certainly was better than the original. Purdey's built ten of these, making eighteen of the Green-style over-unders in all.

So, not all of Purdey's ventures were successful. A line of sporting clothing proved a bust when the "special rain-proof coat" turned out to be more absorbent than proof. In 1927, still recovering from the devastation of World War I, the firm bought some land at Eastcote to use for shooting instruction and to test guns. Unfortunately, the local sewage works was next door, which made the shooting grounds unusable when the wind was in the wrong direction.

Tom Purdey, whose greatest love was trout fishing, carried on the tradition of Purdey tyranny begun by his grandfather. In 1932, a customer who had just purchased a new pair of guns discovered on the opening day of grouse shooting in Scotland that neither would fire. In a rage, he phoned Tom and shipped the guns to London by train. There is was discovered that someone had forgotten to install firing pins. Tom assembled the entire staff for a tongue-lashing and bellowed, "When a man pays this sort of money for one of my guns, he does at least expect the bloody thing to go bang!"

Tom also carried on James the Younger's habit of writing comments in the ledger-book margins about customers who failed to pay their bills. One gentleman, a merchant who lived in Half Moon Street, earned the following opinions from Tom Purdey: "Stinking Bad and a Shit 1936," "Still is, Jan. 13/37," and "More so; Feb. '38."

Despite the cachet of its royal customers (which by then included warrants from Victoria, Edward VII, George V, Edward VIII, and George VI), the 1930s were hard years at Purdey's, as they were nearly everywhere. The Great Depression all but gutted the lucrative American market, and as its effects rippled worldwide, more and more formerly wealthy customers found they could get along without the luxury of a new Purdey gun. Faced finally with only the options of bankruptcy or selling out, the Purdeys sold controlling interest in the firm. With Tom's death in March 1957, the family's managing link with the company ceased altogether.

As it had during the 1914-1918 war, Purdey's secured plenty of work producing military materiel during World War II, though the stress of trying to work during the air raids must have been enormous. A bomb damaged Audley House, though not seriously, in April 1941. Beaumont reports that factory manager Christopher Gadsby awoke the morning after a particularly violent air raid to find that "all his hair had fallen out and was lying on the pillow beside him."

Purdey's prospects after the war were enough to make anyone's hair fall out. The firm was fully prepared to build guns, but almost half of the orders placed during the war had been cancelled by September 1946. A tool-and die-making section that Purdey's had set up during the war offered some diversity, but the economic and political climate of England was such that few "luxury" businesses could see much future.

Once again, the American market made the difference. Beginning in 1949, Purdey representatives made almost annual trips to the United States and returned to London with ever-increasing numbers of orders. The American fondness for the over-under gun inevitably raised that particular issue once again, and this time Purdey's got a stroke of luck.

In 1947, Charles Woodward offered to sell his company, James Woodward & Sons, to Purdey's. Woodward, in business since 1800, built splendid guns – every bit as good, actually, as Purdey's – but it, too, was feeling the post-war pinch. Its fortunes, in fact, were at such a low ebb that the Purdey directors declined to make an offer. In September 1948, however, Purdey did buy the Woodward name, the firm's goodwill, and all rights and materials for manufacturing the Woodward over-under gun – all for £444 14s 6d.

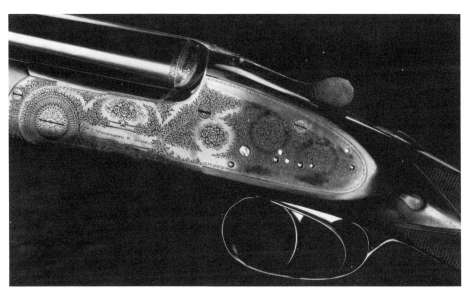

With the purchase of James Woodward & Sons in 1948, Purdey acquired one of the finest over-under guns in the world. The original Woodward design subsequently evolved into the Purdey over-under, which is still available today.

The Woodward was a first-rate gun and just what Purdey needed to satisfy the market for a best-quality over-under. For the first few years, Purdey simply built the Woodward gun under its own name. Ernest and Harry Lawrence adopted the gun as something of a pet project and over time made a number of changes in the original Woodward design: among others, a slightly slimmer reshaped frame, redesigned firing pins, and improved lockwork. Thus the Woodward of forty years ago became the Purdey over-under of today, though it remains essentially the Woodward action – a graceful, back-action sidelock. Even in 12-gauge, it's almost a full pound lighter than the first guns built on Edwinson Green's patents. Beaumont reports that Purdey's had built a total of 266 over-unders, all types included, by the end of 1983.

Now, well into its second hundred years, Purdey enjoys good days once again. The Purdey reputation is such that its guns command the highest prices in England – something near $50,000 for a standard best. Depending upon how you want it decorated, the price goes up from there.

And for your money, you get what you ask for – a side-by-side or over-under in any gauge, precisely tailored to your fit. It can be a gun built strictly in the classic style or in your own style, engraved in any pattern from the traditional rose and scroll that the first James Purdey learned from Joe Manton, to superb gold-work now done by Ken Hunt.

Whether the Purdey name is worth the additional cost is up to you – but you will pay a premium for any gun, new or used, with "J. Purdey & Sons"engraved on the lockplates. Other guns, some made in England and some made elsewhere in the world, are equally good. Nevertheless, there's only one Purdey.

Holland & Holland, Ltd

Harris Holland opened his shop at No. 9 King Street, Holborn, London, in 1835, the year Joe Manton died. Unlike James Purdey or Charles Lancaster or Thomas Boss or any of the others in the first great generation of English gunmakers, Holland never worked for Manton nor for any of Manton's disciples. No record remains to show where he learned the skills, but there is ample evidence that gunmaking was not Harris Holland's primary trade. He was a tobacconist and a would-be professional musician. He was twenty-nine years old when he opened the King Street shop.

He was, though, a keen sportsman, reportedly a splendid shot, and a member of the London pigeon-shooting clubs at Old Red House and Hornsey Wood. From his father, an organ-builder, Holland seems to have inherited a talent for working with his hands, and gunmaking apparently was a hobby. According to Peter King's excellent book on Holland & Holland, titled *The Shooting Field*, Holland's tobacco-shop customers encouraged him to take up gunmaking as a trade. One source has it that the King of Italy provided the financial backing, another that Holland's working capital came from some of his early customers.

In any case, the transition from tobacconist to gunmaker came slowly, for Harris Holland did not describe himself as solely a gunmaker until 1857. Only a handful of Holland guns built during those years remain, most of them percussion hammer guns with bar-action locks.

About 1860, Holland took on his fifteen-year-old nephew, Henry Holland, as an apprentice and in 1866 moved his shop to more fashionable quarters at 98 New Bond Street. Harris Holland had two daughters but no sons; Henry Holland probably became a working partner as soon as his indenture was completed in 1867, although formal articles of partnership weren't drawn up until 1876. By then the firm was operating under the style Holland & Holland.

According to what evidence remains, Harris Holland was a skillful craftsman but not a particularly imaginative designer. His one patent, issued in 1862, covers a hinge-type action with sliding barrels, which Geoffrey

Boothroyd describes as similar to Dougall's lock-fast action, patented two years earlier. Holland apparently did not build many guns on this action.

For all the gaps in the firm's early history, there is no question that both of the Hollands were astute businessmen extremely skillful at finding and supplying markets for best-quality guns. As did Purdey, Westley Richards, and others, Holland sold a great many guns to Indian princes during the days of the British Raj. When Harris Holland died in 1896, the company owned the New Bond Street shop, shooting grounds outside London, and a 15,000-square-foot factory on Harrow Road. Two years later, Henry Holland, now sole owner, moved the gun works a few hundred yards up Harrow Road to the factory where Holland guns are built today.

By the 1870s and '80s, Holland was building guns, rifles, and pistols in a multitude of styles – game guns, wildfowl pieces, smallbore rook rifles, big-bore rifles, even a revolving percussion rifle much on the order of the early Colts. The majority were centerfire breechloaders, although Holland also built a number of pinfire guns and even a few that could be used with either pinfire or centerfire cartridges. There were exposed-hammer actions and hammerless, bar-action and back-action locks. In addition to Henry Holland's own designs, the company built guns on a multitude of patents held by other makers. Quite a few were made on the Climax action patented by William Scott of

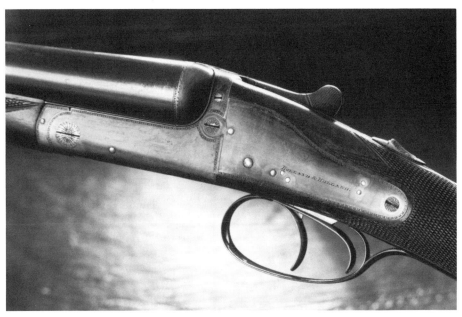

Many of Holland's early guns were of backlock or back-action design.

159

Birmingham. Holland also enjoyed considerable success with a self-cocking hammer gun patented by Thomas Perkes of 4 Duck Lane, Soho.

An almost uncanny ability to recognize good ideas and then to create a market for them was one of the most important factors in Holland's success, and one of the best examples is the Paradox gun.

Ever since shotguns and rifles diverged to become definably different items, some gunmakers have tried mightily to get them back together. That curious human desire to be prepared for anything at any time seems to have prompted considerable effort toward getting a rifled barrel and a smooth-bored barrel onto the same frame.

Even at best, the results have compromised something in handling quality, firepower, recoil, or general usefulness. Like most compromises, they are adequate for most uses without being truly great at any. The Germans cobbled two, three, and even four barrels together and devised ingenious trigger and sear mechanisms to make everything work. The British, more reserved, were content with two barrels and turned out some beautifully built combination guns. Having only two barrels did the least mischief to handling, but for practical purposes, these are single-shot guns. The ideal was a double gun that could handle shot or bullets equally well through the same bores.

Bullets in smooth-bored guns weren't the answer, though the earliest English double rifles used just that. The 12-, 10-, 8-, 6-, and even 4-bore guns that British sportsmen and explorers carted off to Africa and India proved barely adequate against dangerous game and, at fifteen pounds or thereabouts, utterly useless as shotguns.

Similarly, a rifled bore does weird things to a charge of shot. A round pellet has a miserable aerodynamic shape, and rifling simply magnifies its erratic tendencies, sending pellets by the dozen spiraling off from the main swarm, shedding velocity, thinning patterns, and generally upsetting all the advantages that choke-boring imparts.

W.E. Metford, a British civil engineer who essentially fathered the modern concept of rifle boring, found the right track in 1865 with full-length rifling cut no more than .004 inches deep. A few years later, Metford demonstrated that even shallower grooves – which he called scratch rifling – not only lent sufficient spin to a bullet but also would pattern a charge of shot better than any sort of rifling so far yet devised. Not long after, Charles Lancaster perfected oval boring – a smooth, elliptical bore that worked remarkably well with either ball or shot.

But the real breakthrough, the discovery that fostered a whole class of ball-and-shot guns, came from Colonel George Vincent Fosbery.

Fosbery, whose services to the Crown had earned him the Victoria Cross, started with the intention of designing a shotgun that could be used as a rifle. (His predecessors seem to have gone about it the other way around.) He found that a few inches of rifling at the muzzle of an otherwise smooth bore made both a relatively accurate rifle and a fairly close-shooting shotgun.

Fosbery patented the idea in 1885. Holland & Holland bought the patent a year later, perfected the notion, and brought out the famous Holland Paradox. Paradox it was. Into the bore of a tightly choked shotgun barrel, Holland barrel-makers cut a few inches of sharp-edged grooves with a fairly high rate of twist, starting at a scarcely perceptible depth and deepening progressively through the choke cone. These barrels proved quite accurate with either conical bullets or round balls. Bullets were reliably accurate out to about 120 yards; balls, less efficient, were good to about seventy-five or eighty yards. Shot patterns generally were similar to those from shotgun barrels with improved-cylinder choke.

Holland's built Paradox guns in gauges 8, 10, 12, 16, and 20 on both exposed-hammer and hammerless actions. Length of the rifling varied according to bore size, ranging from about four inches in 8-bore to just over two inches in 20.

Weight was the key to the Paradox's practical success. Earlier ball-and-shot guns suffered from being either too heavy for shotguns or too light to dampen recoil from the enormous bullets they fired. In guns built according to Fosbery's patent, bullets met little resistance in the smooth bore, thereby holding down gas pressure and recoil effect, and they passed so quickly through the rifling that felt recoil was not much more than one got from a similarly loaded shotshell. Consequently, muzzle-rifled guns commonly weighed little more than half as much as a fully rifled gun of the same bore.

During the effective life of Fosbery's patent, Holland & Holland had a corner on muzzle-rifled guns in the British market, but the Paradox was so popular that virtually every important English maker – and a few obscure ones, besides – brought out similar guns almost the moment the patent expired: Greener, Jeffrey, Pape, Bland, Cogswell & Harrison, Westley Richards, Army & Navy Stores, Ward & Sons, C.G. Bonehill, William Ford, G.E. Lewis & Sons, and Manton & Company, Calcutta.

Successful as they were, muzzle-rifled guns still compromised much of their usefulness as either rifles or shotguns. More modern, high-intensity rifle cartridges were well on the way in any case. Holland's continued to build Paradox guns as late as the 1950s but only a few, probably for customers who wanted to complete a collection of Holland guns.

By the turn of the century, Holland & Holland was the only maker in England to rival Purdey in both reputation and as a holder of royal warrants.

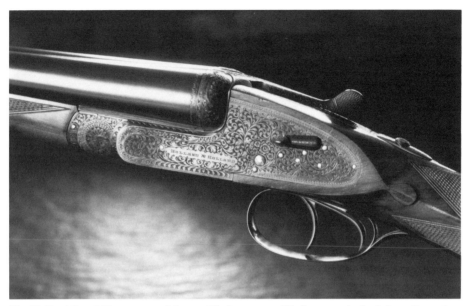

The Holland Royal Ejector, one of the world's finest guns. The lever on the lockplate allows the shooter to remove the locks without using a screwdriver – a system patented by Henry Holland.

Holland's has held appointments as gun and rifle makers to Edward VII and George V of England, to King Alfonso XIII of Spain, the Czar of Russia, and the kings of Sweden, Italy, and Portugal. The firm currently is by appointment rifle maker to H.R.H. The Duke of Edinburgh.

Of all the guns that Holland's built during the halcyon years of the English trade, the classic Holland & Holland is the hammerless Royal Ejector. Henry Holland himself presumably had a hand in developing the action, although none of the literature offers much discussion of how or even exactly when it evolved. Holland's secured trademark protection for the name "Royal" in May 1895.

The important point, in any case, is that the Royal action is less an "invention" than it is the final result of the whole evolutionary process of English gunmaking. The Holland Royal incorporates the best of what went before – the Anson & Deeley cocking system, the Purdey bolt, the Scott spindle and more – combined with Holland's own lockwork and rendered as a thing of elegant, timeless beauty. It is, for the most part, the world standard. You can order Holland-action guns from dozens of makers the world over. With the outbreak of war in 1914, orders for best-quality game and pigeon guns naturally dwindled, even though Holland records show that 160 such guns were finished and delivered from 1915 through 1917. Most of Holland's efforts during World War I centered on sniper's rifles and other military hardware. While no English gunmaker was unaffected by the social and economic changes that bedeviled England in the 1920s and '30s, Holland & Holland appears to have fared better than most, owing no doubt to Henry Holland's ever-incisive mind for business.

Nonetheless, he was growing old. One of his twin sons, Hal, who had been a director of the firm since about 1905, died of tuberculosis in 1921. Holland's other son, Jack, had planned a military career and served with distinction both in the Boer War and in World War I. The horror of the Great War, however, soured his taste for the military, and he resigned his commission in the spring of 1921 and moved to Ireland to breed horses. Henry Holland's health began to fail in the late 1920s, and Jack finally accepted a director's position with the firm in 1927. When Henry Holland died on January 25, 1930, Jack took charge. He proved as shrewd a businessman as his father had been.The second world war naturally brought more military work to Holland's, primarily setting up sniper's rifles, making and installing sights and silencers of various kinds, and boring propeller sleeves for de Havilland airplanes.

And orders for guns and rifles naturally were few in the post-war years. Even when the old markets of Europe and Asia and South America did begin to revive, painfully short supplies of high-quality wood and steel and ammunition made filling orders difficult. Changing political climates in India and the Far East slowly eroded those once-lucrative markets, and like Purdey, Holland soon found that a substantial portion of its future lay in America.

Colonel Jack Holland died in 1958. His son-in-law, Derek Mangnall, succeeded him as chairman of Holland & Holland. The following year, Mangnall and the Holland family and Malcolm Lyell struck a deal that amalgamated Holland's and Westley Richards under a holding company called Holland, Farlow and Lyell Limited.

Lyell had worked for Westley Richards since 1947, managing the Richards shop on Conduit Street in London. He bought the shop as a Westley Richards agency in 1956 and subsequently also acquired the Farlow fishing-tackle shop and W.J. Jeffery (Gunmaker), a company established in London about 1888 and well known for building high-quality guns and, especially, rifles.

The amalgamation brought new energy to Holland's, particularly from Malcolm Lyell. During his twenty-five-year tenure as Managing Director, he would provide the same astute and energetic business sense that has characterized the company since the days of Harris Holland himself, and this, it seems to me, is the key to Holland & Holland's continuing success. Simply turning out an excellent product never has been enough. Holland & Holland has endured the same rough times that have bedeviled every English

In recent years, Holland & Holland has been particularly active in building sets of commemorative guns. Above: No. 3 of The Broadlands Set, four guns built in 1984 in honor of Broadlands, the estate of Lord and Lady Mountbatten. Lord Mountbatten was a Commander of the Royal Navy and the last British Viceroy of India. The left side of gun No. 3 commemorates the Sword of Honour and Freedom of the City of London, decorations presented to Lord Mountbatten.

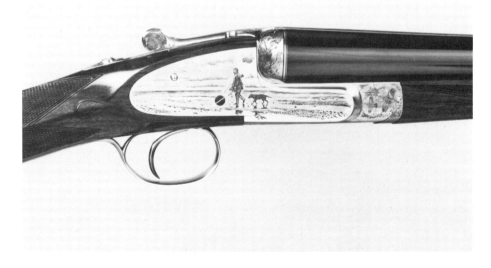

gunmaker, but Holland seems generally to have fared better through it all than most of the others. Shrewd management – the lack of which nearly sent Purdey's down the drain more than once in this century – has made the difference. And it continues to do so in the form of Roger Mitchell, the current Managing Director.

For Lyell and his colleagues, the 1960s were critical, busy years. They moved the Holland shop to larger quarters at 13 Bruton Street in 1960, refitted the Harrow Road factory with better equipment, instituted more efficient manufacturing techniques, began to make better use of the Holland shooting school as a marketing tool, and expanded the Holland marketing efforts worldwide, with particular emphasis on the United States.

One has only to walk through the door of the present Holland showrooms at 31 Bruton Street to see that all the work paid off. In these handsomely decorated rooms, with rows of lovely guns new and old ranked in glass-fronted cabinets, there is a clear sense both of the diversity of Holland's current business and of the tradition upon which it all is founded. You can order a new gun, buy a used one, leave one for repair, or browse through an excellent selection of sporting books (Holland now owns Rowland Ward, the famous sporting publisher), clothing, and accessories.

If you look closely at the guns, you can see even more clearly that Holland & Holland is focused upon the future.

In 1985, Holland bought W&C Scott (Gunmakers) of Birmingham, a purchase that netted not only a line of excellent boxlock guns but also a well-equipped factory and the only remaining barrel works in England other than Holland's own. (Holland bought out the Vickers-Armstrong barrel works in 1963, leaving Scott as the sole supplier of barrels to the entire English trade.) Although Scott guns will still be built, Holland has converted much of the factory to production of best-quality boxlock guns that bear the Holland name.

As I said earlier, the cost of building a best-quality English sidelock gun is high and the selling price even higher. A market for such guns certainly exists, but it's a luxury market and a tiny one even in worldwide terms. It's a highly competitive market as well, and every small gunmaker in the world is literally a hostage to the whims of world economics. Any maker hoping to create some security must look to a broader market, and that means producing lower-priced guns – which is precisely what Holland & Holland is doing.

There is a persistent attitude among many gun-fanciers that only a sidelock can truly meet the highest standards of quality, an attitude that the English gun trade did much to create. Actually, that view has little basis in fact. A fine gun is a fine gun, regardless of what style its action happens to be. Boxlocks are

165

easier to build than sidelocks, and the English trade traditionally did use boxlocks for its lower-quality guns, but that was a matter of choice. There simply is nothing inherently inferior about a boxlock action. In fact, a fine boxlock is a better gun than a poorly made sidelock; we have a world of guns and a hundred years of history to prove it.

Neither of the two Holland & Holland boxlocks – the Northwood and the more expensive Cavalier – is cheap, but both are extremely high-quality guns, and both naturally can be built to the customer's requirements. They are not as highly refined nor as meticulously finished as a Royal Ejector, but they don't cost $45,000, either. Prices fluctuate with the currency exchange rate, of course, and there are import duties as well; as a rough guide, though, you can expect to pay about $9000 for a Northwood and about $13,000 for a Cavalier.

Considering the conservatism of the English trade and a similar conservatism on the part of those who buy English best guns, Holland's move into the boxlock market is a daring venture, made even more so by the fact that Holland has instituted high-tech manufacturing methods to produce them. The boxlocks – and to some extent, all of Holland's guns – are designed and built with the assistance of computer technology.

Along with the notion that a sidelock gun is somehow intrinsically "better" than a boxlock has come a similar idea that a gun must be hand-made in order to be of best quality. The English trade has done much to create this illusion, too, even while violating it at every opportunity.

Actually, relatively few modern guns ever have been literally hand-made, since every gunmaker with any business sense at all has sought to do as much preliminary work as possible by machine. It's more efficient and more economical and doesn't make the slightest difference in the quality of the finished gun. Final fitting and finishing is where handwork is the key, because no machine can match the human hand and eye for that. The real artistry in gunmaking lies in the last few thousandths of an inch, not in the stage where a block of steel or wood is roughed into the shape of a frame or a stock. Look at it this way: If Michelangelo had owned a jackhammer, he sure as hell would've used it – and neither *David* nor the *Pieta* would be any less beautiful if he had.

So, Holland & Holland is now bringing the English gun into the Space Age, taking advantage of the same technology that the Japanese and the Italians have used with such remarkable success. At the old W&C Scott factory, guns now are designed on computer screens, with the data transferred to other computers that drive the milling machines and spark eroders. The parts thus created are still fitted and polished by hand. It isn't how Joe Manton made guns – but only because Joe Manton didn't have a computer.

Along with the boxlocks, Holland has recently added another sidelock gun to its line, one that reaches well back into Holland history. It's called the Dominion, a distinctive, back-action design that Henry Holland used extensively around the turn of the century for both rifles and guns.

Responding to the same market that prompted Purdey's to build them, Holland & Holland made its own foray into over-under guns in the 1950s, producing a total of twenty-five of them before giving up the over-under in 1960 as too expensive to build. Computer technology has reopened that door, too.

In fact, Holland plans to build two new over-unders. One is a back-action sidelock that essentially is a redesigned, improved version of the original Holland over-under. It's to be built in both 12- and 20-gauge versions and fitted with a single trigger (not, however, the old Holland-patent trigger; Piotti now supplies all Holland single triggers). It also will be expensive, as costly at least as a Royal Ejector side-by-side.

The other over-under, still in design, will be a boxlock meant, I'm told, to compete in the sporting-clays market. The price likely will be on a par with the Cavalier boxlock, perhaps $15,000. It should be a beauty.

All of this makes Holland & Holland something of an anomaly in the British trade. The arch-traditionalists may scoff, but the world is not now as it was a hundred years ago. If the tradition is to survive past the turn of the next century, it must do so in twenty-first century terms. Holland & Holland seems fully prepared to take up the challenge. That's how tradition lives on, anyway – by preserving old values while accommodating new times.

Boss & Company, Ltd

Since even before Joe Manton's days, the London gun trade has been a tightly knit community, interdependent and laced with generations of names woven through 200 years of history. Thomas Boss is a fine example.

Boss learned the trade from his father early in the nineteenth century and subsequently spent several years working for Manton at the Oxford Street shop. He hired on with James Purdey in 1817, remained in Purdey's shop until 1821, and set up on his own at 3 Grosvenor Street in 1830. Sometime later, he moved to Clifford Street and then to 73 Saint James Street, Pall Mall, and finally to 41 Albemarle Street in Piccadilly about 1859.

By then, the style was Boss & Company, for Thomas Boss had taken on a partner, a young gunmaker named Stephen Grant. When Boss died about

1865, Grant went into business on his own account. He later became associated with Joseph Lang; their successors formed Grant & Lang and, later still, amalgamated with Henry Atkin's successor to become Atkin, Grant & Lang. By the time it closed down altogether, which was fairly recently, the firm incorporated Churchill, Harrison & Hussey, Lancaster, Watson, and Beesley.

Meanwhile, Thomas Boss' widow took over Boss & Company and brought in Boss' nephew. He, in 1891, took on John Robertson as a partner; Robertson had spent the previous ten years working for the second James Purdey (James the Younger) and eventually became sole owner of Boss & Company. His descendants still own the firm today.

A complex tapestry, the London trade. No Russian novelist or soap-opera script writer could have created a more interesting cast of characters nor intertwined their lives in more intricate ways.

What came out of it, in Boss's case, is a relatively small number of guns that are as carefully crafted as guns can be. In the 1850s and '60s, when Boss and Grant were working together, the London trade was all abuzz with energy and ideas centered on the breechloading gun. No record remains to show whose idea it was, but both Boss and Grant obviously were intrigued with the notion of using a side-mounted lever to operate the fastening system of a break-action gun. Even long after, when Boss and Grant were separate companies and when the top latch was for practical purposes the trade standard, both continued to build side-lever, snap-action guns.

Grant, in particular, has come to be associated with elegant side-levers, in both exposed-hammer and hammerless forms. Boss often used a hammerless side-lever action for its patented try-guns; in fact, if you go to Griffin & Howe in New York today for a stock-fitting, you'll use a Boss side-lever.

While Thomas Boss no doubt established the standards of quality to which all Boss guns have been built, he died long before the breechloader reached its final, modern form. The greatest technical contributions, which unquestionably ensured the firm's survival to this day, came, instead, from John Robertson.

A gifted designer as well as a deft craftsman, Robertson developed one of the earliest intercepting-safety mechanisms for hammerless guns, designed the Boss ejector system, and in 1894 patented the Boss single trigger. Even though functional single triggers had been applied to wheellock guns as early as the seventeenth century and to flintlocks in the eighteenth century, none of the nineteenth-century London makers thought much of them. As H.A.A. Thorn of Charles Lancaster later put it, he did not consider that any single-trigger mechanism "could be relied upon never to go wrong in use." This, even though Thorn himself had designed and patented the Lancaster trigger. James

Purdey the Younger and his son Athol felt the same. None of which, of course, had stopped anyone from trying to make the idea work. Between 1864 and 1910, more than a hundred different single-trigger designs – and as many as eighteen in a single year – earned patent protection in England.

A Purdey actioner named William Nobbs designed a single trigger in 1883. It didn't work, but Nobbs kept at it and came up with a much better design in 1894, the same year that Robertson patented the Boss trigger. Although the mechanics were different, both functioned on the "three-pull" principle. (So, in fact, did a number of others, including the Holland & Holland single trigger, designed by Henry Holland and Thomas Woodward and patented in 1897). All single triggers have to somehow accommodate the phenomenon by which involuntary pressure from the shooter's finger sets off the second shot while the gun is recoiling from the first. Nowadays, this customarily is accomplished by an inertia-block arrangement or by some other means that prevents the second sear from engaging until the trigger is fully released from the first pull. In the three-pull approach, the trigger must actually be pulled three times to fire two shots. At the first shot, the trigger mechanism shifts from the first sear to an intermediate position, out of contact with either sear. The second pull, the involuntary one prompted by recoil, shifts the mechanism again and engages the second sear. The third pull, naturally, fires the second shot.

It sounds complicated, and mechanically it is, but it works well enough, especially if it's very carefully made and fitted. The complexity, of course, is the greatest weakness. Robertson's version, which used a cylindrical gear driven by a watch-spring, comprises a total of fourteen parts. Still, it was a good trigger by turn-of-the-century standards and no doubt contributed something to the popularity of Boss guns. It also contributed to some friction between Boss and Purdey. The problem began in March 1897, when Athol Purdey all but accused John Robertson of copying the Nobbs trigger (recall that both the Robertson and Nobbs patents were issued the same year, 1894). Why he waited nine years to do it isn't clear, but Robertson brought suit against Purdey's in December 1906, asking Mr. Justice Parker in the Chancery Division of the High Court to issue an order restraining Purdey from infringing his patent for a three-pull single trigger.

The case concluded in February 1907, and we have two, somewhat different versions of the outcome. Richard Beaumont says that the court found in Purdey's favor, at least to the extent of ruling that Purdey was not infringing Robertson's patent. Greener, on the other hand, reports that Justice Parker threw out both patents on grounds that they infringed an earlier patent for a three-pull system issued to Jones and Baker. Greener doesn't say which Jones and Baker, although he's undoubtedly referring to William P.

169

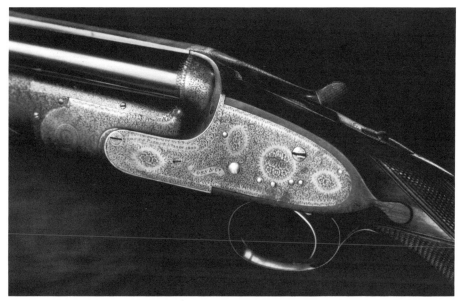

John Robertson, a former Purdey craftsman, patented the Boss over-under in 1909. It was the first truly great British over-under gun.

Jones, a third-generation Birmingham maker who patented a three-pull single trigger in 1883.

In any event, none of it seems to have done either maker any lasting harm. Two years later, in fact, Boss was to reach a milestone in gunmaking history.

In 1909, John Robertson obtained patents for an elegant sidelock gun that probably is the best of all the English over-unders. Besides its exceptionally fine craftsmanship, the Boss, like the Woodward and Purdey guns that followed, has that cardinal virtue of a great over-under – a slender, shallow frame that promotes not only dynamic balance but splendid pointing qualities as well. With side-mounted trunnions forming the hinge and a fastening bolt that engages bites at the sides of the lower barrel, the Boss frame is scarcely taller than the stacked barrels themselves, less than 2½ inches from the trigger plate to the top of the standing breech.

One of the main reasons why a good break-action gun points so well is that it aligns the shooter's hands almost perfectly with each other and with his dominant eye. The barrels literally lie in his left hand, the hand that directs the muzzles, while the shallow frame and gentle angle of the stock wrist positions his right hand on the same plane. This allows eyes, hands, and the rest of his body an easier time getting into sync, and the result is a gun that points with a natural feel, right where the shooter looks. If this sounds like over-refined

170

claptrap, shoot a good double for a while, long enough to grow accustomed to the feel of it, and then pick up a pump gun or autoloader, most of which don't align your hands nearly as well. You'll see the difference immediately.

Besides its intrinsic merits, the Boss over-under is historically significant as well. So far as I know, it was the first high-quality over-under (and maybe the first of any quality) to use the trunnion hinge and to be bolted at the breech face itself rather than on a barrel lump or barrel extensions. If you compare the bolting systems that Beretta, Perazzi, Marocchi, and some others use today, you can see that they're all based on the same principle; look at a Boss and you can see where it came from.

The Boss over-under was an almost instant success, particularly in the foreign markets, and remained so through the 1950s. It never was built in great numbers (Boss probably has made fewer than 10,000 guns of any kind in the past hundred years) but always with great care and attention to every detail. By the early '60s, Boss operated a shop on Cork Street and shooting ground on Barnet-By-Pass Road. Its factory on Lexington Street still turned out game guns and try-guns and single triggers and cartridges. In the following years, though, as competition from Italy all but took over the market for best-quality over-unders, orders for Boss over-unders were few.

Happily, the shooting world has rediscovered it, and the past couple of years have brought enough new orders that its future once again holds promise. Which is good, for Boss guns of every sort deserve all the appreciation they get, and more.

John Wilkes

Fathers passing the arts and skills of gunmaking along to their sons is one of the oldest traditions of the European trade. It's happened among literally hundreds of makers, although the quirks and twists of human affairs are such that companies rarely remain in the hands of the founding families for more than three or four generations. The twelve generations of gunmaking Berettas are the great exception, of course, and probably the oldest family-owned business in the world. But it's the exception, as the old cliché says, that proves the rule.

There are no twelfth-generation English makers, in part because the British trade itself isn't that old, and in part because the twentieth century has been damnably hard on it. Neither of the two most famous names that still survive are owned by the founding families and haven't been for years. Purdey's effectively passed from family ownership in the 1930s, Holland & Holland in the 1960s. There are, however, two British firms still owned and managed by direct descendants of the founders. William Powell of Birmingham, now in the sixth generation of Powell directorship, is one. The other is John Wilkes of London.

You can find the current John Wilkes, the fifth gunmaker to bear the name, at 79 Beak Street in Soho, under the sign, now faded by more than sixty years of London soot, that reads JOHN WILKES, GUN & RIFLE MAKERS. In the tiny front room, with its racks of guns and clutter of cases and cartridges that nearly reach the ceiling, you feel as if you've stepped out of the twentieth century and into the London that Charles Dickens knew.

The shop hasn't been on Beak Street, or even in London, quite that long, but the firm itself is older than any of Dickens' novels, founded when John Wilkes' great-great-grandfather set up shop in Birmingham about 1830.

His aim was to build rifles for the British military to use in tending and expanding an enormous world empire. With England continuously involved in wars and conquests from the Orient to the Crimea, the demand was such that by the early 1860s Wilkes employed a staff of several hundred, turning out rifles for the British government and supplying foreign armies as well – including both the Union and the Confederacy during the American Civil War. ("We did build guns for both sides," John told me, "but our sympathies were with the South; otherwise, we wouldn't have accepted their money. There's still some of it around here someplace.")

In a tradition reportedly begun by the first John Wilkes of all, a flamboyant political reformer born in London in 1727, the oldest sons of each generation are named John and second sons Tom. So, by 1866, the second gunmaking John Wilkes had taken over the firm and for reasons that no one ever knew, brought it nearly to ruin.

He simply failed to show up at the Birmingham factory one morning. The following day, his brother Tom and son John discovered that John Wilkes had cleared out the firm's banking accounts, mortgaged the business for every additional shilling he could raise, and boarded a ship bound for America.

The Wilkeses managed to keep the gun works afloat while Tom headed off to America, both to raise some money and to pursue his errant brother. He worked at Colt's for a while and then at the Singer Sewing Machine Company – and probably had to deal with some confusion whenever he inquired the possible whereabouts of one John Wilkes, since that was two-thirds of a name known to virtually everyone in the country as the assassin of President Lincoln.

In any case, the family's recollection has it that Tom made his way as far west as St. Louis, where he learned of a man who advertised himself as John Wilkes, Gunmaker. He found the premises but not the man himself and reportedly gave up the search. By the time he arrived back in Birmingham, the Wilkes fortunes were turning for the better, thanks to the continuing demand for military arms and no doubt helped along by the Franco-Prussian War of 1870-71, but the firm never would be as large as it was before.

Sometime during the 1880s or '90s, the Wilkeses developed both business and family relationships with James Dalziel Dougall, the Scottish maker who had invented the famous Lock Fast breechloading action and who had opened a London shop at 59 St. James's Street in 1864. Dougall and Wilkes formed a partnership to manufacture smokeless powder, a partnership that probably continued until Dougall's death in January 1896. Although its origins were rooted in military weaponry, Wilkes built at least a few sporting guns and rifles almost from the beginning, probably upon requests from military officers. As the century came to a close, demand for sporting guns increased throughout the trade, and by 1894 John Wilkes had opened a London shop, at 1 Lower James Street, Soho, to accommodate the demand. For the first year, it went under the style of Wilkes & Harris. Harris was a bookkeeper, not a gunmaker, and his tenure was brief; in 1895, the firm became John Wilkes, as it remains today.

The business did well in the twenty years between the great wars, building boxlock and best-quality sidelock guns and rifles and bolt-action magazine rifles. For a few years, Wilkes marketed its own shot cartridges under two trade names: Doughty and Tom-Tom, the latter clearly a pun on the traditional family name. The address changed a couple of times in the 1920s, first to Gerrard Street, then to Broad Street, Golden Square, and finally, about 1925, to Beak Street.

The fourth John Wilkes had a particularly clever mind for unusual, specialized weaponry and during World War II supplied a great variety of it to British undercover forces and to resistance groups in Europe – including a pistol of his own device that could be fastened to a man's wrist or inside a coat pocket and fired by a remote trigger.

In the post-war world, it was business as usual, as much of the usual business, at least, as could be drummed up in a slack market. In the '50s and '60s, Wilkes filled what orders for bespoken guns that came along (including some for other makers who no longer had the staff or the facilities to build guns on their own), built boxlock guns for front-shop inventory, and did repair work. The fourth John Wilkes died in 1968, succeeded by the current owners, John and Tom, who now

Twenty-bore game gun built by the fifth John Wilkes. Founded as a maker of military rifles more than 150 years ago, John Wilkes now builds only best-quality game guns in the classic London style.

manage the business as a simple, co-owner partnership.

In the late 1970s, faced with a future that looked anything but auspicious, John Wilkes did what some other English makers have done and began making periodic trips to the United States to see what orders might come of it. Through the good offices of some mutual friends, I met John during one of his early visits, and we've kept in touch in the years since. Happily for the firm, they seem to have been good years, as quite a number of Americans have discovered that superb workmanship is both available and more affordable than the Purdey or Holland catalogues might suggest.

The response has been good enough, in fact, that the staff of six gunsmiths, including John and Tom Wilkes, both of whom are master gunmakers, now builds only best-quality sidelock guns in the London style, and orders are in place that will occupy several years to come.

As I said, the little Beak Street shop is like a world out of time. The front room will hold perhaps four people if two of them take turns breathing. Beyond lies the repair room/office, where John's daughter manages the books and the telephone and where minor repairs are carried out. The real shops are in the two rooms above, at the top of a steep, narrow stairway; there, if you're invited up, you'll find some very simple machinery, workbenches, and a litter of hand tools, all overlaid with a patina of dust, ancient gun oil, and shavings of steel and wood. Mixed in are barrels and frames, stock blanks, trigger guards, stray parts, mountings, and guns in various stages of completion. It looks like a gunshop ought to look.

When my wife and I stopped by during a day in London last winter, John was working on a set of best guns for an American customer. The frames, just back from Ken Hunt's engraving shop, hung on an upstairs wall, their lovely scroll and gold inlay almost glowing in the fading afternoon light from the window. From the floor rack in the center of the room, John handed me a 10-gauge still aborning, the stock headed up and rough-shaped, the action bristling with slave screws, awaiting the filer's touch. And then a 28-gauge that, even half-finished, felt as delicate as a fine old sword.

But for Susan, ever the sensible part of us and ever gentle with my preoccupations, I'd probably be there still.

William Evans, Ltd

Like many another English gunmaker, William Evans has all but passed out of sight beyond the scrim of history. He worked at Purdey's in the early 1880s, but no record remains to show whether he went there as an apprentice or a journeyman. In any case, he left in 1883, the same year that Purdey's moved from Oxford Street to Audley Street, and set up shop on his own account at 63 Pall Mall. And he was crossways with James Purdey the Younger almost straightaway.

The trouble stemmed from Evans' practice of engraving his guns "William Evans (from Purdey's)." It was not at all uncommon for makers to use the names of famous former employers in their advertising – for obvious reasons. The first James Purdey himself did so, noting on his earliest case labels that he was "from J. Mantons." The practice was so widespread that it became almost a tradition in the English trade, and, in fact, it's still done today.

The gunmakers whose names were being used generally faunched and fumed, branding the practice unethical and claiming that it amounted to unauthorized use of a trade name. The ethical argument has some merit, but such claims are protected by law so long as they're true. Moreover, as Frederick Beesley (who customarily cited his own previous employment with Purdey) pointed out, "it must be admitted that it is by the technical knowledge and skill of those who work for them that the 'well-known firms' sustain their well-deserved reputations."

Beesley – who was a far better gunmaker than a writer – has a point: it's the shop men who actually make the guns, regardless of whose name appears on the finished product.

None of which cut the least ice with James Purdey the Younger, who does not seem to have been a man much given to the finer shades of argument. A number of Purdey craftsmen went out on their own in the 1880s; most used the Purdey name, and James the Younger grew wroth, particularly at William Evans. Perhaps it was Evans' habit of noting the Purdey connection on the guns themselves. (Henry Atkin did, too.) Using a former employer's name in advertising, on stationery, or case labels is one thing – paper is perishable – but guns are something else entirely, made to last, meant to be used and seen. James consulted his solicitor in the matter. What he heard was not what he wanted to hear; since William Evans actually had worked at Purdey's, he was perfectly free to say so in any way he chose. Purdey workmen probably had a rough go of it for a few days after that meeting.

Evans, on the other hand, apparently did quite well, for at some point he obtained royal patronage, from Queen Victoria's third son, Arthur, Duke of Connaught. That alone says something for the quality of Evans' work. Second-rate makers don't get royal warrants, despite the whining of the anonymous gentleman from Brighton who wrote to Purdey's in January 1885, complaining about the "man named W. Evans selling guns of *very inferior*

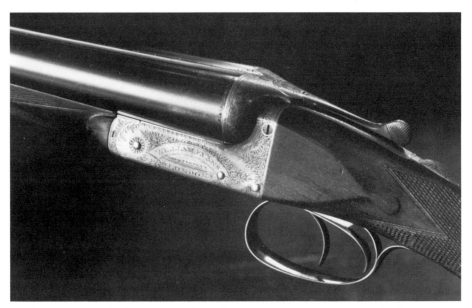

William Evans never hesitated to cite his previous employment with James Purdey & Sons, even to the point of engraving "from Purdey's" on the guns he built.

Birmingham make and having 'from Purdey's' engraved on them." The italics are his, although James no doubt shared the opinion. From this point, the trail of William Evans grows dim, though he clearly weathered the wrath of Purdey and sailed on into some prosperity. At some point, he obtained a patent for a single trigger. According to advertising from the early 1920s (by which time William Evans probably was either retired or deceased), the shop remained at 63 Pall Mall and dealt in guns and rifles, hammer and hammerless, new and used, by Evans and other makers. The firm still held a warrant as gunmaker to H.R.H. Duke of Connaught and operated a private shooting ground at South Harrow.

Somehow, the company managed to survive the disasters that have befallen the British trade over the past fifty years. The shop now is at No. 67a St. James's Street, and there you can have a new William Evans gun or rifle built to order, either a handsome boxlock or a sidelock in the London style. Both are of excellent quality.

The Brighton man who in 1885 accused Evans of selling "inferior Birmingham" guns also noted that "two young friends were led away by his advertisement and bought guns." Nothing about the guns themselves, then or now, suggests that they made a mistake. In fact, a couple my own young friends visited Evans while in London just a few weeks ago, and they're considering the same thing. There are many worse choices that a young man could make.

Sir Ralph and the Monstrous Horrendum

Sir Ralph Payne-Gallwey, Baronet, of Thirkleby Park, Thirsk, was a famous game shot of the late Victorian Age. He was an amateur in the strictest old sense of the word, almost a caricature of a turn-of-the-century British sportsman, consumed by his pastimes, earnest to an extreme. He was an inventor of shooting gadgetry – of cartridge bags and shooting sticks and game counters – and a writer of serious-minded, if sometimes murky, treatises on shooting, such as *High Pheasants in Theory and Practice*.

In 1896, Sir Ralph had this to say:

> ...as a rule, that 'monstrous horrendum' a ready-made, reach-me-down Birmingham gun, is fit for neither man, nor bird, nor beast, and is a mere unwieldy log of iron and wood when compared to the perfect article produced in London.

The point of Sir Ralph's little diatribe wasn't so much an attack on the Birmingham gun trade as an argument for the notion that a shooter will do better work with a custom-fitted gun than with one built to standard dimensions. He's quite right about that, but his approach did nothing to soothe the already-scratchy relations between the Birmingham and London trades. The attitude that Birmingham guns are inferior to those built in London is long-standing and, in fact, still exists; it's true in some cases, utter nonsense in others.

With iron ore and coal deposits nearby, Birmingham has been a manufacturing center since the Middle Ages. The earliest record of guns – "musquets," actually – being built there dates to the 1640s, and Birmingham makers were supplying weapons to the armies of William and Mary by 1693. By 1770, the Birmingham trade comprised thirty-eight gun and pistol makers, six gunlock-makers, and five barrel-makers. During the Napoleonic Wars, between 1804 and 1815, Birmingham turned out 1,827,889 finished arms, 3,037,644 barrels, and 2,879,203 locks.

Taking its cue from American industry in the 1850s, the Birmingham trade was the first in England to adopt the techniques of mass-production and interchangeable parts. More than 4,000,000 military gun barrels were made and proofed in Birmingham between 1854 to 1864, a period that includes both the Crimean War and the American Civil War. From October 1861 through 1864, the Birmingham trade contributed 733,403 weapons to the American conflict, supplying, as we've seen, both the Union and Confederate armies.

By the turn of the nineteenth century, most of the components used throughout the English gun trade came from Birmingham – locks, barrels, furniture, and all. In 1830, for instance, only one barrel-maker remained in London. This symbiotic relationship made good economic sense for everyone; it offered ready markets for the items that the material men – those who actually made the various parts – produced, and it provided a source of high-quality components that London and provincial makers could assemble into finished guns.

A useful relationship but never a particularly cordial one. Chartered by King Charles I in 1637, the Worshipful Company of Gunmakers of the City of London exercised all but complete political control over the entire English gun trade. The charter authorized the Company to establish rules of proof, and further laws enacted in 1670 made illegal the sale of any unproved weapon in and around London. Anyone, in other words, could make guns, but none could be sold in London, where the vast majority of British wealth was centered, unless approved by the Gunmakers' Company.

The legal requirement that all Birmingham-built guns had to be shipped to

Sir Ralph Payne-Gallwey, dressed for wildfowling.

179

London for proof before they could be dispatched to their customers naturally created an enormous bureaucratic bottleneck, particularly considering the vast numbers of military weapons being produced. As early as 1707, the Birmingham makers unsuccessfully petitioned the government for authorization to establish a proof house there. Private proof houses were organized in Birmingham in the latter eighteenth century, but they did little to change the situation.

Finally, with Britain simultaneously fighting the Napoleonic Wars in Europe and the War of 1812 in America, both of which required weaponry on a massive scale, the whole thing became so absurd that Parliament capitulated and in 1813 officially established the Birmingham Proof House.

Besides military arms, the Birmingham trade offered well-built, inexpensive sporting arms – certainly inexpensive by London standards – and the London makers had long been resentful of the competition. So long as the London Proof House was the only one in England, they felt relatively secure, but when the Birmingham trade gained co-equal power of law, the Londoners waxed testy indeed. Momentarily losing its collective head, the Gunmakers' Company backed a bill in the House of Commons to require that no one but the actual manufacturer could put his name on a gun. This was meant to stop the fairly common practice in which entrepreneurs stamped their own names and London addresses on Birmingham-built guns. The Birmingham contingent countered by pointing out that it would then become illegal for bona-fide London makers to put their names on guns made from Birmingham components. Since virtually all of the London makers did exactly that, they dropped the matter like a hot rock.

Even as the London trade grew more and more dependent upon the Birmingham shops and factories, it remained rancorous toward the Birmingham gun, seldom losing an opportunity to at least imply vast differences in quality between its own product and the Monstrous Horrendum. And to a great extent, the Londoners succeeded, mainly through the simple, natural human response to snob appeal. Even if Sir Ralph didn't intend his remarks to be quite as vicious as they sound, taken out of context, his castigation of the Birmingham gun accurately reflected an attitude that remains quite strong even today.

Because a London address was almost as important as a high-quality product, a great many Birmingham makers opened London shops. Westley Richards, in fact, became so widely associated with the London trade that it scarcely was thought of as a Birmingham firm. William Powell, on the other hand, does not appear to ever have had a London address. These, along with W&C Scott, are the only Birmingham gunmakers still in business today.

William Powell & Son, Ltd

Powell claims the earliest founding date, 1802, when William Powell and master gunsmith Joseph Simmons set up shop together at 44 High Street. The Bailey and Nie directory of the Birmingham and provincial gun trade lists Joseph Simmons as a partner in Simmons & Howell at that address in that year; "Howell" probably is a typo for "Powell." The earliest listing for William Powell himself is 1822, at 3 Bartholomew Row. In 1832, he took over Simmons' old shop at 49 High Street and at some time within the next few years moved to Carr's Lane, where the firm still is located. Since 1847, the style has been William Powell & Son.

Like the other Birmingham makers, Powell almost certainly built military weapons, but the firm clearly was interested in sporting guns as well. Its first important contribution to the evolution of the gun came in 1864, with a patented snap action using a top lever that the shooter pushes up rather than swings to the side. It's a strong, simple system that Powell used successfully for years, adapting it to hammer guns of both pin- and centerfire type and to both boxlock and sidelock hammerless actions.

Over the next twelve years, Powell earned patents for several other innovations, including half-cock locks, "loaded" indicators for hammerless guns, a spring-loaded fore-end latch, and a cross-bolt fastening system operated by a conventional top lever.

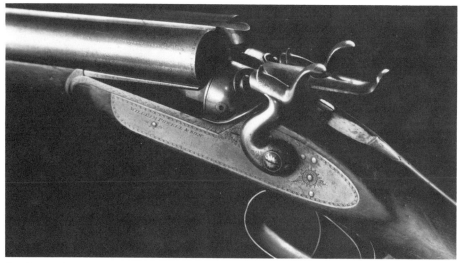

Bar-in-wood snap-action gun by William Powell. In Powell's 1864 patent, the top lever operates on a horizontal pivot; to open the action, the shooter pushes to lever up rather than to the side.

The firm obtained no further patents after 1876 and seems thereafter to have remained content building guns on established designs, both its own and those of others. Powell guns of every period, from the 1860s to the 1980s, show all of the craftsmanship and handling dynamics that a best-quality gun should.

The current line includes both sidelock and boxlock ejector guns at a price range from about $9000 to $25,000. Powell also offers a Heritage series built, I believe, on Italian actions. These include a sidelock and a boxlock; the boxlock version can be ordered as a standard gun, a round-action, or with Richards-type detachable locks.

For some reason, William Powell is often described in this country as "the Purdey of Birmingham." It's probably meant to be complimentary, but it strikes me as a note of faint praise, like describing some cheap but flossy clunk as "the poor man's Porsche." What it really says, to my ear, anyway, is that the old prejudice against Birmingham guns is with us still. Birmingham guns, and William Powell in particular, are better than that.

Westley Richards

It began about 1747, when Thomas Richards opened a shop at 53 High Street. He was a silversmith and, among myriad other items, made silver gun furniture. When he died in September 1779, Theophilus Richards took over the business and continued to trade under the Thomas Richards name until

Although the current firm of Westley Richards was established in 1812, the family's tradition of fine craftsmanship dates to the mid-eighteenth century, when Thomas Richards worked as a silversmith in Birmingham. The Anson and Deeley boxlock action, patented in 1875 and first manufactured by Westley Richards, provided the basic mechanical concept for self-cocking, break-action guns worldwide.

1784. Theophilus probably was Thomas Richards' son, and he, too, was a silversmith, jeweler, and cutler.

In 1799, Theophilus Richards set up as a gun and pistol maker at 26 High Street. The relationships are not fully documented, but Theophilus Richards appears to have had two sons – the elder also named Theophilus and the younger, born in 1788, named William Westley. Theophilus I died in 1828, presumably succeeded by his elder son. When Theophilus II died in 1833, the business came to an end.

The Richards family influence upon gunmaking, however, did not, for William Westley Richards had set up his own gun- and pistol-making shop at 82 High Street in 1812, just as the United States declared war on Britain. With the British army engaged in both the Napoleonic wars in Europe and the War of 1812 in North America, business was brisk. Among other military arms, Richards built a number of double-barreled cavalry pistols that were used in the American conflict.

William Westley Richards was an ambitious, inventive man and one who clearly recognized the importance of the London market. In 1815, he opened a shop at 170 New Bond Street, London. The firm ultimately would be the most famous of the Birmingham gunmakers, although it's difficult to say which contributed more in the early days – the quality of Richards' guns or the man he hired to run the London shop. William Bishop, as a contemporary described him, was a "large roomy man…a right reverend and episcopal figure" dressed always in black with gleaming white shirt-front and cuffs and a tall black, broad-brimmed hat. Peter Hawker called him "Uncle." Everyone else called him the Bishop of Bond Street.

London gentlemen, drawn by Bishop's lordly bearing and easy manner, soon found the Bond Street shop an excellent place, as Hawker says, to get "a good gun at a few hours' notice." Hawker, who apparently wasn't as troubled by the Monstrous Horrendum as Sir Ralph later would be, also observes that a good ready-made gun is better than one bespoken of a third-rate maker.

William Richards was no third-rate maker. Owing to his place in history, he naturally worked with muzzleloading guns, but his creativity placed him at the leading edge of innovation during the period when the flintlock evolved into the caplock and when the early breechloaders began to appear. Between 1821 and 1841, he earned five patents on designs relating to percussion primers and priming mechanisms. Other patents over the next fifteen years covered actions and other features for revolvers.

Though he remained an active designer almost until his death in 1865, William Richards retired in 1840, to be succeeded by his son Westley, born August 8, 1814. Westley Richards would play an even greater role in the evolution of English gunmaking.

Like his father, he possessed both a broad interest and a wonderfully creative mind. The twenty patents he eventually earned cover percussion caps, rifle actions, gunstocks, break-action guns, rifle sights, cartridges, and handguards. Commenting upon the extent of Richards' contribution, an anonymous writer in a 1902 issue of *The Birmingham Magazine* says:

> Every military rifle adopted by the Government since 1852 has been improved at the hands of Westley Richards and Co. To Westley Richards the Government were indebted for the solid drawn metallic rifle cartridge, adapted for the small Gatling gun, and also for the production of the Enfield rifle. Mr. Richards was also associated with Sir John Whitworth [actually Sir Joseph] in the production of the Whitworth rifling.

Westley Richards sporting rifles ultimately became as famous as the military guns. King Edward VII, while still Prince of Wales, shot his first tiger in India with a Westley Richards.

Sporting guns, too, earned a share of Richards' attention. He patented a snap-action design in 1858, a slide-forward hinge action in 1861, a top-latch fastening system with a doll's-head rib extension (possibly the first such system ever) in 1862, a modification of the doll's-head fastener in 1864, and, in 1866, an ingenious hammer and striker system that works equally well with either pinfire or centerfire cartridges.

In the 1860s and '70s, Westley Richards built a number of bar-in-wood guns. In this design, sometimes called "isolated sidelock," the action bar is reduced in size and enclosed in the stock so that the wood extends along the underside of the gun all the way to the hinge. The lockplates are entirely surrounded by the stock, hence the bar-in-wood name. William Westley Richards is sometimes given credit for inventing the arrangement, but it actually was developed by Charles Moore of 77 St. James's Street, London, in 1827. In any event, the bar-in-wood is an unusual though quite handsome gun, and a great many makers built them, including Purdey, Thomas Horsley, MacNaughton, and others.

Westley Richards retired in 1873, although like his father he continued to experiment with gun designs. When he died on May 27, 1897, Westley Richards & Company, Ltd. was one of the best-known and most highly respected gunmakers in the world. Though Richards himself certainly played a major role in the firm's success, the capstone to it all came from John Deeley.

Deeley was born in 1825 and began working at Westley Richards in 1860. When Richards retired, Deeley took over management of the firm, and before he, in turn, retired in 1899, he added at least seventeen additional patents to the Westley Richards repertoire. Many of his designs also were patented in the United States. Deeley's projects generally were collaborations – with James Edge, F.J. Penn, Leslie Taylor, William Anson. English patent No. 1756, issued jointly to William Anson and John Deeley on May 11, 1875, describes the most important of them all, the one that changed the course of gunmaking worldwide, for with that design Anson and Deeley created the boxlock action.

It's impossible to overestimate the significance or the impact of the Anson and Deeley action, because it literally ushered in the modern gun. The cocking principle, operating on leverage created by the barrels as they pivot on the hinge, can be applied to any sort of lockwork and now is to be found in virtually every break-action gun in the world. The Anson and Deeley lockwork is marvelously simple and perfectly efficient, and it, too, is a world standard.

By the turn of the century, the Anson and Deeley gun was built worldwide, on license from Westley Richards. Some makers simply copied the original, others developed variations on the same principle. Deeley himself continued to refine the idea, first with an intercepting safety that also has become widely used among the world's gunmakers. Deeley and Leslie Taylor patented a further improvement in 1897; this one has remained associated with Westley Richards ever since.

One of the advantages of a sidelock over the typical boxlock gun is that it's easy to remove the sideplates to clean the locks or replace springs and firing pins and lock parts. If you have the proper screwdriver and a spare spring or two, you can even make some repairs in the field. Holland & Holland developed a means for detaching sideplate locks by hand, to make it easier still.

On the other hand, you have to remove the trigger guard and the stock just to see the lockwork of a box-frame gun, and replacing parts usually requires a hammer and drift pins besides. It can be a chore.

Even though well-made locks rarely break down, being able to quickly get a gun back into working order is a refinement that has some merit in it, particularly in the case of a heavy rifle when you're a long way from a gunsmith and dealing with game capable of stomping you to marmalade. Deeley and Taylor, in a design patented in 1897, devised a boxlock action with hand-detachable locks. It's a brilliantly simple affair; the floor plate is removable, exposing the lockwork from underneath. The locks themselves comprise a cocking lever, tumbler, sear, and mainspring all attached to a small steel plate rather than to the gun frame. With the floor plate off, you can lift the locks out of their slots in the frame and install new ones in just a few seconds. By the turn of the century, the hand-detachable locks made Westley Richards rifles, already quite popular, into the darlings of African and Asian hunters.

Fitted with a single trigger designed by the American Allen Lard, a Westley Richards hammerless ejector gun with hand-detachable locks won a Special Award for artistic design, workmanship, and finish at the Paris Exhibition in 1900. It was well deserved.

Leslie Taylor succeeded Deeley as managing director at Westley Richards in 1899. By then, the firm owned a large factory and shooting grounds at Bournebrook, near Birmingham, and another shooting school at Hendon, outside London. It probably was the only Birmingham maker ever to operate shooting grounds around London. Customers included the Prince of Wales, the Duke of Edinburgh, the Duke of Cambridge, the Marquis of Queensbury, Viscount Curzon, Lord Hood, the Earl of Essex, the Duke of Somerset, and an equally long list of Indian princes as well.

As I mentioned in discussing Holland & Holland, Westley Richards & Company was liquidated in 1946 and subsequently purchased by a Birmingham businessman. In April 1948, Malcolm Lyell took charge of the London shop, then located at 23 Conduit Street. At the end of 1955, the owners decided to close down the London business, which Lyell purchased and operated as Westley Richards (Agency) Company, Ltd. When Lyell amalgamated with Holland's in 1959, Westley Richards became once again solely a Birmingham firm.

Now, much of the machinery and factory space at Bournebrook is devoted to tool and die manufacture, but gunmaking has its place, too. At the moment, Westley Richards offers an excellent sidelock gun in the $20,000 range, a boxlock built on a Scott action and marketed as the Connaught, and detachable-lock rifles. And for a price close to that of the sidelock, you can buy the most famous Westley Richards of all – a box-frame Anson and Deeley gun with hand-detachable locks: the well-known "drop-lock."

More than any of the still-surviving Birmingham gunmakers, Westley Richards reflects something of how the twentieth century has savaged the English trade. As it always has, Richards still turns out a diverse range of products, but the economic significance of those products has undergone an ironic reversal. A remarkable variety of military and sporting arms once formed the foundation of everything; any other items that Westley Richards might have manufactured were peripheral to gunmaking. Now, it's gone the other way. The tool and die business supports the gunmaking, and guns undoubtedly account for a minuscule portion of the firm's financial profile.

It isn't that Westley Richards is no longer serious about gunmaking, but rather that the world gun market has left a painfully narrow window for the English trade as a whole. In the face of what amounts to nearly overwhelming competition, it's a wonder, actually, that Richards is still able to build guns at all. In the past, the company's welfare rested wholly on the splendid quality of its guns; like the present, the future isn't likely to be so accommodating. And that's a great pity, because the splendid quality is still there.

W&C Scott

Sir Ralph Payne-Gallwey's distaste for the Birmingham gun reflected a more parochial point of view than the good baronet probably realized. No doubt Sir Ralph would have been astonished to know that the best-known English gunmaker in the world market of the late nineteenth century was not a London firm but rather a practitioner of the Monstrous Horrendum. To the rest of the world in the 1890s, the most familiar name from the English gun trade was that of W&C Scott.

William Scott was a Suffolk man who went to Birmingham in the 1810s. The earliest record of his work in the gun trade shows him as a gun- and pistol-maker at 79 Weaman Street in 1820. In 1834, he married Mary Susan Middleditch, moved his shop to Court 5 Russell Street, and founded the firm

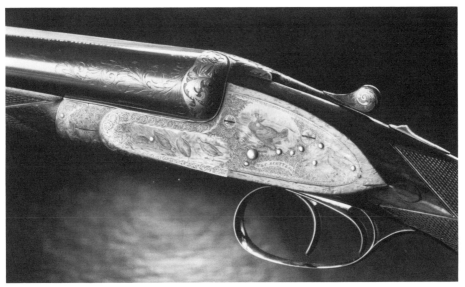

At the end of the nineteenth-century, W&C Scott was the best-known English gunmaker in the world. All Scott guns, from plainly finished boxlocks to this beautifully built Premier sidelock, are of extremely high quality.

that still bears his name. His brother Charles joined him in 1840, and the two set up at 11 Lench Street as W&C Scott (Gunmakers). William Scott's two sons – William Middleditch, born 1835, and James Charles, born two years later – joined the company in the mid-1850s, and the style changed to W&C Scott & Son in 1858.

Almost from the beginning, Scott set out to found its reputation on high-quality guns, and the market responded in kind. By 1864, the firm was prosperous enough to build a new factory at 123 Lancaster Street. Its success owed much to the inventive mind of William Scott's elder son.

Between 1865 and 1884, William M. Scott earned a total of fourteen patents for various gun actions, cocking indicators, stocks, and the like. All of them contributed something to the company's continued growth, but one in particular secured Scott a niche in the evolution of the gun itself.

The English trade as a whole seems to have almost instantly recognized James Purdey's sliding underbolt, patented in 1863, as an important breakthrough in gun design. While some makers experimented with various underlever arrangements adapted to the Purdey bolt, William M. Scott devised a way of connecting the bolt to a top lever and included the design in his first patent, granted October 25, 1865. The Scott spindle, as it's usually called, still is a standard part of Scott guns. Other makers adopted it as well, so widely, in fact, that by the turn of the century almost every maker in the world who used the Purdey bolt used the Scott spindle, too.

Scott also designed a barrel lump that could be adjusted with a screwdriver to compensate for wear in the hinge joint. To enhance the bolting system, he designed several variations on the rib extension/cross bolt system, which he used in conjunction with the Purdey-type underbolt. In some of these, the cross bolt extends out of the frame when the action is open; in others, the top bolt is concealed inside the frame. All of them are extremely durable.

William M. Scott succeeded his father as head of the company in 1866 and shortly proved that his ability to establish markets was every bit as good as his ability to produce the guns to supply them. He opened a London shop at 7 Dorset Place in Pall Mall (later moved to Great Castle Street), but his vision extended far beyond. Through frequent visits, he opened substantial European markets for Scott guns, especially among pigeon shooters. He also began traveling to the United States in the late 1860s and over the next few years set up a network of gun dealers that reached clear across the country. As a result, Scott sold more guns in America during the 1880s and '90s than anywhere else in the world.

American trapshooters were fond of the Scott guns, both during the live-pigeon days and later, when glass balls and clay targets began to take over the game. Adam Bogardus, one of the great American pigeon and exhibition shots of the late nineteenth century, used a Scott with two sets of barrels, one in 12-gauge, the other 10. At the same time, Italian pigeon shooters were winning the most prestigious European matches with Scott guns. Scott naturally recognized the marketing value of it all and frequently mentioned such accomplishments in its advertising and factory literature. Scott won recognition in other ways as well, garnering more than a dozen awards at trade exhibitions throughout the world.

As the century drew toward its close, both of William Scott's sons were growing old. Charles Scott succeeded his older brother as head of the company in 1894, although Charles, too, was approaching retirement. In 1897, W&C Scott merged with another old Birmingham firm, Philip Webley & Son, established in 1838. Although it had built sporting guns and rifles as well as military arms, Webley was best known for its revolvers, and after the merger (which also included acquisition of Richard Ellis & Son, yet another Birmingham maker) the new firm was named The Webley & Scott Revolver & Arms Company, Ltd., shortened in 1906 to Webley & Scott, Ltd.

Webley and Scott continued to operate as essentially separate businesses until 1899. After that, under centralized management, Scott's London office was closed down and the showrooms combined with Webley's at 78 Shaftesbury Avenue.

With an output that now included sporting guns, rifles, revolvers, pistols, and military weapons of all sorts, Webley & Scott was in an excellent position to meet the turmoil of the twentieth century. Production of sporting guns naturally ebbed and flowed according to world events, but even during the 1950s, generally a slack period for the English trade, Webley & Scott built as many as 1000 guns per year. They were meant to serve as well-made guns available at affordable prices, and they were exactly that.

Scott had long been the largest manufacturer of double guns in England, and before 1940, scarcely more than ten percent of them were sold under the Scott name. The rest, either as finished guns or as barreled actions, went to other makers. After Holland & Holland bought out Vickers-Armstrong in 1963, Scott was the only barrel-maker left in England. The firm continues to supply the trade with barreled actions

The next twenty years brought more changes of ownership. R.H. Windsor, Ltd., bought Webley & Scott in 1958 and a year later sold it to Arusha Industries, Ltd. Webley & Scott bought W.W. Greener in 1965 and for a while built a single-barrel trap gun under the Greener name. It was based on a Martini-type action and enjoyed a brief flurry of interest in the United States.

Webley & Scott once again courted the American market in the late 1960s with a line of well-made and moderately priced boxlock guns imported through Abercrombie & Fitch. Harrington & Richardson later became the official American distributor, but the guns never made much impact here.

The Harris & Sheldon Group of Companies, a British conglomerate, bought Webley & Scott in 1973. Production of sporting guns under the Scott name had been declining for several years and continued to do so until it amounted to fewer than 300 guns per year in the late '70s. In 1979, the company decided to convert all its resources to producing Webley & Scott air rifles and air pistols, which still enjoyed a strong market. Harris & Sheldon, however, saw another option.

In 1980, almost ninety years after it ceased to exist as an independent firm, W&C Scott (Gunmakers) was reborn. Twenty-six craftsmen, most of whom had worked in the shotgun division of Webley & Scott, were installed in a new factory, named Premier Works, on Tame Road in Witton, and in the first year they completed more than a hundred guns under the old Scott name.

By 1983, the Scott line comprised five boxlocks and a sidelock. Four of the boxlocks were called Bowood DeLuxe, Chatsworth GrandeLuxe, Kinmount, and Crown – double-trigger ejector guns in the British style. The differences among them are a matter of wood quality, engraving, and finish.

The Texan, the fifth model, built specifically for the American market, also is a boxlock but fitted with decorative sideplates. With beavertail fore-end, pistol-grip stock, single trigger, and, for God's sake, a longhorn steer engraved on the bottom of the frame, it's hardly an attractive piece of work. The sidelock, called Blenheim, is a handsome bar-action gun in the classic style.

Production of W&C Scott guns has continued since Holland & Holland bought the firm in 1985, although Holland has converted much of the Premier Works to producing guns under the Holland name. Scott still is the largest barrel-maker in the United Kingdom and continues to export barreled actions to other countries.

For all the rumor, innuendo, and sheer nonsense that's been inflicted on the Birmingham gun trade over nearly 200 years, it hasn't fared so badly after all, certainly no worse and in some ways better than the London trade. If the gunmaking environment is not as rich or as varied as it once was, it's largely a result of economics and foreign competition. Any shortcomings in the Monstrous Horrendum are more apparent than real.

John Dickson & Son, Edinburgh

Though the Scottish gun trade never was as large nor quite so famous as the English, it has a long and distinguished history, with roots going back at least to the sixteenth century. For 200 years or more, Scottish makers were best known for their distinctive, highly ornate Highland pistols.

By the middle of the nineteenth century, however, the trade in sporting guns and rifles prospered, and the roster of best-quality Scottish makers includes some highly respected names: David Murray of Stonehaven; Charles Playfair of Aberdeen; Alexander Martin, W. Horton, James Dougall, and George Coster, all of Glasgow. The best-known makers worked in Edinburgh, the most important gun-making center in Scotland: William MacLaughlin, James MacNaughton, Daniel Fraser, Alexander Henry, Joseph Harkom, James Wallace, Agnew, and most famous of them all, John Dickson. Now, only Dickson remains.

The first John Dickson, who was born in 1794, began his apprenticeship in 1806, with James Wallace of 187 High Street, Edinburgh. Wallace later moved to 63 Princes Street. Geoffrey Boothroyd reports that Wallace and Dickson may have formed a partnership about 1830. If so, it was short-lived, for Dickson and his son, also named John, set up shop on their own at 60 Princes Street in 1840, under the style of John Dickson & Son.

Wallace, in turn, took on a partner named Agnew and appears to have sold out to Agnew in 1842. In 1849, Agnew sold out, apparently to Dickson, and Dickson moved back down Princes Street to the old Wallace – Agnew shop at No. 63.

Having begun, naturally, with muzzleloading guns, Dickson built his first breechloader, a 14-gauge pinfire, in 1858, followed in 1859 by another pinfire gun with underlever bolting. Through the 1860s and early '70s, Dickson experimented with snap-action breechloaders, building guns on patents held by a number of other makers – Brazier, Westley Richards, Thomas Horsley, Bastin-LePage, Lancaster, Jones, and possibly Purdey. Records describe at least one snap-action, built in 1865, as being of Dickson's own design, whatever that may have been.

The next design of Dickson's own, however, is more certain, for it would become one of the most famous actions ever built.

Actually, it wasn't entirely Dickson's own. In 1879, James MacNaughton designed a hammerless action in which all of the lockwork is mounted on the trigger plate, not unlike the arrangement that George Gibbs and Thomas Pitt had jointly patented several years before, nor, in principle at least, is it unlike Edwinson Green's hammerless gun first produced in 1866. Also like the Gibbs

191

& Pitt guns, MacNaughton's featured a long top lever that served both to operate the fastening system and cock the locks.

Something about the idea caught John Dickson the Younger's fancy, and between 1880 and 1887 he entered a series of patents on a similar gun. German makers, too, liked the trigger-plate locks, which they called the Blitz action. None of them, however, came even close to matching what John Dickson created.

Dickson's called it the "round action," after the smoothly rounded action bar. The round-action frame is immensely strong, since no steel has to be removed to accommodate lock parts, and because of this inherent strength, the frame can be made relatively small, which contributes both light weight and a graceful appearance. In fact, the Dickson round action strikes my eye as one of the most elegant and beautiful non-sidelock guns ever built. (I say "non-sidelock" because the trigger-plate design is not a true boxlock but rather something in between sidelock and boxlock, much like some of Dan Lefever's Automatic Hammerless guns.)

The Dickson ejector mechanism, unlike most, is entirely contained within the frame. The action is fastened by a Purdey-type underbolt.

The round action is literally a Dickson signature, and Dickson's has built it in a variety of forms, some with sidelevers on the order of Stephen Grant's

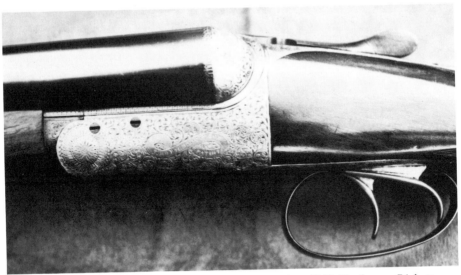

John Dickson & Son has been building guns in Edinburgh since 1840. The famous Dickson Round Action is one of the most elegant guns ever made. Since the lockwork is mounted on the trigger plate, the frame itself is relatively small, and Dickson guns are lightweight and highly dynamic. (Photo courtesy of Dr. Tom Bright.)

guns, others with top levers, even a few with decorative sideplates. In some, the action bar is partially covered by the stock. The craftsmanship, always, is exceptional.

The round action also proved versatile enough to accommodate designs other than the traditional side-by-side double gun. The first of these was a three-barrel patented in February 1882 by John Dickson and Arthur Murray.

Around 1880, the enormous numbers of game birds available on the great English shooting estates and the Scottish grouse moors prompted a flurry of interest in greater firepower, and guns with more than two barrels were ordered from a number of makers. Edwinson Green built some with a third barrel set between and above the other two. Henry A.A. Thorn of Charles Lancaster patented three different four-barrel guns in 1881 and 1882.

Dickson's version may have been created at Murray's behest, for the first two were built for him. The patent specifications cover three variations: two barrels side by side with a third on top, two barrels side by side with another centered below, and three barrels all in the same plane – a side-by-side-by-side, so to speak.

And that's how Dickson built it, as a horizontal, three-barrel, three-trigger ejector gun with a side-lever. The barrels are fitted with two lumps, and the fastening system comprises two double-bite Purdey bolts. Most, if not all, of the Dickson three-barrels were made in 16-gauge to keep the weight of the barrels down to a reasonable level. Even with 28-inch barrels, though, the guns generally weigh less than seven pounds, thanks to the choice of 16-bore tubes and to the lightweight round-action frame.

The multibarrel fad was not widespread, and it was mercifully brief. Serious shooting men realized that having more than two barrels demanded a tradeoff in weight and balance and concluded that a matched pair of double guns was a better choice. No one built many of the multibarrel guns; Dickson made only a dozen three-barrels.

Almost equally few but infinitely more useful are the Dickson over-unders, made in the 1930s. These, too, were built on the round-action frame; essentially, they are round-action, top-lever side-by-sides rotated ninety degrees, so that the lever is on the right-hand side, the action bar is on the left, and the barrels pivot to the left instead of downward. A scale of wood is fastened to the right side of the barrels to match what is virtually the standard splinter fore-end on the left. It's a somewhat asymmetrical, rather odd-looking gun, but it weighs no more than a conventional Dickson side-by-side and handles just as well. And because it's not built with the typical U-shaped over-under action bar, it's as shallow-framed as an over-under could possibly be.

The last member of John Dickson's family retired from the firm in 1923. Soon after, the shop moved from its old quarters on Princes Street to Hanover Street and later to 21 Frederick Street, where it is now.

Dickson's success continued while other Scottish gunmakers failed, and as they did, Dickson's bought them one by one: MacNaughton, Harkom, Mortimer (a London maker who relocated to Edinburgh), Henry, and Martin. In the Alexander Martin purchase, which happened about 1960, Dickson's also acquired a young apprentice named David McKay Brown. Brown completed his apprenticeship at Dickson's and remained on the staff before setting up shop on his own in 1967. In the meantime, he learned to make the Dickson round action and does so today.

And so, for that matter, so does John Dickson & Son – the same gun that first appeared more than a hundred years ago, built with the same flawless craftsmanship and showing the same elegant grace. In some ways, the Dickson is a sleeper, overshadowed by more famous British guns, but it only takes one to make a lasting impression. No matter what its vintage, you'll never forget the first Dickson gun that you hold in your hands.

Into the Future, Out of the Past

It doesn't take a particularly broad view to recognize what extraordinarily rich and fertile ground the English gun trade once occupied, nor do we have to probe very deeply to get a sense of the vitality that flourished during the halcyon years, from about 1850 until the shattering horror of the Great War. Similarly prosperous gun trades have existed elsewhere, and at least one of them still does. But none has ever had a more far-reaching nor longer-lasting influence.

One of the most fascinating aspects of the English trade is how thoroughly intertwined it all was, like a vast tapestry woven in multiple dimensions, in which each major thread touches every other, so that almost any English gun implies virtually the whole tradition. For instance, the gun lying on the desk beside me now, the same one I'm holding on the back of this book's dust cover.

From across the room, you could recognize the style as London best, but even at arm's length, you'd be hard pressed to say who built it. If you have a particularly sharp eye for English guns, your first guess might be James Woodward, because the fences are filed in the fluted, "umbrella" style that Woodward often used. The engraving style is no clue at all; it's the traditional

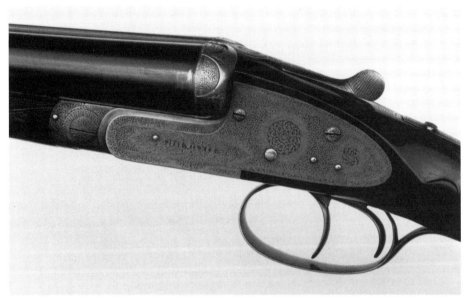

This John Wilkes game gun, built in the 1930s, synthesizes nearly the whole English gunmaking tradition.

rose and scroll that has decorated English guns for 200 years. But look closer and a whole gunmaking tradition comes alive.

The name on the sideplates is John Wilkes, and on the rib is the address: 79 Beak Street, London. It's the No. 1 gun of a matched pair built in the 1930s by the fourth John Wilkes, father of the John and Tom Wilkes who still work in the Beak Street shop today. Somewhere in the world, there's another just like it, different only in bearing the numeral 2 inlaid in gold on the top latch, the breech end of the rib, and on the fore-end pipe.

The man they were made for asked for 29-inch barrels, uncommon but not particularly unusual. He also asked that the fences be sculpted in the umbrella style; so far as John and Tom recall, these are the only guns Wilkes ever made with fences filed that way. And for reasons that we'll never know, the original owner even specified the serial numbers. They're in the 24000 range, far out of sequence for the 1930s and in fact still out of sequence, since the Wilkes chronology has only reached about 19000 even now. But those were the numbers he wanted on his guns, and those are the numbers he got.

So, a London gun of fifty-odd years ago. When it was built, the John Wilkes firm had been in business for just over a hundred years and had been involved in both the Birmingham and London trades. The action is bolted by a double-bite Purdey bolt with a third fastener in the standing breech, a mechanism that dates back to 1863, invented by a gunmaker whose career began with Joseph Manton. Between the bolt and the top lever is a Scott spindle, invented by William Middleditch Scott of Birmingham in 1865.

The barrels are engraved "Sir Joseph Whitworth's Fluid Pressed Steel." Joseph Whitworth was born at Stockport in 1803. By 1850, he was working as a machine-tool manufacturer in Manchester. He also was much interested in rifles and military ordnance and held several patents, including one for the hexagonal-bore Whitworth rifle, introduced in 1854. Over the following years, he opened a number of retail shops in both Manchester and London.

Whitworth, who was created a baronet in 1869, was a major supplier of rifle barrels to the trade. Greener tells us that the introduction of choke boring was a prime factor in the change from Damascus to fluid-steel gun barrels and that about 1875, when "Whitworth steel was giving great satisfaction for rifle barrels, a leading London gun-maker decided to adopt it for shot-gun barrels." Unfortunately, he doesn't say who that London maker was, but it may have been James Purdey the Younger, who used Whitworth tubes exclusively except for a brief period in 1898 when a steel-workers strike temporarily cut off the supply.

In any case, Greener goes on to say:

> Of the steels used for shot-gun barrels, the best known is Whitworth's fluid compressed steel. This is a cast steel; the ingot whilst in a liquid or semi-liquid state is submitted to pressure, with a view to eliminating blow-holes...it is generally allowed that Whitworth steel is of excellent quality, and it has been used for barrels for so many years that its superiority for that purpose may be taken as fully proven.

By the turn of the century, a number of American makers – among them Lefever, Parker, and L.C. Smith – offered Whitworth barrels for their highest-grade guns. Even by the mid-1930s, Hunter Arms used Whitworth tubes as standard fare for Monogram, Premier, and DeLuxe grade L.C. Smiths.

Joseph Whitworth & Company, Ltd., eventually was bought out by Vickers and, later still, by the British Steel Corporation.

The ejectors in my Wilkes gun are made after Thomas Southgate's patent of 1893, one of the two ejector systems most commonly used in the English trade. The other is John Deeley's design, patented in 1886.

Deeley also contributed the cocking system that Wilkes and nearly every other gunmaker in the world has used: cocking levers fitted through the action bar, pivoted on the same axis as the hinge joint, and actuated by leverage from the barrels.

The lockwork, too, is a classic design: bar-action sidelocks with intercepting safety sears. The plates are stamped inside with the name JOSEPH BRAZIER, ASHES.

Joseph Brazier was a gunlock-maker and a gun- and pistol-maker in Wolverhampton, near Birmingham, who first set up in business in 1827. In 1834, he established his gun works on Great Brickkiln Street and named it The Ashes; presumably, there were ash trees on the property. From 1849 to 1874, the company style was Joseph Brazier & Son; afterwards, it was Joseph Brazier & Sons. The Braziers apparently were a sizeable family, as Bailey and Nie list six gunlock-makers of that name as working in Wolverhampton during the nineteenth century.

Joseph Brazier exhibited gunlocks and accessories at the Great Exhibition of 1851 and, later in the 1850s, earned patents for such items as a rammer for percussion revolvers, a spring clamp, and a lock vise. In 1876, Brazier began manufacturing Anson and Deeley-type guns and actions under license from Westley Richards and in the late 1880s manufactured a game counter invented by Sir Ralph Payne-Gallwey, which was marketed as the Gallwey Brazier Improved Game Scorer. One of Brazier's sons and William Cashmore, a well-known Birmingham gunmaker, in 1896 jointly patented a safety for hammerless guns.

By the end of the century, Brazier was a major supplier of gunlocks to the English trade. Sometime after 1900, the firm sold out to Edwin Chilton.

Chilton, too, was a Wolverhampton lockmaker and apprenticed with John Stanton, the man who in the 1860s and '70s perfected the rebounding gunlock. Chilton went into business on his own about 1873, and within a few years, he also was an important supplier to the trade. Frederick Beesley, who invented the Purdey self-opening action, used Chilton locks. W&C Scott used them, too, along with Chilton-made ejectors.

Joseph Brazier locks were highly respected in the gun trade, and Chilton both maintained the quality and continued to use the Brazier name until Chilton's finally closed down in 1977.

So, the various parts of one typical, best-quality English gun touch, one way or another, the mainstream history of the gun trade from the turn of the nineteenth century right up to the day it was finished, from Joseph Manton to the fourth John Wilkes. Its mechanics and aesthetics will continue unchanged so long as the English gun trade continues to exist. Small wonder, then, that every time I pick it up, I feel as if I'm shaking hands with gunmakers long dead, in touch with the whole tradition.

LES BEAUX FUSILS DE CHASSE

Though the modern sporting gun reached its evolutionary zenith in nineteenth-century England, its origin reaches back to seventeenth-century France. As I said in an earlier chapter, the sport of *tir au vol*, literally "shooting on the wing," was a French export that reached England with the Restoration, in 1660.

The French trade in sporting guns dates at least to the early fifteenth century, when a barrel-making industry began to flourish in St. Etienne. Eventually, St. Etienne would become the center of French gunmaking (and it remains so today), but the most important of the early makers naturally worked in Paris. According to Greener, the Paris trade reached its peak in the mid-seventeenth century, about the time that King Charles II returned to England and there delivered both the sporting gun and *tir au vol* into the hands of history.

If Greener's comment on the Paris trade is meant to imply that French contributions to gun-making dwindled after 1660, it has more to do with the old, peckish rivalry between the British and the French that it does with historical fact. Greener knew better anyway.

Not only did the double-barreled fowling piece reach England by way of France, but so did the hinge-action breechloader, the self-contained cartridge, and the snap-action concept of bolting.

There is no question that French guns found their way to England in considerable numbers between the Restoration and the Great Exhibition of 1851. In 1662, English diarist Samuel Pepys noted seeing "a gun to discharge seven times, the best of all devices I ever saw..." And again, in 1664: "There were several people by, trying a new fashion gun...to shoot often, one after another, without trouble or danger, very pretty." The guns that Pepys saw almost certainly were French.

The first breechloaders that the English saw were French, too, and the English took toward them a somewhat predictable attitude. About 1850, Peter Hawker wrote: "Let me caution the whole world against using firearms that are opened and loaded at the breech – a horrid ancient invention, revived by foreign makers, that is dangerous in the extreme." William Greener, W.W. Greener's father, similarly thought the whole idea of breechloading guns was utter rubbish; in *Gunnery in 1858*, he describes breechloaders as a "specious pretence" that "cannot be made sufficiently durable to yield any reasonable return for the extra expense and trouble attending their fabrication."

The following year, J.H. Walsh, writing under the pseudonym "Stonehenge," referred to the pinfire breechloader as the "French crutch gun."

How much of this was honest opinion and how much was nationalistic prejudice toward things French? In British slang, syphilis had long been called "the French disease" or "French gout," so you can decide for yourself.

The gun that prompted all the flap was Lefaucheux's pinfire, which appears to be the first break-action gun ever built. It was not, however, the first breechloader; that distinction belongs to Samuel Johannes Pauly. Pauly was Swiss, born in 1766, and served in Bonaparte's Armies of the Eagles as a sergeant major in artillery. He moved from Geneva to Paris in 1808, set up shop as a gunmaker, and presently invented a breechloading action for a pouch-type cartridge with a percussion primer inside. (He also hired a young Prussian named Johann Nikolaus von Dryse as an assistant. When von Dryse returned to Prussia in 1824, he took the Pauly action with him, tinkered with it through several improved versions, and in 1836 obtained a patent for what shortly would become the famous needle gun adopted by the Prussian Army in 1841. As such, it was the precursor of the modern bolt-action rifle.)

Pauly continued to work on breechloading actions and in 1812 patented a concept that would have a lasting effect on French gun-making – an action comprising fixed barrels and a hinged breechblock, designed for use with centerfire cartridges. It was, moreover, a hammerless action, with two hammerlike cocking levers.

Pauly moved to London about 1814 and in 1816 secured an English patent for his action. Pauly's successor in Paris, Henri Roux, and Roux's successor, Eugène Pichereau, both continued to build Pauly-type guns for several years.

Another Parisian gunmaker, Robert, invented a variation on the Pauly action in 1831. Like Pauly's, Robert's breechblock hinges on trunnions fastened to either side of the barrels, so that the shooter lifts the block from the rear and swings it forward to expose the breeches. Unlike Pauly's design, the Robert cocks automatically as the breechblock is lifted.

The whole notion of fixed-barrel guns obviously appealed to the French. The Darne, probably the most famous of all French guns, is a variation on the same theme. The English, however, never did warm up to the idea, and it remained for Eugène Pichereau's successor, Casimir Lefaucheux, to truly change the course of gunmaking.

It's impossible to say exactly why the English responded to Lefaucheux's break-action after the Great Exhibition of 1851 and not before. There is no question that Lefaucheux guns found their way to England during the years between the early 1830s, when the patents were granted in France, and the

Exhibition itself. In fact, there probably were quite a few of them in England, especially after 1836, when Lefaucheux switched to the pinfire system, and again after 1846, when Houllier patented a much improved pinfire cartridge. The most likely explanation is simply that English gunmakers clung to the "English" gun (in those days, a caplock muzzleloader) until English shooters began to recognize the obvious advantages of breechloaders. From 150 years' perspective, the subsequent carping about "French crutch guns" from some quarters of the English trade sounds more like stodgy conservatism and sheer prejudice than considered opinion.

Being forced to adopt a French idea, especially a good one, clearly was a bitter pill for some English makers, but the enormous burst of creativity that followed was clearly more than enough to soothe whatever abrasions the British national pride may have suffered.

Even though English accomplishments largely eclipsed all others during the latter nineteenth century, the French trade certainly did not wither away. Hundred-year-old French guns are hardly abundant in America these days (nor are new French guns, for that matter), but one doesn't need to see many specimens to realize that French gunmakers have always been splendid craftsmen. Shooting in England last year, I met a young Frenchman whose company I enjoyed immensely and whose appreciation of fine guns helped fuel several hours of conversation. In the course of it, as shooting men everywhere are wont to do, he brought out his own gun, which once belonged to his grandfather. The maker's name I didn't recognize, but fine quality speaks for itself. It was a trim sidelock, beautifully fitted and finished, its snap action operated by an underlever that curved gracefully over the trigger guard. It was well used and obviously well loved, light and lively and elegant in every detail.

I asked François what he knew of the maker. Very little, he said, a now-obscure St. Etienne craftsman from the turn of the century. I remarked that he clearly was a very fine craftsman, whoever he was, and that it was a lovely gun.

"*Ah, oui,*" François said, smiling, "*un bijou de famille.*" An heirloom. Translated literally, it means "a jewel of the family." True enough, in any sense.

Darne and Bruchet

By the latter nineteenth century, the city of St. Etienne, near Lyons in southern France, had become to the French gun trade what Birmingham has long been to the English. In both cities, the gun business amounted to full-scale industry, ranging from mass production of sporting and military arms to smaller specialty shops supplying the trade with barrels, locks, actions, springs, stocks, and all the myriad other parts that go into a gun. St. Etienne has its own proof house, established in 1741, and its own guild system. By the mid-twentieth century, it was the center of the French trade.

Literally dozens of gunmakers have worked in St. Etienne and have come and gone in the flux of history. One of the longest-lived, and certainly the one best known in America, was established in 1881 by two brothers, Regis and Pierre Darne, under the style F. Darne Fils et l'Aïné.

Regis Darne was a designer whose sense of the gun clearly sprang from the very earliest breechloaders, from Pauly's fixed-barrel, moveable-breech designs created at the turn of the nineteenth century. While Pauly was content to simply hinge his breech block to the barrels and lift it like a hatch cover, later disciples of the fixed-barrel gun experimented with all sorts of mechanisms by which the breech could be moved. In Darne's first gun, produced in 1881, the entire frame – standing breech, lockwork, triggers, trigger guard, hammers, bolting lever, and all – was designed to rotate a quarter-turn clockwise to expose the chambers, while barrels and stock remained stationary.

It sounds weird, and in fact it looks weird, but it obviously worked, since it survived for a surprisingly long time; it was replaced in 1891 by a hammerless version of the same action, and that one remained in production until the entire French gun trade began building military weapons in 1914.

The gun that truly earned Darne a place in history first appeared in 1894 – another fixed-barrel piece but this time one that featured a sliding rather than a pivoting breech.

In profile, the Darne doesn't look radically different from more conventional guns, although the stock extending under the frame, the long, sloping, triangular breech, and the absence of a top lever combine to give it a somewhat sleeker appearance than most. Seen from the top, the Darne looks like a gun wearing a bow tie or one that's sprouted ears just behind the fences.

These ears are the equivalent of a break-action gun's top latch. To open the action, the shooter grasps them with thumb and finger, lifts, and pulls backward. A lever, flush-fitting and hinged at the rear, lifts out of its slot in the breech, disengages the fastener, and the whole top of the breech slides backward a few inches. Push the lever forward, and the system works in reverse, sealing the chambers and locking the breech into place.

It's as simple as that, although simplicity in a gun often is the result of having solved some extremely complex problems. The most difficult problem

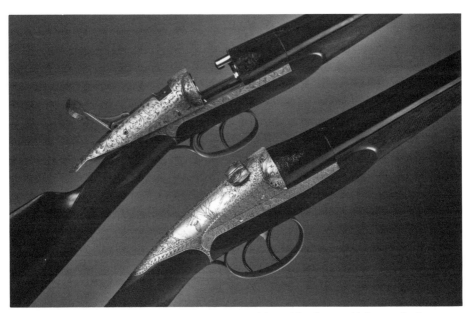

The Darne's pedigree extends back to the first French breechloaders – which were the first breechloading guns of all. Darne-patent guns are still manufactured by Paul Bruchet.

in designing a gun like the Darne is in the bolting system. The breech block has to slide easily once the action is unbolted, but it also has to lock up firmly and withstand the full force of recoil. A sliding breech, in other words, has to perform two diametrically opposite functions and, if it's to work properly, has to perform them equally well. Designing a bolting system that works isn't the hard part; bolt-action rifles and repeating guns also have sliding breech blocks, and their designers have solved the same problem in a variety of ways.

The hard part is finding a way to fasten the action that requires the least motion and effort on the shooter's part. As other types of guns demonstrate, it can be as simple as pushing and turning a rifle bolt, or else it requires the complex mechanism of a pump or semiautomatic – neither of which is appropriate for a two-barreled game gun.

Regis Darne solved the problem brilliantly. Closing and bolting a Darne gun requires only a single motion – pushing the lever forward – so it's simpler in that regard than even a turnbolt action. The mechanism itself, in turn, is simpler than that of a repeater.

At the heart of it is a lever inside the breech block, linked to the top lever by a toggle. This internal lever itself is the main bolt, bearing like a buttress against the frame when the action is closed. When the top lever is pulled back, the toggle simply lifts the bolt up into the sliding breech and out of the way.

As a secondary bolt, Darne designed a heavy, round rib extension, projecting from between the barrels; this fits into a hole in the breech face, and as the main bolt pivots into place, it raises a vertical lug into a notch in the bottom of the rib extension. It's hard to imagine a sliding-breech fastener that's simpler or one that works any better.

And work it does. By the early 1970s, the Darne was available both in 10-gauge and in a 12-gauge version bored for three-inch cartridges, either of which is capable of rendering as much punishment as any action needs. I have not handled a great many Darnes, but I've fooled with some that have digested thousands of rounds, and I've yet to find one with a loose breech. Operating the action applies very little friction to either the bolt or the frame surface it bears against, so there is virtually no opportunity for any part of the fastening system to wear.

Nevertheless, Regis Darne clearly took great pains to account for every detail. A double gun's barrels are fastened together at a converging angle so that shot charges from both will shoot to the same point at a given distance. Cartridges in the chambers therefore do not rest at precise right angles to the standing breech. On the Darne's breech face are two flanged steel discs that enclose the cartridge rims. The faces of these, generally called obturator discs, are milled at a slight angle so that each cartridge base is exactly parallel with the breech block.

Nearly everyone who writes about the Darne makes a great fuss about all this, pointing out that the flanges enclose the cartridge rims in case one should crack under gas pressure, effusing over the low recoil because cartridge cases don't rap the breech face, marveling at how you don't hear cartridges rattle in a closed Darne, and generally taking such a gee-whiz attitude that you begin to wonder why every gun doesn't have obturator discs.

The fact is, no properly built gun needs them, not even the Darne.

Those who apparently have never seen a cartridge rim crack seem to believe it's a disaster that threatens life and limb. Actually, it happens fairly often among shells that aren't made with integral base wads. Gas seeps back around the base wad and sometimes the brass rim ruptures and allows some gas to escape. Some brands of cartridges are notorious for this after they're reloaded a couple of times. But if the gun is tight and the action on-face, the shooter likely won't ever know it's happened until he sees the empty hull.

To insist that a Darne gun recoils less because of the obturator discs is princess-and-the-pea nonsense. A fixed-breech, or locked-breech, gun recoils as much as it recoils, obturator discs or not. There is some additional set-back if the cartridge case is able to move in the chamber, but if there's more than a few thousandths of an inch excessive headspace, the cartridge won't go off because the firing pin isn't long enough to crush the priming chemical against the anvil. And a cartridge case traveling a few thousandths of an inch does not create set-back to a degree that any shooter can feel.

It's true that there's enough headspace in most guns, including most best-quality guns, to allow cartridges to rattle with the action closed – or, more accurately, to allow *some* cartridges to rattle, since rim thickness among shotshells, like everything else in gundom, is a matter of tolerances rather than absolute dimensions. If it were a serious problem, it would have been universally solved a long time ago.

But the Darne's obturator discs do serve a purpose, two purposes, actually, and one really does have something to do with recoil. Regis Darne obviously recognized the potential weakness inherent to a sliding-breech design and added the discs as a means of ensuring the most even distribution of recoil force against as much of the gun's total mass as possible. Set-back is a factor, not a serious one with heavily wadded ammunition fired in a carefully made gun, but it does represent a small additional stress on the bolting system; Darne solved that by designing his gun with slightly less headspace than usual, so that there's no room for even a thin-rimmed cartridge to set back under recoil. The toggle linkage in the action has enough camming force that a thick rim simply gets compressed a bit.

All told, Regis Darne's attention to detail in augmenting the durability of his action is more admirable in itself than all of the breathless, and specious, claims that you're likely to read. The bottom line is that Darne's concern for recoil was in behalf of the gun, not the shooter. No gunmaker has any control at all over the cartridges that are stuffed into one of his guns – and despite the nonsense you might hear about six-pound Darnes recoiling less than seven-pound guns of some other design, you may be assured that heavy loads are going to kick smartly, no matter what.

The flanges, too, serve a real purpose, a simple one that has nothing to do with fairy tales about the horrors of cracked cartridge rims. They do offer a bit of additional support to the case heads and do help seal the breech, but that isn't the main reason why they're there. Without the flanges, the Darne's extractors wouldn't work reliably.

The typical extractor system of a break-action gun – an extractor plate mortised into the barrel itself – works so well that we scarcely give it a thought. The tiny, clawlike extractors of repeating guns are far more prone to malfunction, mainly because they're so small and require spring tension to maintain their purchase on a shell case. Darne extractors naturally are of the hook type, which pull rather than push empties out of the chambers; mortised plates would require an ungodly amount of Rube Goldberg machinery in a fixed-barrel gun. The Darne hooks are good ones, more efficient than the typical repeater's, but no hooks work very well unless the shell head is held tightly against the breech bolt. Otherwise, since it's being pulled out by a grasp on only the merest edge of the rim, a case can easily slip away from the hook, and the farther out of the chamber it is, the more likely it is to slip.

So, the flanges around the obturator discs are there to ensure that the extractors keep hold of fired cases until they're free of the chamber.

Even though Darne literature described the guns as having *ejecteurs automatiques*, they aren't the typical sort. A spring-loaded stud protrudes slightly from the breech face near the top of each obturator disc. Once an empty is fully extracted and the case mouth is no longer supported by the chamber, these studs disengage the case heads from the extractors' grip; the shooter simply gives the gun a slight roll to one side or the other, and the hulls fall away. It's quite a simple system and works perfectly well.

In hand, the most striking characteristic of Darne guns is their weight. A typical 12-gauge weighs about six pounds, a 20 about half a pound less, and a 28-gauge barely more than five pounds. One reason for such light heft is that a Darne comprises proportionately less steel and more wood than a conventional double gun; another is that, like most European makers, Darne built specialized bird guns tailored to European game loads and knew very well how to trim every excess ounce without compromising safety, durability, or handling quality.

Darne barrels are constructed on the monobloc principle, with the barrel work as meticulously done as everything else that went into a Darne gun. By about 1960, Darne was one of only two St. Etienne makers doing their own barrel work in-house. Traditionally, Darne barrels were proved at the heaviest level used by the St. Etienne proof house.

Although you could order a gun built with a conventional flat rib, the ultralight Darnes carried a *bande de visée plume*, or "feather rib" – a deeply swamped affair that lies well below the tops of the barrels through most of its length. Since it was used without a bottom rib or fillet, it shaved a few ounces from total gun weight. A lot of European shooters are fond of swamped ribs; most Americans aren't, simply because we're not accustomed to them. For shooting, it doesn't really matter, or it shouldn't, since you ought to be looking at the target instead of the rib, anyway.

French sportsmen liked the Darne immediately, and the company thrived. In 1915, Darne accepted a contract from the French government to manufacture Lewis machine guns for the army and in 1917 began manufacturing a machine gun of its own design. Darne's interest in military arms continued for many years after the war, eventually including production of aircraft guns, an anti-tank gun, and several light machine guns.

By 1928, Darne had turned out more than 100,000 game guns. As patents expired, other makers copied the design. In the late 1920s, one clever Belgian maker named Charles Leve even turned the Darne action into a sort of repeater, designing a double shell carrier that fit into the action table. As the shooter opened the action after firing the first two shots, the carriers lifted automatically, bumped the empty cases out of the way, and presented two fresh rounds for the breech block to push into the chambers. An altogether ingenious idea, it offered the firepower of a repeater without affecting the gun's balance, since the extra rounds were stored under the action and not in a magazine tube slung under the barrel. Leve also managed to carry the whole thing off without deepening the action body to any great extent.

Darne guns never made a great impression on the American market, but they did make a respectable showing, championed in the 1960s by a few American gun writers, notably Roger Barlow and John Amber. By the late '70s, however, competition from Japan and a sluggish world economy combined to bring *Etablissements Darne*, as the company was then called, to a standstill.

When the Darne shops closed down in 1980, Paul Bruchet, who for some years had managed a portion of Darne production, bought the machinery. By 1984, Bruchet, his son, and several other former Darne craftsmen were installed in new quarters at 25 Rue des Armuriers, St. Etienne, and had begun building guns where Darne left off.

The current guns are Darnes in all but name. The Bruchet guns are built on order only, one at a time, and the quality is fully as good as Darne's ever was.

Like its predecessor, the Bruchet is available in all of the standard gauges from 12 to .410-bore, including 24-gauge. As a bespoken piece, all details are the customer's choice.

The Bruchet is significant for its historical value as well as for its intrinsic merit. To shoot a Bruchet is to handle a piece of history, to touch a pedigree that reaches back to where the modern breechloading gun began, to demonstrate the truth of that fine French axiom, *Le plus ce change, le plus c'est la même-chose*.

Georges Granger

While Darne, Bruchet, and a few others have chosen to follow gun-making traditions that are peculiarly French, other French makers subscribe to the classic London form, building fine sidelock game guns with exceptional skill and artistry. To my mind, the best of them all is Georges Granger.

According to Don Zutz, Granger is successor to Henri Guichard, a well-known St. Etienne gunmaker and himself successor to Aime Coeur Tyrode, who began working in St. Etienne in 1902. Granger (which is pronounced *Grawn-ZHAY*) learned the trade during twenty years with Guichard. He clearly learned it well.

There is nothing unusual about the design of a Granger gun. It is a sidelock of Holland-style action, right down to the hand-detachable locks that are something of a Holland signature. More than likely, it will have a straight-hand stock, splinter fore-end, two triggers, and the other characters of a best-quality English game gun. It might be engraved in rose and scroll, after the traditional London pattern; in the more open, rosette style that the French call *rosace*; in game scenes cut in the *bulino* style; or in some baroque fancy originating from an engraver's imagination.

In any case, it will be just the way some customer asked for it, since Granger guns are built solely on order and strictly to customer requirements. It also will be executed – in every detail, inside and out – according to standards of craftsmanship of which there are none higher anywhere in the world.

Such consummate skill has earned Granger himself considerable recognition, including nominations as Best French Worker in 1968, Master Craftsman in 1978, and Laureate of Artistic Professions in 1979. If you ever have a chance to handle a Granger gun, you'll see why.

Some gunmakers simply stand out even among the best, and Georges Granger is one of those. The same standard of performance applies in the Granger shop now that applied under Joseph Manton in London 200 years ago: Only the best is acceptable. Like most of his countrymen, Manton didn't think much of the French, but he would have approved of a gun by Georges Granger.

Armurerie Vouzelaud

St. Etienne is the center of the French gun trade but not exclusively so. As in nineteenth-century England, France traditionally has had its share of provincial gunmakers. There are fewer of them now, but the provincial trade has life in it yet.

Armurerie Vouzelaud (pronounced *voozeh-LOW*) has been at home in the

Vouzelaud Model 315 EGL, an extremely well-made boxlock gun with decorative sideplates virtually indistinguishable from a true sidelock.

village of Brou – about seventy miles southwest of Paris – since 1888, passed down generation to generation, father to son, still family-owned. Under management of the current generation, the brothers Alan and Hubert, Armurerie Vouzelaud has become to France something of what Abercrombie & Fitch once was to America – purveyors of fine guns, its own brand of cartridges, and shooting gear of all kinds. The company also operates a shooting school. Best of all, Vouzelaud builds guns under its own name, and they are excellent, in quality and in value alike.

Built on frames and barrels supplied from St. Etienne, Vouzelaud guns are available in both standard and made-to-order form. All are Anson and Deeley-type boxlocks, incorporating Purdey bolts and Holland-system ejectors. A Purdey-type third fastener is available on request.

Vouzelaud calls them the Model 315 series, and the differences among them are largely cosmetic. There are two standard box-frame guns, models 315E and 315EL. The 315E is built in 12, 16, and 20 gauges. The frame is lightly engraved and color-case-hardened; the furniture is blued. The 315EL frame is a bit more artfully filed, finished in French gray, and engraved in rose and scroll. It, too, comes in 12, 16, and 20 gauges, with 28-gauge and .410-bore versions available on special order at higher prices.

The sideplate models are lovely things. Frames are filed in classic sidelock style, and the decorative sideplates are so cleverly executed that you'll swear you're looking at a true sidelock gun. The studs and screw-ends, which are gold-plated, are exactly where they ought to be for Holland locks, and there's scarcely any way to tell just by looking that there are no lock parts fastened to the other side of the plate. The first Vouzelaud I tested fooled me completely, and I described it in a *Sporting Classics* column as a genuine sidelock. We live and learn.

Not even the trigger pulls offer a clue – which isn't to say that boxlock triggers can't be good ones, but among side-by-sides the really exceptional triggers usually are on sidelock guns. Not so in the case of Vouzelaud. The sears are light and crisp, obviously adjusted with considerable care, and a pleasure to shoot.

The sideplate guns, the models 315EGL and 315EGL-Special, also come in standard versions – as 12, 16, and 20 gauges with 28-inch barrels, straight-hand stocks, splinter fore-ends, and double triggers – but you can order one made up in almost any configuration and any gauge you want.

The differences between these two are almost entirely cosmetic, although the Vouzelaud catalogue indicates that the EGL-Special is built with monobloc barrels. The EGL is engraved with bouquets and scroll in the London pattern. On the guns I've seen, the scroll is rather larger than you'll find on most best-quality guns, but there's certainly little room to quarrel with the execution. Two of Vouzelaud's artists are certified Master Engravers. The EGL-Special typically is decorated with *bulino*-style game scenes accented with scroll. The work is quite good, though not exceptional by world-class standards. You can get better *bulino* engraving, but not at the price of a Vouzelaud.

Vouzelauds aren't cheap – the sideplate models start at $7500 or so – but they offer excellent value. You can spend more money and end up with less gun. With gun prices and currency-exchange rates in constant flux, it's hard to know even from day to day what a fine European gun is likely to cost. Sidelocks certainly aren't getting any cheaper, and a number of makers are putting a lot of first-class craftsmanship into best-quality boxlocks. Vouzelaud is irrefutable proof that it can be done with great success.

SPANISH BEST

Although it has hummed along nicely for 500 years, earning respect and reputation in Europe, the Spanish gun trade hasn't made much headway in the American market. Until the 1950s, in fact, the average American shooter scarcely knew there was a Spanish gun trade, and even then, the guns that began to show up in this country generally made something less than an auspicious impression.

In those days, a few Spanish names appeared in the Foreign Guns sections of *Gun Digest* or *Shooter's Bible* – Sarasqueta, Arizaga, Zabala, Ugartechea, Aguirre, Aranzabal, all of them old-time Basque gunmakers of excellent skill, all capable of building shotguns that could stand their ground in almost any company. Some of the better-known American gun writers spoke fondly of them. Jack O'Connor liked his Arizaga side-by-sides; Elmer Keith thought well of Sarasqueta; Charles Askins, Jr., has always been a great admirer of Aguirre y Aranzabal or AyA, as the firm is best known.

Of the good ones, only AyA caught onto the American market to any great extent, even though some big importers contracted house-brand guns from the Spanish trade. Stoeger, for instance, sold a series of guns under the trade-name Zephyr; they were built by Victor Sarasqueta. But by then, the mid-1960s, the best of all Spanish makers were virtually unheard of in this country, and American gunners were taking an exceedingly dim view of any piece with an Iberian name.

And rightly so. The problem wasn't that the Spanish couldn't build good guns; the problem was that few of them were showing up here. Instead, Spain's share of the American market was occupied almost exclusively by cheaply made double guns sloppily cobbled together from decidedly third-rate materials. Low price was the only thing they had going for them, but even at that they offered no real value. Consequently, the reputation of the Spanish gun trade on this side of the Atlantic took an enormous black eye. Through it all, AyA remained a worthy sleeper, but it suffered by association, appreciated only by those who recognized a good gun under the tarnish of prejudice. The whole thing was unfortunate, and Spanish guns aren't entirely free of it yet.

The situation has shown some improvement, though, largely because the market for good shotguns is not only quite healthy but also considerably less parochial than it was twenty-five years ago. In those days, the American industry was still relatively diverse and fairly prosperous, and British and

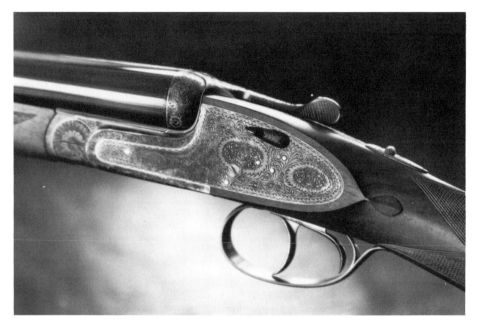

Grulla sidelock, with hand-detachable locks.

German guns were the premier imports. But the American industry declined, American shooters began to realize that most German guns, while certainly rugged, show virtually none of the exquisite style and grace endemic to truly first-rate game guns, and prices for English guns escalated almost out of sight. All that created a niche soon occupied by foreign-built guns that could demonstrate high quality at reasonable prices. The Italian makers were the first beneficiaries. The Spanish may well be the next.

As in every other country except Italy, the segment of the Spanish trade devoted to best-quality guns is a diminishing fraternity. Once there were two dozen or more Spanish shops that could turn out excellent game and pigeon guns built to order. In 1987, there were five. Now there are four. With the demise of Diarm, a conglomerate that comprised Arizaga, AyA, and eighteen others, the custom trade now rests solely with Pedro Arrizabalaga, Grulla Armas, Armas Garbi, and Arrieta y Cia.

What the four have in common is an unshakeable devotion to the classic gun. My good friend Terry Wieland, a first-class writer whose work-in-progress book on the Spanish gun trade will be must reading for any student of the gun, puts it this way: The Spaniards' particular gift is not a flair for innovation, but rather a matchless ability to duplicate the best work of others. Considering that their model is the classic London gun, duplication is no small task.

And there's more to it than simply copying a style. Terry explains it as adoption of a principle – a firm belief that a proper shotgun is in all respects a reflection of the sort of Platonic ideal that evolved in England during the eighteenth and nineteenth centuries. A proper gun, therefore, is a sidelock double trimly stocked and engraved in London scroll, certainly in nothing more rambunctious than acanthus. Garbi and Grulla do some work in the chiseled, high-relief German style – perhaps because it's also popular among some British guns these days. Arrizabalaga, on the other hand, stays entirely with London scroll and acanthus.

Arrieta is the maverick. Its guns mechanically are no different from those of Arrizabalaga or Garbi or Grulla – which is to say that they're no different from the typical English sidelock gun of Holland-style action with Purdey bolts. What sets Arrieta apart from the others is a willingness to depart from the British mold in finish and decoration, a willingness to be modern in ways that must give its traditionalist peers the shivers at times. Only from Arrieta can you order a fine Spanish double gun with frame and sideplates finished in deep black with gold-wire inlay around the contours or the same gun finished in French gray with no engraving at all.

Like the majority of current Italian makers, none of the four best Spanish makers is a particularly old firm. Arrieta was founded about 1928 by the father of the current owners, Jose and Victor Arrieta. As early as 1915, a firm called Hijos de J. Arrizabalaga was making revolvers in Eibar, but the current firm of Pedro Arrizabalaga lists its founding as 1940. Grulla (which is Spanish for "crane") grew out of an earlier firm called Union Armera. Garbi got going in 1959; the name is an acronym made from the initials of the five gunmakers who founded the shop.

In keeping with the nature of handmade guns, none of these makers has a particularly high annual production. Arrieta is the largest, employing twenty-odd craftsmen who build 500 to 1000 guns each year. Garbi averages about 100, Arrizabalaga about 180.

With few exceptions, what they build is a best-quality gun in the London mold. Some offer quite a few different models – Arrieta thirteen and Grulla fourteen – but for the most part they are different only in decoration. Grulla makes one model that has monobloc rather than chopper-lump barrels, is machine-engraved, and lacks the Holland & Holland-type assisted-opening mechanism of other Grulla guns. Both Arrieta and Garbi also build one machine-engraved model each, but all the others are hand-made from start to finish.

Arrieta builds some guns to inventory specifications and exports them to America, but the rest of its annual output – and all that of the others – are guns made to order. None of the best Spanish guns are expensive by English standards, particularly now that the price of a new Purdey begins at about $50,000; any of them represents a splendid value.

As Terry Wieland points out, some makers do not value their names as much as they ought to and are perversely willing to put their stamps on crudely built boxlock guns made on contract for the low end of the European market. Yet those same makers are extremely proud of the good guns they build, and rightly so. The gunmaking world, like life, would be dull without some contradictions.

Other makers, Garbi and Arrizabalaga in particular, not only will refuse to deliver a gun that fails to pass an extremely close final inspection, but actually will decline an order for a gun that doesn't fit their concept of what a best-quality gun should be and how it should be decorated. Neither will build a gun without engraving it. Similarly, if you want your gun stocked with anything but fine walnut, someone else will have to build it. Garbi and Arrizabalaga will not.

Whether the Spanish gun trade ultimately will succeed in mitigating the abysmal reputation it earned in America years ago remains to be seen. Much of the rest of the world is fond of best Spanish guns. The English buy a substantial number of them every year. In a story published in *Guns* magazine about twenty years ago, Charles Askins reported that Holland & Holland was negotiating with Aguirre y Aranzabal for an agreement under which AyA would build Holland's guns. If that's true, it was a short-lived idea, but Spanish craftsmen now are working in virtually every English gun shop.

Even if the best Spanish makers never fully achieve the recognition in this country that they deserve, it won't be because no one is trying.

ITALIAN RENAISSANCE

Trompia Valley is a narrow groove in the foothills of northeastern Italy, hewn by the Mella River. Through most of its length, which isn't far, there is scarcely a square yard of naturally level ground. It's a difficult place to grow crops, and in any case, the growing season is short. Unlike other valleys in that part of the world, Val Trompia doesn't even grow first-rate grapevines. But inhospitable as it might be to agriculture or the luxury of a good local wine, Val Trompia is a piece of geography upon which nature bestowed a particular gift.

The valley slopes are laced with rich veins of ore that yield nearly pure siderite, iron carbonate. It contains some phosphorus and a healthy dose of manganese and produces a tough, lightweight iron that's easily worked. In the days before steel, such amiable metal was immensely useful, and ore was being dug and smelted in Val Trompia as early as the Middle Ages, perhaps even before.

With all that going for it, Val Trompia can lay a fair claim to being the oldest gun-making district in the world. It's a claim that Suhl, Antwerp, Augsburg, and Nuremburg might well dispute, but Val Trompia unquestionably is the oldest arms-producing district to remain an important center even today. Brescia, at the southern end of the valley, and Gardone, a few miles north, are home to some of the finest gunmakers in Italy.

By the middle of the sixteenth century, an arms industry already thrived in Trompia Valley, supplying arquebuses, muskets, pike heads, breastplates, and myriad other items of military hardware to the courts of Europe. Gun barrels were a particular specialty among Val Trompian craftsmen, but the area was unique in that it could produce guns more self-sufficiently than any other place in the world. Ore and wood could be transformed into a finished gun without ever leaving the valley and without any component being imported.

So pervasive was the Val Trompian influence upon arms-making that national museums all over Europe and Asia contain guns locally manufactured but fitted with barrels signed by the *maestri da canne* of Gardone. And the Val Trompian influence remains, having endured countless wars and endless political turmoil, having survived all the ebb and flow that fortune can deal out over nearly five hundred years. Like William Faulkner's vision of the ultimate triumph of man himself, the Italian gun trade has not only endured but prevailed, for now, as the twentieth century draws to a fitful close, Val Trompian craftsmen are building the finest guns in the world.

Armi Beretta

The Italian ascendancy is a recent phenomenon, by and large, although one current maker can trace its lineage virtually throughout Italy's long gunmaking tradition. Putting an exact date to the origin of Armi Beretta probably never will be possible. Some evidence leads as far back as 1450. Bartolomeo Beretta was a working Gardonese barrel-maker in the 1530s. His second son, Giovannino, was by 1577 a master maker with his own shop. Because both tradition and law held that only the son of a master could himself become a master, the current Beretta company considers 1530 its founding date. A few years more or less scarcely matter, because Beretta's continuation as a family-owned business through at least twelve generations makes it the oldest of all the world's current gunmakers. It may in fact be the world's oldest industrial enterprise of any kind.

In any case, Armi Beretta now is one of the three or four pre-eminent gunmakers in the world.

Except for brief periods of precedence for one or the other, Beretta always has built military and sporting arms simultaneously. Indeed, from the fifteenth through the eighteenth centuries, the superb Gardonese barrels, lightweight and wonderfully strong, were the heart of the finest sporting guns built everywhere in the world.

Almost without exception, the Gardonese barrels were smooth-bored. Beretta made no rifled barrels until the beginning of World War I – which meant that military and sporting barrels could be made interchangeably, with no alteration of technique and without interrupting production. Since everything was built by hand anyway, the shop could fill military orders and switch to sporting guns without stopping for breath.

Beretta's guns followed the same evolutionary stages as all the rest, from matchlocks to wheellocks to flint guns. And like all the other makers of muzzleloading guns, Beretta experimented with breechloading designs. Giovanni Antonio, the third generation of gunmaking Berettas, in 1641 presented the Venetian government with a breechloading cannon of his own device. After testing it, the government awarded Beretta 200 ducats, a twenty-year annuity of ten ducats per month, and promptly forgot about the whole matter.

The Venetian Republic, which governed nearly the whole of northern Italy from 1426 until the rise of Napoleon, took a protectionist view of its industry, certainly including the arms trade in the Trompia Valley, and even though the valley itself was periodically wracked with internecine social struggle, the

Pietro Beretta Model 503EELL sidelock over-under.

national economy remained stable. The gunmakers freely carried on their work, their rights of trade supported by the government. After 1797, when Napoleon annexed Lombardy and dismantled the old republic, Val Trompia was governed by the French, and the arms industry turned virtually all its resources to supplying weapons for Bonaparte's Armies of the Eagles.

Eighteen years later, Napoleon went down in final defeat, and Lombardy became part of the Austrian Empire. The market for military arms instantly dried up. For the gunmakers in the Trompia Valley, the world was a new and somewhat hostile place. The obvious course was to renew the civilian markets, but those were in sad disrepair. The vast Oriental market, to which the Val Trompian makers traditionally had supplied gun barrels, was gone altogether. Most of the others had been usurped by the French, English, and Belgians. To make matters worse, the European economy was sluggish, and the Austrian government was hungry for taxes.

Beretta's position was no better than anyone else's. The family still had its workshops, but without some means of competing on a broad scale, its prospects were dim. As sometimes happens, the right man was in the right place at the right time.

Pietro Antonio Beretta was born June 18, 1791, heir to eight generations of gun-making tradition. Like his forebears, he had all the skills of a master barrel-maker, but he also owned an astute sense of how to meet the demands of a largely uncertain future. Almost before the cannon smoke had cleared from the battlefields at Waterloo, Pietro Beretta left the Trompia Valley to gather the threads of a tattered market.

He met with wholesale dealers, retailers, and importers all over Italy. Inevitably, there soon was some demand for martial arms from the Hapsburgs in Austria and their allies, but was scarcely a trickle compared with the old days of the Venetian Republic. No doubt Pietro Beretta was pleased that his workshops were turning out barrels of any kind, but he was shrewd enough to know that the Val Trompian industry and the Berettas in particular could hardly hope to prosper without a strong showing in sporting guns. His pursuit of that market, won largely through the network of contacts he forged over the next few years, would in time form the foundation upon which the company still stands.

Even the name he gave it in 1832 remains today – *Fabricca d'Armi Pietro Beretta.*

He would not live to see it come to full flower, but Pietro Beretta virtually assured the firm's future. In 1850 he bought back a smithy that his father had sold in 1814. The two buildings, with their forges and workshops, were important enough, but along with them came the rights of use for such canals and watercourses as might provide both transportation and a source of power. The full significance of the purchase would not become apparent for more than a generation.

Pietro Beretta died in 1853, and in due course, control of the company devolved upon his son Giuseppe. Here, too, was a man who knew that merely manufacturing barrels or locks was no assurance of survival in a world grown increasingly complex. He strengthened and expanded the marketing network his father had put together and transformed Armi Beretta from what still was essentially a barrel shop into a full-fledged manufactory.

The gunmaking industry in the Trompia Valley had always been largely cooperative. The Gardonese masters made barrels; craftsmen in other villages made locks, springs, mountings, screws, and other metal parts; most guns were assembled, stocked, and finished in Brescia. By about 1870, Beretta had consolidated all phases of gun manufacture into one operation. With that, Armi Beretta became unique. In an 1878 letter to the Neapolitan newspaper *La Borsa*, Giuseppe Beretta claimed that his firm "alone possesses the remarkable quality of total production: that is, it brings to its premises raw iron and wood, and sends out finished guns…"

The majority of them, by about 1880, were sporting guns, although Beretta continued to pursue military contracts. A few statistics clearly show where

Giuseppe Beretta was headed. From 1850 to 1860, Beretta produced about 300 sporting guns each year; by 1881, annual production comprised 8000 finished shotguns and nearly 2000 double-barreled pistols. Moreover, the firm annually sold about 2500 pair of barrels and accompanying parts to other gunmakers. The factory employed 200 people that year, and the production rate was high enough that a good deal of work was contracted out to other shops around Gardone.

Beginning about 1873, primary emphasis went to breechloading shotguns, and before the decade was over, they were being sold in every corner of Italy, in Greece, Turkey, Tunisia, and Egypt. The 1887 catalogue lists more than 100 different shotguns. About seventy are breechloaders of either centerfire or pinfire type; some fifty of these were of Beretta's own make, the others Belgian and English imports. There are sidelocks of various designs, with bolting systems ranging from top-lever snap actions to underlevers with wedge bolts.

The first hammerless guns appeared in the catalogue of 1893, and these included boxlocks as well as sidelocks. The vast variety of Beretta sporting guns would continue to flourish until the beginning of World War I, when the firm made its first serious – and as it turned out, prophetic – foray into the design and manufacture of automatic weapons. The results of that make a story in itself, for Beretta continues to occupy an eminent place in the international military-arms industry.

The demand for sporting guns naturally dwindled after August 1914, only to revive shortly after the Treaty of Versailles. By then, Armi Beretta was in new hands.

Giuseppe Beretta died in June 1903, and leadership passed to his son, the second Pietro. In less than thirty years, building upon what his grandfather and father had begun, Pietro Beretta brought the firm into international status. To ensure that production could keep pace with the world markets he so successfully curried, he expanded the factory, installed new machinery and, taking advantage of the water rights the first Pietro had purchased long before, built two generating plants on the Mella River to secure his own source of electric power.

The proliferation of sporting-gun designs abated somewhat between the two world wars, but there was variety enough to reach almost every niche in the market. Breechloaders naturally predominated, but muzzleloading percussion guns remained in production until 1923. The 1938 catalogue even featured a special insert offering pinfire guns, ranging in finish from plain to lavishly ornate. As early as the mid-nineteenth century and probably even before, Beretta had built a number of over-under muzzleloaders. No doubt sensing the

219

impact that John Browning's Superposed would have in the future, Pietro Beretta introduced his own version in 1932, called the Model SO. The name still is used for Beretta's best-quality sidelock over-unders.

Even with so great a diversity of types, virtually all of the Beretta double guns built in the twentieth century share a common basic design. Beretta began using the monobloc system about 1903 and has used it ever since. The breeches of both barrels, the barrel lump, and rib extension are milled integrally from a single block of steel. The breeches are counter-bored to accept the barrels. The block is heated to about 350 degrees Centigrade, and the barrels, their chamber-ends lathe-turned for sleeving, are inserted. As the block cools, the shrinkage, combined with a special-alloy solder, bonds barrels and breech as firmly as if they'd been machined all of a piece.

Of itself, the monobloc system doesn't necessarily produce a stronger gun than one built the more traditional way, but it does offer some practical manufacturing advantages. If a break-action gun is to open, close, and lock up properly – and continue to do so for several human lifetimes – it's critical that the breech, barrel lump and bolting bites all fit together in precisely the right way. Assembling them as separate parts is a demanding job; if they're all made in one piece to begin with, the task is simpler, requires less exacting handwork for fitting and essentially amounts to lower cost for the level of quality.

The monobloc system obviously isn't the only way to build a high-quality gun, but it's an excellent way to build one that doesn't cost your left arm and your firstborn.

Providing quality is something that Armi Beretta does very well indeed. Any Beretta is an admirable piece of work – whether an assault rifle, a pistol, a pump or autoloading shotgun, or a meticulously finished best-quality double. The difference between a bespoke game gun and a production side-by-side or over-under is largely a matter of cosmetics and wood. Everything else, the steels and the functional mechanics, is identical. To my mind, that makes the less-expensive Berettas among the best buys on the world market.

And it's the world market that really tells the tale of Beretta's success. American sales of sporting guns are respectable but not remarkable; it's just the reverse nearly everywhere else. Over the past twenty years, the Italians have all but taken over the market for top-quality target guns, and Beretta is pre-eminent in almost every country except America. You don't see all that many Berettas on the firing lines at the big-time American tournaments, but don't let that fool you. The rest of the world shoots more Berettas than anything else.

The reason is simple: Beretta builds a superb gun from a deep understanding of what a gun ought to be, a commitment to building it that way, and from having been around long enough to figure out how to do it.

Abbiatico & Salvinelli

As the twentieth century approaches its final decade, the gunning world is only now beginning to appreciate the full extent of what Italy has contributed in the past twenty years toward advancing the standards of gunmaking excellence. Fine Italian guns certainly are not under-appreciated by those who know them well, but in general, it seems to me that Italian achievements in gun design and in sheer craftsmanship generally are overshadowed by the extraordinary work of Italian engravers. Simply put, much of the gunning world is so bedazzled by Italian engraving that it fails to recognize the intrinsic quality of the gun underneath.

Italian engravers always have been superb artisans, but their current reputation is largely the work of Mario Abbiatico. Both sons of gunmaking families, Abbiatico and Remo Salvinelli served apprenticeships in the Val Trompian gun trade before setting up shop together in Gardone in 1967. For the first ten years, *Fabricca d'Armi Mario Abbiatico e Remo Salvinelli* – or FAMARS, as it's commonly known – built guns in a range of quality from knockabouts to first-class bespoken game guns. The market for best guns proved sympathetic enough that the two partners decided about 1977 to forego everything else. The following year, Abbiatico published *Grande Incisione su Armi d'Oggi*, nearly 300 pages devoted to the theory and practice of modern firearms engraving. The book brought Italian engraving to many new eyes around the world, and the engravers at FAMARS brought the actual work into a lot of new hands.

Thus the world discovered *bulino*. I never have been able to find the word in any Italian dictionary, but an Italian-trained engraver tells me that a *bulino* is a small wooden-handled engraving tool meant to be wielded solely by hand. In any case, the word has come to denote the style itself, of which Abbiatico has this to say:

> Only one hand is used in *bulino* work. The big difference between this and the [hammer and chisel] method is that the tool is driven by the hand, not by a hammer. The sensitivity of the hand allows greater precision and gives better results – pressure and depth of cut can be more carefully controlled, a smoother, more graceful flow of groove and line are achieved by a master of this style.

The *bulino* technique originated with printers in the days when copies of bank notes and fine documents were pulled from a painstakingly engraved tablet of stone or, later, metal. *Bulino* often is called "bank note" style. The Italians were the first to apply it to guns.

In any case, *bulino* engraving is a mind-boggling affair. It amounts literally to pictures, with all the subtle shading of a halftone, cut into steel – cut, not scratched nor etched, cut. Every line, no matter how microscopically fine, results in a minute shaving of steel on the engraver's bench. And every value of contrast in a piece of *bulino* work is the result of a cut. No artificial color is applied. The image is purely a function of light reflected or absorbed by the surface of the steel, and if you were so inclined, you could ink a *bulino*-decorated gun, press a sheet of paper to it, and pull off a print.

In the hands of a master, the keenly pointed *bulino* can create an image almost as realistic and as complex in tones and shades as any photographic emulsion. At its best, *bulino* can be astonishing.

Provided, of course, that pictures on guns are your cup of tea. They aren't mine. I can appreciate the technique and the artistry, and I can handle a game bird or a dog, provided they're kept small. Nongame wildlife on any gun moves me not at all, nor do human figures, particularly the enormous crowds that some customers have seen fit to order. It's a matter of taste; yours may be different from mine.

So pervasive has been the impact of the *bulino* style that even some normally conservative English makers have gone half mad on it. In 1984, Holland & Holland made up a set of four guns to commemorate the Game Fair at Broadlands, once the home of Lord Mountbatten. All four are *bulino*-engraved with portraits of the estate house, Lord and Lady Mountbatten (with Mahatma Ghandi, in one case), and members of their family. It's all flawlessly done, but I can't for the life of me see that any of it has the slightest thing to do with a gun. The impact of both the decoration and the gun are diminished, to my mind. Lord only knows what's next – maybe a *Peanuts* cartoon strip, for all I know. If Abbiatico & Salvinelli can order a forty-two-figure tableau depicting the signing of the American Declaration of Independence to be engraved on a gun, then anything is possible.

The Italian engravers, though, are so bloody good at *bulino* work that it's hard to fault even the most outrageous nonsense. They also are bloody good at scroll and at every other style.

By 1980, Abbiatico & Salvinelli had settled on three basic shotgun forms – an over-under, a hammerless side-by-side, and a hammer gun, all of them sidelocks. Of the first two, symbolic of the state of fine guns these days, the side-by-side is a classic London look-alike, and the over-under is graceful, strong, and simple – as only the Italians can make an over-under.

The hammer gun, too, shows a fair share of the innovation that Italian makers have brought to gunmaking. It essentially is a hammerless action in

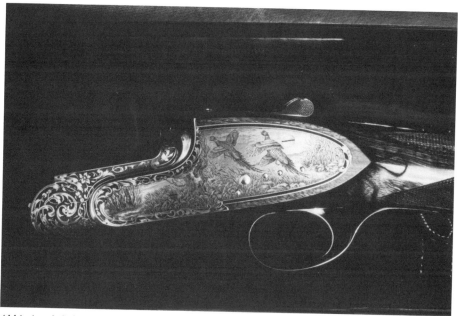

Abbiatico & Salvinelli over-under.

Italian artisans have introduced the rest of the world to bulino *engraving. This Rizzini 20-gauge was engraved by Firmo Fracassi.*

FAMARS self-cocking hammer gun.

that both hammers are self-cocking, and it's a single-trigger gun. A strikingly handsome piece. FAMARS also has built a number of four-barrel guns, each with two external hammers and two concealed inside the frame, all of them activated by a single trigger.

Just as FAMARS was making its mark on the shooting world, Mario Abbiatico died of cancer in 1984; he was only fifty, and his contribution to gunmaking had nowhere nearly reached its end. Under Remo Salvinelli's management, the company continues as before.

Lovely as they are, FAMARS guns have not earned the best reputation among professional pigeon-shooters, to whom mechanical excellence and reliability are absolute requirements. Many of them complain that the guns break down far more frequently than they should. I don't own an Abbiatico & Salvinelli, never have, but several of my friends do, and they, too, seem to experience an unusual number of mechanical problems – broken springs, pins that unaccountably loosen, the sort of thing that leads you to question the quality of materials.

It certainly is difficult to fault FAMARS craftsmanship, and the guns enjoy an extremely high reputation as investment pieces. No one seems to question the worth of an Abbiatico & Salvinelli as a work of art. To understand why that's the case, all you have to do is look at one. You'll find it hard to look away.

Armi Perazzi

But for Daniele Perazzi, best-quality Italian guns might have remained little more than a footnote in the American market, despite the efforts of Beretta and others. Perazzi apprenticed in the Val Trompian trade, worked for a while with Ivo Fabbri, and set up his own shop in 1961. By 1964, every competition shooter the world over knew his name.

It happened through Perazzi's acquaintanceship with Ennio Mattarelli, a splendid shot and gifted designer who wanted a gun for the 1964 Olympics in Tokyo. Mattarelli had a head full of ideas about how an international-style trap gun should be made, and he found in Perazzi just the man to render them in steel and wood. Mattarelli won the gold medal, the two men subsequently formed a partnership, and by the mid-'60s, Armi Perazzi was turning out some of the finest target and live-pigeon guns in the world.

The majority of Perazzi's early converts were European shooters. That the guns took a bit longer to catch the American fancy had less to do with their intrinsic merit that with the general mindset of American target shooters.

As Don Zutz rightly points out in *The Double Shotgun*, the 1960s saw a substantial change in how the American clay shooters approached the games. For several generations, only the most serious-minded of them were willing to spend much money for high-quality guns tailored for targets. Few, in fact, owned a target gun at all, and if they did it usually was a Winchester Model 12, a Remington Model 31, or an autoloader. Winchester offered the Model 21 in trap and skeet versions; Browning did the same with its Superposed. A few really serious types shot Krieghoffs at trap and skeet.

All of the target doubles were by contemporary standards hellishly expensive, and the man who owned one might as well have had "Hotshot Target Shooter" embroidered on the back of his shirt.

But the American economy prospered in the 1960s, and more and more casual shooters decided they could compete with the champions if they had guns like those the champions shot. Zutz puts it well: "People who just a couple of years earlier would have shuddered at the thought of spending $300 on a double, suddenly began spending $3000." Browning enjoyed the first fruits of the new attitude, as did Winchester's Model 101, but the one that finally blew all the others away was Perazzi.

One of the first things Ennio Mattarelli and Daniele Perazzi did after establishing their partnership was to start thinking about a trap gun for the 1968 Olympics in Mexico City. They already had the '64 Tokyo gun, which was on the market as the Perazzi Mirage – first-rate barrels, a frame with more steel than a Subaru, flawless ejectors, and a superb trigger that was part of an ingenious arrangement by which a shooter could drop out the trigger/striker assembly and slip in a new one in a matter of seconds.

Considering Mexico City's high altitude and relatively thin atmosphere, Mattarelli designed what at the time was an extraordinarily tall rib, which got the shooter's line of sight as far as possible from the shimmer of heat waves coming off the barrels. Its real advantage, as Mattarelli well knew, was that it lowered the barrels in relation to the shooter's shoulder, permitting an extremely high-combed stock that could be mounted low on the shoulder and therefore deliver noticeably softer recoil. The MX-8, as the gun came to be called, kicks just as much as any other in foot-pounds of energy, but since the barrels are in line with the shoulder, the recoil tends to come straight back and doesn't whip the muzzles around. That means you don't get socked on the cheekbone and also means less muzzle jump to overcome for the second shot.

There would have been something poetic about it if Ennio Mattarelli had taken a second gold medal at Mexico City, but he didn't. What he did was show the target-shooting world the gun of the future. Now, twenty years later, everybody who builds serious target guns offers high ribs. Then, only Perazzi and Al Ljutic made them. The gun Mattarelli used in '68 had a screw-in choke tube in the bottom barrel; these days, there are screw-in chokes in almost everything that shoots.

Medals notwithstanding, the MX-8 brought Perazzi to the forefront of target-shooting worldwide. In 1970 Ithaca Gun Company began marketing the guns in America, and as trapshooters like Dan Bonillas and Ray Stafford began using them to set new all-time records, demand in the American market bloomed like dandelions.

In the early '70s, Perazzis were imported in three models: Competition I, a basic target gun built in both trap and skeet versions; the Mirage, which Ithaca and Perazzi positioned in the world market as a live-pigeon gun; and the MX-8, offered as the ultimate high-tech competition piece. Ennio Mattarelli worked up yet another Olympic trap gun for the 1976 games in Montreal, this one called the MT-6. It didn't take the gold (Don Haldeman won the trapshooting medal with a Krieghoff), but the MT-6 took Perazzi innovation a step further by having screw-chokes fitted in both barrels. If memory serves, it was the first factory over-under so built.

The Ithaca-Perazzi relationship lasted until 1978. After that, Winchester marketed the guns for a couple of years, until Perazzi U.S.A. was established about 1981. By then, a steadily worsening economy was cutting into the gun market, and the '80s brought some lean and difficult years. Flagging sales prompted Perazzi to bring out the MX-3 as an economy model. "Economy," of

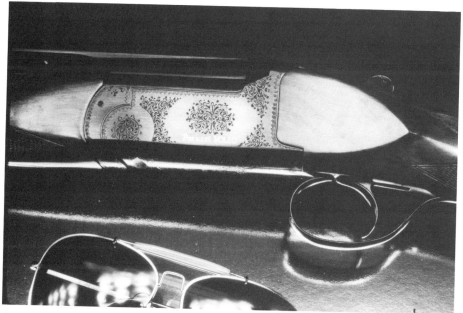

Special Perazzi MX20 game gun, commissioned as a limited-production gun by Pachmayr Ltd.

course, is a relative term when you're talking about a gun that sells for more than $2000, but the MX-3 has sold in respectable numbers, that's what it was meant to do.

Aside from the splendid quality of materials and workmanship that goes into them, the Perazzi over-unders have two innovative features that hold vast appeal for competitive target and pigeon shooters. The triggers are mechanically excellent to begin with, but the quick-change feature is a gem. The lockwork is fastened to the trigger plate, and the whole assembly slides into the bottom of the frame where it's held in place by a spring-loaded latch. If the lock should go awry, or if the shooter wants a trigger with different characteristics for some particular purpose, he simply can push the safety button forward to release the catch, drop out the lockwork, and put another in its place. Some of the lower-priced Perazzis don't have the quick-change locks; all of the best-quality target guns do.

Buttstocks are similarly interchangeable. The drawbolts are fitted with allen-type heads, and a stock wrench – which looks like a screwdriver with a long, allen-type blade – comes with every new gun. All you have to do to swap stocks is push the wrench through a small hole in the center of the buttpad, loosen the bolt, pull off the stock (there's no trigger-guard tang to fool with), and put on a different one the same way. Trap and pigeon shooters love it, because it lets them use one gun and still have the advantage of stocks tailored to the demands of each different event. It's also gives handy access to the lockwork of a Perazzi that doesn't have the quick-change trigger.

The dark side of it is that the wood-to-metal fit of the typical Perazzi over-under is abominable. The inletting and heading-up are excellent, but the wood is always oversized, simply because every stock is made to fit every gun. So, while the head of the stock snugs nicely to the frame, it also sticks out all around, by a sixteenth-inch or more in some places. Some people don't mind, and it has some obvious advantages, but gun wood that isn't perfectly flush with the metal looks like veriest hell, to my eye. A Perazzi is such a handsome gun otherwise that having the stocks worked down is worth the trouble, at least to me.

Judging from the guns that appear on the American market, you'd be inclined to believe that Perazzi builds nothing but over-under target pieces. Not so. Over-unders certainly make up the majority, but Armi Perazzi will make virtually any sort of break-action gun you want: boxlock or sidelock, over-under or side-by-side. You'll seldom see a fine, built-to-order Perazzi sidelock game gun in this country, but if you do, its splendid quality will catch your eye. The price tag likely will put a catch in your throat, as well; a best-quality Perazzi smallbore can cost upwards of $50,000. That kind of money puts Perazzi on a par with Purdey, Holland, Piotti, and others. The quality does, too.

Fabbri

Every country with even a reasonably prosperous trade in bespoken guns can present a few makers whose work shares the pinnacle of quality, craftsmen and artists of such consummate mastery that it's impossible to define by any objective standards which is "best" or even "better." Perfection is, after all, an absolute.

Nonetheless, everyone who truly fancies best-quality guns has some favorites, some makers whose work for one reason or another resonates our appreciative senses in a fuller chord than others'. Among Italian makers, the one who strikes that chord for me is Ivo Fabbri.

He is a mechanical genius, for one thing, an inventive, free-thinking mind on the order of a John Browning or a Dan Lefever, as diverse of interest as an Ansley Fox. He is an automotive engineer (formerly at Fiat) turned gunmaker, possessed of an artistic sense as deep and as integrated as that of anyone who ever built a gun.

Fabbri's technical innovations actually have more to do with manufacturing methods than with gun design. Fabbri side-by-sides, like everyone else's, follow the London best mold; the over-unders are not radically different from those of other fine Italian makers. Most of the machines on which these guns are milled, however, reportedly are of Ivo Fabbri's own design, and the milling is so precise as to require only minimal handwork to achieve perfect final fit.

Annual production is quite low, perhaps two dozen guns or fewer, and every one is built with meticulous attention to every detail. The side-by-sides are made on a Purdey-type action. (Fabbri, in fact, supplies Purdey with single triggers.) Barrels are bored from billets of exceptionally fine – and exceptionally expensive – steel made by Paolo Ferrone of Milan. Fabbri stockwork is utterly flawless. Engraving customarily is done by the finest Italian artisans – by Gianfranco Pedersoli, Angelo Galeazzi, Firmo Fracassi, and others of that ilk. Whether it's decorated with scroll, *bulino*, acanthus, or floral, a Fabbri gun is a visual symphony.

They're all beautiful, but the ones that send the shivers up my back are the over-under sidelock pigeon guns. It takes some doing to make an over-under match the sheer elegance of a fine side-by-side, but Ivo Fabbri can. The profile is as trim as a high-fashion model's, the frame as gracefully sculpted as a seashell.

Exquisitely finished guns are such a pleasure to look at that we can get sidetracked by appearance. Precise craftsmanship and clever design can be similarly misleading. That Ivo Fabbri can design machines capable of milling gun parts down to a gnat's whisker contributes something to the final quality of the product, but it doesn't ultimately make the difference. If machining were the key, the Japanese, with their computer-controlled laser-scan tracers, would have a lock on the world gun trade.

Actually, there is no single key, no prime element from which all others follow. Form and function are more deeply integrated in a fine gun than in any other object of human creation. If you handle enough best-quality guns, you begin to realize that there's a certain, distinctive feel about them, a characteristic that's easier to sense than it is to describe. It has much to do with balance, with the way a gun's weight is distributed between a shooter's hands, and the way the mass of it responds to the force imparted by his muscles. It also has much to do with form and how closely the various shapes of a gun agree with the human physique. It's the quality that the late British gun writer G.T. Garwood ("Gough Thomas") had in mind with the word *eumatic*, which he coined to describe a state of perfect compatibility between the nature of a

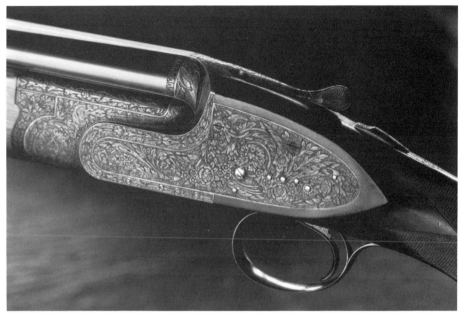

Ivo Fabbri sidelock over-under pigeon gun.

tool and the human body that uses it.

All truly great guns have an extremely high eumatic quotient and none, to my mind, higher than that of a Fabbri pigeon gun.

At a box-bird shoot not long ago, I struck up a conversation with a fellow gunner. That he was a serious pigeon shooter was clear both from his performance in the ring and from the Fabbri under his arm. Our talk inevitably turned to guns, and when I mentioned my great admiration for Fabbri, he very graciously asked if I'd care to shoot his for a while.

The gun he handed me was as lovely as a gun can get – a sidelock over-under richly engraved in scroll with a tiny, perfectly executed gold pigeon inlaid on the bottom of the frame. As do many European pigeon guns – and as all sidelocks should, in my view – it had two triggers. The owner was a man of about my size, so the gun fit me fairly well.

Those who've done a good bit of it tell me that *columbaire* – pigeons launched by hand inside a 300-meter circle – is the most difficult shooting there is. They may be right, though I find shooting box birds in a thirty-meter ring sufficiently demanding for my meager skills. Even so, I never shot anything so well as I did the next three pigeons when my turn came around. I've never fired a gun that handled more effortlessly and pointed more precisely where I looked, nor one that has that magical element of "feel" in greater measure. At thirty-two yards rise, every bird came down dead as a brick, and each time the second barrel was unnecessary insurance, required by the rules of the game.

I handed it back with sincere thanks and profound regret, picked up the Krieghoff I'd been using, and lost the next six-bird race to Steve Smith. Smitty still thinks it was his shooting that made the difference; what he doesn't know is that I didn't see any of those birds, not even the four I killed. I was seeing other things instead, mentally shuffling through every possibility short of committing a felony, looking for something that might put together the wherewithal to place an order with Ivo Fabbri.

Fratelli Piotti

Even though four generations of the family have made them, Piotti guns were little-known in America until the late 1980s. It's been a happy discovery, for Fratelli Piotti – or Piotti Brothers, as it translates – builds some of the finest guns in the world.

Ownership now rests with the founder's grandsons, Araldo and Fausto, and someday will pass to their sons, who are master craftsmen now active in the trade.

Piotti has built game guns since the beginning and has long been a darling among Italy's professional pigeon-shooters. In the late 1960s and early '70s, Piotti guns took a number of European and world target-shooting championships, including a gold medal at the 1972 Olympics. Today, virtually all of the world-class Italian pigeon shots who use side-by-sides have them built either by Fabbri or Piotti. And Fratelli Piotti holds a royal warrant, by appointment gunmakers to Queen Beatrix of the Netherlands.

Respectable credentials, these, although nothing demonstrates the splendid quality of the guns better than the guns themselves.

Other than a few boxlocks made as inventory guns for export, Piotti at present builds only best-quality sidelock side-by-sides made to order. It's a relatively small shop – twenty-one craftsmen – with an average output of seventy to eighty guns per year. The catalogue lists several models: Piuma and Westlake boxlocks; Monte Carlo, King, Lunik, and Monaco sidelocks. The differences among them are entirely a matter of finish and largely serve to establish base prices. Actually, Piotti will build a gun to virtually any specification, within certain limits, that a customer requests.

Piotti is unusual among Italian makers in that it buys no parts ready-made from the Val Trompian trade. Only steel billets and stock blanks come into the Piotti shop, and only finished guns go out. The only exception is that Piotti guns, like those from most of the best Italian makers, are sent to the engravers guild for decoration.

The sidelocks are built on a Holland & Holland-style action, frames and lock parts machine-milled to half-millimeter tolerances, then filed and fitted by hand. The steel that Piotti uses is extremely fine-grained and polishes to such a high luster that parts almost look as if they've been plated. They haven't. Like Ivo Fabbri, Piotti uses only Paolo Ferrone steel for its barrels – and they are the only two Italian makers to do so exclusively.

Some aspects of Piotti quality are apparent only to the closest look. The bridle, a part central to the structure of a side-plate lock, probably is the one lock part other than springs that's most likely to break, because it has to absorb considerable stress as the lock operates. In fastening the bridle to the plate, Piotti has devised a clever variation that provides extra support where the stress is greatest.

As with other best guns, a certain degree of Piotti quality is measurable more by what doesn't happen than by what does. As part of the family's insistence upon using only materials of the best quality available, Araldo Piotti has an impromptu test of his own for gauging the quality of stock blanks. Piotti mainly uses Circassian walnut for stocks, bought as three-year-old blanks and seasoned for an additional two years before it's used. By the time a blank gets to the stocker, it's a valuable item, considering the cost of storage and handling added to a purchase price that was substantial to begin with.

As the first step, the stocker saws the blank into a profile roughly the shape of a gunstock and then inlets and fits the frame, a process the British call "heading-up." It's a highly critical operation in functional terms, because the stock-head takes a terrible beating; if the frame and the stock-head don't mate snugly with one another throughout the maximum extent of their bearing surfaces, then recoil slams the frame against the wood at every shot. If the tangs and sideplates are more closely fitted than the frame itself, they become wedges. Sloppy heading-up is the prime cause of split stocks.

Even a well-headed stock can split if there's some internal flaw in the wood. A lot of wind-shakes and checks and cracks don't show up until the stocker begins the actual shaping, and some don't show up at all until the owner fires a few dozen or a few hundred shots, since guns customarily are sent to the proof house without their stocks.

So, as soon as a gun is headed up and before the stocker does any shaping, Araldo Piotti simply drives the butt of the blank against a concrete floor,

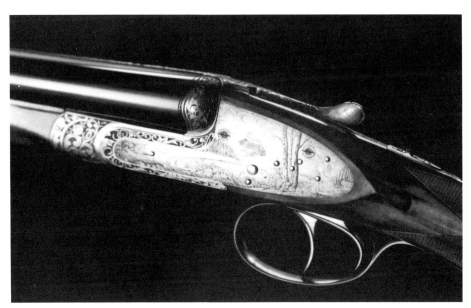

Fratelli Piotti Model King Extra.

perhaps a dozen times. If the wood cracks, it goes to the scrap heap; the stocker would, too, if his work were the cause, but Piotti stockers know their craft better than that.

Unorthodox, it is, and at times expensive in terms of pricey blanks that don't get used, but Piotti's test makes economic sense. With a blank put through what amounts to a proof process early on, the stocker doesn't waste his time on a flawed piece of wood.

But why such pounding, which stresses the wood far more than any amount of shooting ever is likely to do? Araldo Piotti simply shrugs: "It's better that a flaw should show up here, in the shop, than in the hands of the customer."

Economics is one thing, and no gunmaker can survive without a healthy sense of it. An unyielding commitment to the highest possible quality, though, is quite another, and without that, best guns cannot exist at all.

Armi Marocchi

Had American shooters not taken a serious interest in best-quality target guns nearly a generation ago, a number of first-rate Italian makers would have remained virtually unknown in this country. Perazzi is the most obvious example, followed at some distance by the excellent guns built by Renato Gamba and marketed by Dynamit Nobel of West Germany under the trade name Rottweil. Farther yet behind, Armi Marocchi is only now beginning to make some headway toward recognition in the American market.

Marocchi certainly is no newcomer, having built guns since 1922, and it continues still as a family business, largely in the hands of Piero Marocchi, the founder's son, and Mauro Marocchi, the third generation of gunmaking Marocchis.

During its nearly seventy years, Armi Marocchi has built everything from fine side-by-side game guns to over-under target guns, combination rifle – shotguns, rimfire rifles, and even air guns. According to company literature, its design for a CO_2-powered gun mechanism won an Oscar Award at the 1957 International Exposition of Inventions.

Armi Marocchi currently is a sizeable operation by Italian standards, employing about fifty people, and it supplies a substantial number of barreled actions to the trade. Its offerings are diverse, including a line of inexpensive, machine-engraved, boxlock field and target guns. These are sturdy, if not particularly well-finished pieces that feature a cross-bolt fastener. The system is stout enough that Marocchi uses the same action for an over-under gun that combines a 12-gauge barrel with a rifle barrel chambered for several rimmed cartridges – 5.6 x 52mm, 6.5 x 57mm, 7 x 57mm, and 7 x 65mm.

At the other end of the scale, Armi Marocchi offers a made-to-order, Holland-style sidelock game gun that's as meticulously built as any in the world.

Best of all, though, Marocchi builds a line of over-under target and pigeon guns that arguably are among the finest in the world and that fill an extremely important niche in the world gun market. Perhaps better than any other guns, the Marocchi Contrast series demonstrates the advantages of the Italian guild system of gun-making and its ability to reconcile extremely high quality with excellent value.

The Italian gun trade today functions much as the English trade did a hundred or even fifty years ago – as a thriving, diverse community of craftsmen rich in creative talent. There are a great many gunmakers but only a handful who fashion their guns entirely in-house. For the most part, it is a community of specialists – lockmakers, stockers, barrel-makers, and others whose expert craftsmanship is available to the trade in general. It is a system vastly different from that of the American arms industry, which in modern times has sought to maintain proprietary distinctions among products and which consequently has suffered all the ills inherent to that approach.

In what I'll call the industrial system – as opposed to the community or guild system – there is little sharing of expertise. In a guild system, a gunmaker usually buys his locks or his barrels or his single-trigger mechanisms from a specialist who makes only that component. In a healthy trade, moreover, a maker can choose among several specialists for the same item, and he can choose according to different criteria – quality, cost, a particular design, or some other factor. The point is that each maker doesn't have to reinvent the gunlock in order to avoid infringing someone's patent.

In the industrial system, each maker not only has to manufacture every part but also has to employ a full complement of specialists whose job it is to continually reinvent the gun. In the American industry, for instance, every company had its own single-trigger mechanism, each slightly different from the others and not all of them equally good. If you wanted a Parker gun, you had to accept the Parker single trigger; you couldn't buy a Parker with a Kautzky trigger, even though it was better, because Fox owned the Kautzky design.

One of the worst effects of the industrial system is that the gunmakers accrue a lot of overhead costs in attempting to be different from everyone else, and they must pass those costs along to the customer. Therefore, a certain proportion of the price the customer pays has nothing to do with the quality of the gun he's buying. The guild system generally offers a much closer relationship between cost and value; you have to pay for what you get, of course, but you can get exactly what you want.

To an extent, the guild system promotes uniformity among guns, particularly those of highest quality. The best designs tend to be duplicated by the majority of craftsmen and eventually, as patents expire, become standardized throughout the trade. The end result is the sort of Platonic ideal that becomes the "standard" or the "typical" gun, just as the classic English game gun, as it evolved a hundred years ago, now is the standard of its kind worldwide.

What happened to the side-by-side in England during the last century is precisely what's happening to the over-under in Italy right now. Just as the English took the French fowling piece and developed it to the point where it offers virtually no further latitude for improvement, so the Italian gunmakers have quietly transformed the gun that John Browning first brought into the modern age. In the past thirty years, the Italians have made the finest over-unders ever built, and I daresay that the ultimate form of the over-under, the standard to which all gunmakers everywhere will aspire, will not be greatly different from what the Italian makers are building today.

We may in fact already have a good example of what that ideal over-under is likely to be – the Marocchi Contrast.

Marocchi developed the Contrast specifically for the competition-shooting market. At the heart of it is a wonderfully simple action that demonstrates just how far the Italian designers have come. Since Daniele Perazzi's guns have played a major part in defining what we now recognize as a best-quality over-under, comparisons are inevitable, invited, in fact, by the guns themselves.

Marocchi and Perazzi actions are remarkably similar. Both use extremely simple lockwork, virtually identical in principle. Marocchi locks are fastened to the frame and are driven by coil springs; Perazzi's are mounted on the trigger plate and use leaf-springs. Marocchi mainsprings act directly on the hammers, while Perazzi uses a toggle linkage between spring and hammer. In both, sear angles are highly efficient and hammer-fall is quite short, which promotes smooth, crisp triggers and very fast locks.

The cocking systems are identical – a flattened steel slide actuated by a camlike tongue fastened to the fore-end iron. The Marocchi cocking piece engages the hammers directly; Perazzi's system uses intermediary cocking cams mounted at the front of the trigger plate.

Fastening systems, too, are identical. Both guns use double bolts mounted about midway up the standing breech. These engage lugs on either side of the lower barrel. Both also have heavy bosses milled inside the action bar, with complementary bearing surfaces machined at the sides of the breech, so that recoil stress is well distributed throughout the frame.

Both guns use monobloc breeches, and both use notch-and-trunnion pivots at the hinge. Marocchi trunnions are milled as part of the monobloc breech; Perazzi's are the more conventional sort, machined as part of the frame.

Marocchi uses a brilliantly simple ejector system, identical to that of the Rottweil, with all parts contained in the monobloc. Perazzi ejectors are slightly more complex, with the sears fastened to the fore-end iron. (Current Perazzi ejectors are much better than they used to be, in the days when the ejector stops were slim, delicate pins. Back then, a fair number of trapshooters got an unpleasant surprise when they opened their Perazzis and saw the ejector plate, stem, plunger, and spring fly off along with the empty cartridge case.)

To round out the Contrast's usefulness as a serious target gun, Marocchi adopted the Perazzi system for quickly changing buttstocks.

My point in this comparison-contrast exercise is not to detract anything from Perazzi but rather to argue that Marocchi represents all but one of Perazzi's most important virtues distilled into an equally handsome, equally well-built, equally functional gun at about two-thirds the price. Perazzi's interchangeable trigger group, which Marocchi does not have, is an important

Future arms historians may well consider the Marocchi Contrast action to be the classic over-under, just as the English sidelock of a hundred years ago is now considered the classic side-by-side.

advantage, but only at the highest levels of competitive target and pigeon shooting, and even then it's most important for the latitude it offers in using different triggers, with different characteristics, in the same gun. It's nice to think about having a handy replacement if a lock should break down in the middle of a high-dollar shoot, but you can grow old and gray waiting for a Perazzi lock to break.

Or a Marocchi lock, for that matter. I've shot a Contrast at both skeet and sporting clays for three seasons now, shooting that has accounted for more than 40,000 cartridges, and the first malfunction of any kind has yet to happen. Not that 40,000 rounds necessarily is any great number (one of my shooting partners has put almost five times that many shells through his Perazzi Mirage), but it's enough that any inherent flaws in design, workmanship, or materials ought to show up. I fully expect that I'll still be waiting for the first malfunction when my Contrast has digested as many shells as Joe's Mirage has.

The Contrast is built in several forms, all of them essentially target guns – skeet, trap, and live pigeon – and all in 12-gauge only. The America model comes as a high-ribbed trap or pigeon gun and as a single with the barrel in either the over or under position. The frame can be black or French gray, decorated with some Italianate floral engraving on the frame.

In the Contrast Cup series, frames are color-case-hardened, finished in

French gray, or deeply blacked. My gun is blacked and the steel highly polished; a friend owns a similar gun, also blacked, but with a matte finish. Presumably, you can order it either way. The Cup guns are decorated with simple line engraving around the contours and a nicely cut rosette on either side of the action bar at the hinge. (All lettering on the Contrast frame and barrels is cut rather than stamped; it's a nice touch.)

If you want a more highly decorated gun, the Contrast Prestige series offers excellent wood and engraving that can be rose and scroll, floral, incised floral, or game scenes in the *bulino* style. I've seen only a few highly engraved Marocchis, but the quality of the work has been uniformly excellent.

My taste in gun decoration leans heavily toward the traditional, but one of the handsomest – and certainly one of the most striking – Prestige-series Marocchis has a highly polished, blacked frame that's outlined with thin, inlaid gold wire. Marocchi calls it Black Gold. It's simple, restrained, and thoroughly elegant. I've seen a sidelock side-by-side Marocchi decorated the same way, although the effect isn't as successful on the side-by-side as it is on the over-under. On the Contrast frame, which is beautifully sculpted to begin with, the Black Gold decoration is stunning.

Contrast buttstocks are available in several styles, including straight-hand, half-hand, a variety of pistol grips with or without a palm-swell, and Monte Carlo combs. All dimensions naturally can be made to order.

All told, the Contrast is everything that a best-quality over-under ought to be. The action could readily be adapted to a lighter-weight game gun or scaled down to smallbore size. Whether Marocchi ever does that will depend entirely upon the gun market. The Contrast itself certainly shows no lack of merit.

The greatest problem with a Marocchi gun in this country is finding one. Competition Arms of Lafayette, Louisiana, imported the first North American Marocchi in 1979, succeeded in the early '80s by LT Imports of Chicago. Sales, unfortunately, have been such that the importer cannot justify a large inventory, and virtually all Marocchis imported now are live-pigeon guns built on special order. The Frigon Trap Gun, the house brand of Frigon Guns in Clay Center, Kansas, is built by Marocchi, though not on the Contrast action. A few Contrast skeet and trap guns show up on the used-gun market now and then. All told, the current inaccessibility is a great pity, because the Marocchi is a splendid gun.

I said earlier that Perazzi has done much to define our current concept of a best-quality over-under. What Marocchi has accomplished, it seems to me, is a major step toward defining what we will in time come to recognize as the classic over-under. Similar as the two guns are, it's important to understand that the Contrast is not a "copy" of the Perazzi – just as a Piotti isn't a "copy" of a Holland & Holland, even though most people can't tell one from the other at a casual glance. Terry Wieland's point about the best Spanish guns applies universally: There is an enormous difference between copying a style and adopting a principle. For the side-by-side gun today, that principle is British; for the over-under tomorrow, it almost certainly will be Italian. If the vagaries of economics and the gun market work out the right way, it could well be a Marocchi Contrast.

More than once in this chapter, I've drawn comparisons between the Italian gun trade of the late twentieth century and the English trade of the late nineteenth century. Perhaps I've belabored the point, but it seems to me an extremely important one, because out of that wonderful gunmaking environment of Victorian England came the finest guns the world has ever known, guns that still are the standards by which guns everywhere are judged.

Time inevitably has lent a certain obscurity to what Geoffrey Boothroyd calls the "vintage years" of the English trade. We look back, using the guns themselves as a medium with which to see through time, and we look back with a certain wistfulness, wishing for a closer, more sharply focused view. Like the cave-dwellers of Plato's parable, we see shadows dancing on the walls and try as best we can to perceive in them the realities of a

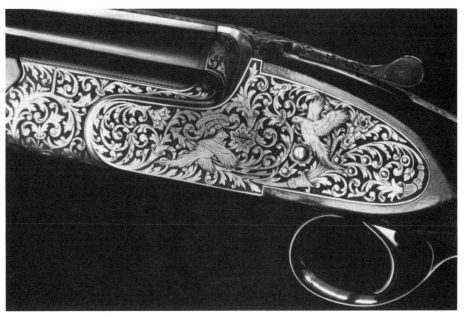

Fabio Zanotti sidelock over-under.

world now vanished into history, leaving only its artifacts behind.

But even if we cannot return to Victorian England, we still can see the same forces at work, in northern Italy. The most incorrigible Anglophiles are likely to take issue with the proposition that the finest guns built in the world today are built in Italy, but there's no denying the hard evidence.

Nationalism is hardly the point, anyway. The point is that we have an opportunity, probably unique, to actually watch history repeat itself. Any student of the gun interested in seeing evolution taking place would do well to study the Italian trade. It's all there, from the great manufactories of Beretta to the modest workshops of Piotti and Rizzini and Zanotti and Bertuzzi, where human hands continue to work the alchemy that brings dross to life as a fine gun.

GERMANY

The great coal fields that stretch almost unbroken from Wales eastward to Polish Silesia have been a prime factor in the rise of European arms industries. Where the veins are particularly rich and accessible and accompanied by equally dense deposits of iron ore, arms trades have flourished for centuries, long before the various central-European city-states and principalities evolved into even the precursors of modern countries.

No one knows how or when gunpowder was first used to propel a missile. Berthold Schwartz, a fourteenth-century German monk, often is credited with the discovery, but modern research has raised serious questions about whether Schwartz even existed, much less performed the legendary experiment with mortar and pestle that many early historians (W.W. Greener among them) cite as the origin of firearms in Europe.

There is no question, however, that "hand gonnes," as small, cannonlike arms were called, were fairly well-known in Europe by about 1325. It is equally certain that the gunlock underwent the major steps of its early evolution in Europe. Gun trades were established in central Europe at least as early as the fourteenth century. Greener tells us that gunsmiths in Suhl organized their guild in 1463. Dutch gunmakers founded a trade in Ferlach, Austria, in the sixteenth century. Active trades developed in Augsburg, Nuremburg, and the Ruhr valley as well.

With its long history of precision craftsmanship in general and gunmaking in particular, you might expect the story of the German gun trade to be a chronicle of splendid achievement in sporting guns. In fact, it isn't. German makers have contributed far more to the development of the sporting rifle than to the gun, while German game guns have by and large followed principles established elsewhere, particularly France and England, leavened by some adaptations according to what seem peculiarly German views on how guns ought to be made. In these adaptations lie both the virtues and the shortcomings of German guns.

As in other countries, available game and the traditions of pursuing it have done much to shape the nature of the German gun. German hunting traditionally has been less specialized than elsewhere, often including fur and feather in the same bag, ranging from grouse to roe deer, from hare to duck. Just as most of the general-purpose sporting dogs have originated in Germany, so the German sporting gun has evolved along multipurpose lines. Nowhere else, for example, has the combination gun ever been so popular or so widely built.

Since German hunters have for the part pursued wingshooting as part of a more general sport, it's easily understandable why the classic German game gun is part rifle, part shotgun. Which also is the reason why German gunmakers have done relatively little toward refining the shotgun in its own right.

This isn't to denigrate in any way the excellence of a German combination gun. If a pair of shotgun barrels and a rifle barrel or two wrapped up into a single package is the most useful gun for the shooting you do, then a German gun is the one to have. But no drilling, no matter how beautifully built, is an ideal bird gun by anyone's definition.

Even without a rifle barrel attached, German guns often come off second-best compared with the best specimens made elsewhere in the world. Craftsmanship is not the problem; some German guns are as skillfully and as meticulously crafted as any guns built anywhere. The problem is more subtle, more often a matter of style and aesthetics.

German gunmakers have always been preoccupied with strength. Under the earliest German rules of proof, established in 1891, the test for nitro-powder guns required a proof load of double the normal powder charge behind one and one-third times the normal shot charge. That is an enormously heavy load, probably the severest proof test required in any country in Europe, and it illustrates what seems to be a pervasive German concern for durability.

The guns illustrate this, too. The simple Purdey-type underbolt has proven itself sufficiently stout for even big-bore Express rifles, and yet few German makers have seemed to trust it, preferring instead to augment an underbolt fastener with a Kersten top bolt. Some German guns, in fact, have more fasteners than lock parts, and while they are undeniably strong, they often are unnecessarily heavy.

The same penchant for overbuilding levies an aesthetic price as well. Even the best of the modern German guns – a group that includes Merkel, Krieghoff, Franz Sodia, J. P. Sauer, and Simson – are far from handsome. Frames tend to be disproportionately thick and blocky, partly because they have to accommodate a multitude of fasteners and partly because of what I can only take to be a Germanic preference for straight lines, square corners, and variously shaped bulges. That concept of design works well for the Mercedes-Benz automobile and the Hasselblad camera; it does not work well for a gun.

Even when they're built to light weight, the contrast between slim barrels, trim stocks, and tall, bulgy frames gives most German guns – over-unders especially – a gawky look.

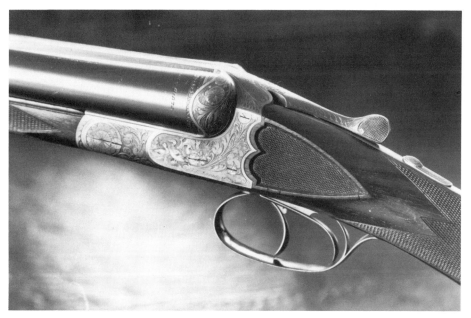

J. P. Sauer 20-gauge boxlock. Notice the heavier, relief engraving common to many German makers.

German styles of decoration don't move me much, either. Engraving patterns run heavily toward oak leaves, coarse scrollwork, and deeply incised game scenes, and the same motifs often are repeated in stock carving. In small, restrained doses, German-style decoration can be extremely handsome, but it's often done in such rococo excess that the disharmony of it all is simply overwhelming. Even done with consummate skill (and some German engravers are consummately skillful), it's often too much. Poorly done, it's a disaster. One current German over-under, for instance, is decorated with what presumably is meant to be a German shorthair pointing a pair of flushing grouse; it looks, unfortunately, like an unhappy coonhound chasing chickens.

Some of the best – and handsomest – German guns were built for export to the United States around the turn of the century. These bore the name Charles Daly and were house-brand guns imported by Schoverling, Daly & Gales of New York City. Although some very early Daly guns reportedly were built in England and Belgium, the most famous of them came from Suhl, from the workshops of H.A. Linder, established in 1874.

The Linder-made Dalys are splendid boxlocks, carefully built and beautifully finished. Like other German guns, they were treated to a multitude of fasteners – an underlug, a rib extension and top hook, and side clips on the fences – but Linder somehow put it all together in an attractive package.

They came in four grades: Superior, Empire, Diamond, and Regent Diamond, the differences among them solely a matter of engraving and wood. Ownership of Schoverling, Daly & Gales changed a couple of times between the end of World War I and about 1930, and the final change brought an end to the best of the Daly guns. The Charles Daly name has since been used on some Belgian-built over-unders, on guns made in Japan, and more recently on guns built in Italy – none as well-built as those that Linder made. If you're thinking of buying an old Daly, look for the word *Prussia* stamped on the water table. If it's not there, check for German proof marks. If you find one or both, chances are it's a Linder gun.

Among current German makers, Merkel and Krieghoff are most active in the American market. Both are old, respected firms. B. and E.A. Merkel, two brothers, began building guns in Suhl about 1920, under the style Gebruder Merkel. Since 1949, Merkel guns have been built by VEB Fahrzeug- und Jagdwaffenwerk Ernst Thalman, also of Suhl. At present, the line comprises more than a dozen different models of over-under and side-by-side guns in both boxlock and sidelock designs.

The boxlocks are built on the Blitz-type trigger-plate action; the sidelocks are Holland & Holland style. The side-by-sides are fastened by Purdey underbolts combined with Greener crossbolts, the over-unders by Kersten crossbolts. One model of over-under has a double underbolt in addition to the Kersten fastener.

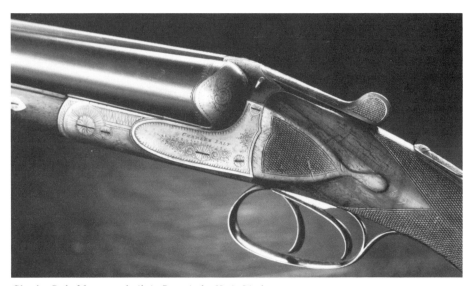

Charles Daly 20-gauge, built in Prussia by H. A. Linder.

Like many German over-unders, Merkel uses the Kersten bolting system.

The Kersten system essentially is the Greener cross-bolt principle applied to an over-under. Instead of a single rib extension, the Kersten designed uses two, one on either side of the upper barrel. There's no question that it's immensely strong, but a gun with Kersten bolts is a pain in the neck to reload quickly – or at least it is for me. The big extensions are knuckle-skinners when you load the bottom barrel, and they make tipping a cartridge into the top barrel all but impossible.

Merkels have enjoyed modest popularity in the United States for thirty years or more. They always have been extremely well built, but even the sidelock side-by-sides suffer aesthetically from too much steel in the frames and from being angular and stodgy where they ought to be smooth and graceful. The over-unders are designed with a barrel lump and hinge pin rather than trunnions, which makes them tall-framed. The Kersten bolts make the top of the frame fairly broad. You can hardly quarrel with the workmanship, but pretty they're not.

Heinrich Krieghoff also was founded in Suhl in the 1920s. The firm moved to Ulm, West Germany, following World War II. Krieghoff is best known in America for its splendid target guns built on patents from the Remington Model 32, but it also builds a line of side-by-side and over-under game guns. As with Merkel, the craftsmanship is excellent, the aesthetics less than entirely pleasing.

245

I realize that I'm being rather hard on German guns for reasons that are largely a matter of personal taste and, as such, certainly open to debate. My intention is not to gore anyone's favorite ox, but the aesthetic nature of a best gun seems to me fully as important as its functional mechanics. In my academic days, the relative importance of form and content was a favorite subject for arguments among my students and my colleagues alike. Perhaps that gives you an idea of the levels of excitement that the academic world embraces, but it's a serious issue to anyone seeking to understand the significance of art, and it applies to guns fully as much as it does to poetry or painting.

In fact, I can scarcely think of any item meant to serve both a practical and an aesthetic purpose in which form and function are more closely related than in a fine gun. There is something about the act of shooting, something as expressive as ballet, that a fine gun enhances in ways that a lesser gun cannot. This is true when the target is as mundane as a clay disc; when it's a game bird, the connection goes even deeper.

Someone, I don't remember who, summed it up perfectly: It just doesn't feel quite right to shoot a beautiful bird with an ugly gun.

BELGIUM

High Quality from the Lowlands

Fifty-odd years before the birth of Christ, Caesar's legions reached the lowlands of western Europe where they engaged and defeated Celtic tribes who called themselves Belgae. Annexed to the Roman Empire as part of Gaul, the southern lowlands remained under Roman rule for nearly 500 years, and during that time, their coal and ore fields gave rise to industries that would play a long, important role in European history.

The coal fields and ore deposits were particularly rich along the River Meuse, where the central-European highlands begin to rise, and there, where the River Ourthe joins the Meuse, the city of Liège evolved as an industrial center. Over the following centuries, the southern lowlands came under a succession of political rule – by the Franks, the Dukes of Burgundy, the Hapsburgs, the Spanish, the French, The Netherlands, and finally, in 1830, to independence as the country of Belgium. By then, Liège was one of the principal arms-making cities of the world.

Geography was a key factor. The Meuse was a main artery of trade, and Liège lay also on the major land route of trade connecting France and Germany and England. Since the end of the fifteenth century, the city itself had been recognized as essentially independent and politically neutral, which certainly helped foster trade with all sides in the minor wars that continually flared and subsided among the nations around it.

The Liège arms trade dates at least to the fifteenth century and probably is even older. By the seventeenth century, it was a major source of military arms for Prussia, England, and Russia. In 1672, the Prince Bishop of Liège issued an ordinance establishing what now is the oldest existing proof system in Europe.

Like Gardone, its Italian counterpart, Liège supplied thousands upon thousands of barrels for everything from military muskets to fine sporting guns. By the nineteenth century, gunmakers worldwide, including those in England and the United States, got most of their barrels from Liège, and the fine Belgian Damascus tubes set standards of excellence that few others could match.

Like other arms industries of similar size, the Belgian trade naturally produced export guns in vast numbers. From about 1880 through the 1920s, the American market was literally awash with cheap Belgian guns sold under a bewildering variety of trade names. The H. & D. Folsom Arms Company of New York City was a major distributor of both Belgian-made guns and similar pieces built in this country by Crescent Arms Company of Norwich, Connecticut. At the same time, dozens of American hardware companies and mail-order houses also sold Belgian imports as house-brand guns. Simply listing the various trade names would amount to a small book in itself; Folsom alone used more than 200 different names, usually referring to "gun companies" that never existed except on paper.

Years ago, a fair number of these, commonly called "contract" guns, still existed, and even now I get an occasional letter from someone who wants some information on Grandad's old gun, stamped Mississippi Valley Arms or Harvard or Chesapeake Gun Company or T. Barker or Nitro Bird or Kingsland Special or some other name. If you own an old single-barrel or double by a gun company you never heard of, chances are it'll have Belgian proof marks.

The contract guns were cheaply made and cheaply sold, and most of them fell apart after a few years' use. Like the cheap Spanish guns that came on the American market in the 1950s and '60s, the Belgians served a purpose but they did little to enhance the reputation of the Belgian gun trade. With the exception of the Belgian-built Brownings, only a few really good Belgian guns found their way to the United States.

The earliest of these were built by Auguste Francotte and imported by Abercrombie & Fitch. Francotte is an old firm, founded in Liège in 1805 as a

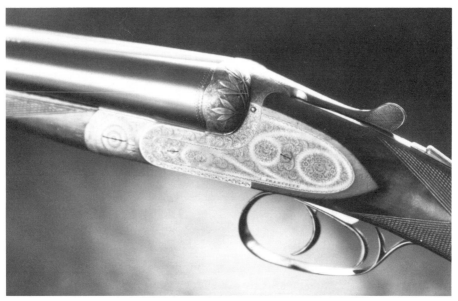

Auguste Francotte is one of Belgium's oldest and finest gunmakers. This is a sidelock made in the classic London style.

producer of military weapons. When it turned to sporting guns, the company set out to compete among the highest levels of quality in the European trade. From 1877 to 1893, Francotte maintained a shop in London, and while it probably didn't steal much custom from the best English makers, British shooters had a high regard for the guns. There was good reason for it. They're hard to come by these days, but the old Francottes are lovely guns, the quality of their craftsmanship and finish on a par with many of London's best.

The Belgian trade is neither as large nor as diverse as it used to be, but a few makers continue to build best-quality guns, nearly all of them according to principles of the English game gun. Francotte offers superb game guns built to order, either on an Anson and Deeley-type boxlock action or as a bar-action, London-style sidelock.

Lebeau-Courally, which reportedly was founded in 1865, makes side-by-sides in both boxlock and sidelock styles. The boxlocks use Anson and Deeley-type actions, and the sidelocks are built after the Holland & Holland image. Lebeau-Corrally's over-under is made on the Boss patents. All of them are beautifully made.

Forgeron also has for some years built splendid boxlock and sidelock side-by-side guns. A few years ago, Don Zutz reported that Forgeron himself was approaching retirement and that the future of the firm was in some doubt. I haven't been able to determine whether it remains in business at this writing, but Forgeron guns certainly are available on the secondary market. Finding one would take some work, but the guns more than justify the effort.

In the United States, the most famous Belgian guns of all are those designed by John Browning and built by Fabrique Nationale d'Armes de Guerre. From the turn of the century until the 1960s, when Winchester established a gun factory in Japan, the Brownings were unique – guns of American design manufactured in a foreign country and sold primarily in the United States. The dozen or so Browning arms manufactured in Belgium included only two shotguns; of those, the one most appropriate to this discussion is the Superposed.

It's impossible to overestimate the impact that John Moses Browning has had on firearms of the twentieth century. He was by no means the only man to recognize new design concepts, but no one ever has nor probably ever will match either the scope or the success of what he accomplished almost single-handedly. In the sixty-odd years since his death, the arms industry worldwide has by and large followed principles first conceived in his busy mind and first brought to concrete form by his hands. It's no exaggeration to say that John Browning did not simply bring firearms design into the modern age, but rather that he created the modern age.

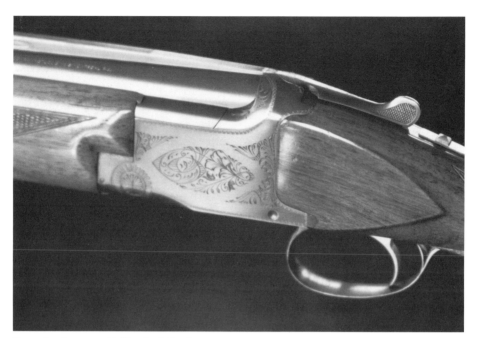

Browning Superposed, Standard Grade.

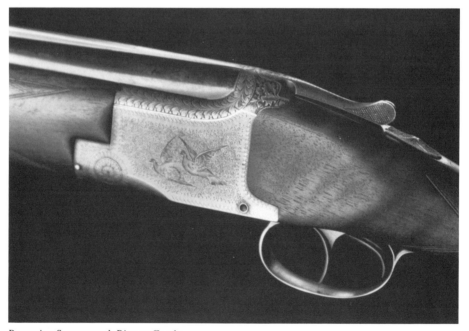

Browning Superposed, Pigeon Grade.

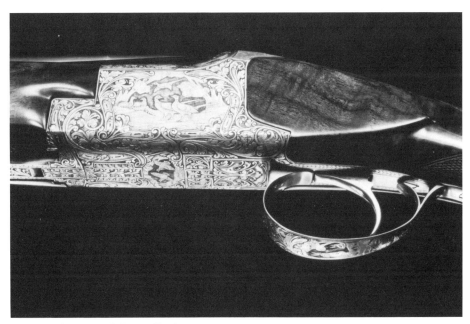

Browning Superposed, Diana Grade.

But progress, Browning once remarked to one of his sons, is not just a matter of getting farther and farther from a starting place. "We are making guns," he said, "that shoot farther, harder, faster, and calling it progress. But if we limit the meaning to movement toward a destination where the most pleasure and satisfaction are to be found, then this progress we brag about is just a crazy, blind racing past the things we are looking for – and haven't the sense to recognize. And in the matter of guns, that makes me crazier than most."

Crazy like a fox, perhaps, but John Browning took seriously the notion that pleasure and satisfaction are qualities that do not necessarily pertain to guns meant solely to shoot farther, harder, or faster. And at the end of his life, he turned his genius back in time. The Superposed was his last gun, and if a break-action, two-shot sporting gun seems an odd finale for the world's greatest inventor of automatic arms, there is a symmetry about it that made perfect sense to Browning himself. He was well aware that he had created fearsome engines of war and, like others whose inventions embodied both benefit and destruction, had waged a private struggle with his conscience because of it. Hunting and trapshooting were his keenest pleasures; in them he found both renewal and respite. His creative urge was irresistible. He invented machine guns and automatic rifles and pistols because he had to. He created the Superposed because he wanted to.

Browning began tinkering with the idea for an over-under gun about 1922. Always shrewd in spotting unfilled niches in the firearms world, he must have known that some American shooters were showing an interest in English over-unders and concluded that an American version would find a ready market. Obviously, he was right.

He filed the first application for patents on the new gun in October 1923, followed by another application in September 1924. After the patents were issued on March 30, 1926, he turned the drawings and the pilot model over to his son Val, who delivered them to Fabrique Nationale in Belgium.

Browning had a long-standing relationship with the Belgians, dating from March 1902, when he contracted with FN to manufacture his Auto-5 shotgun. Val, in fact, had been living in Liège since the end of World War I, serving as the Browning engineering representative. By the autumn of 1926, FN was getting tooled up for the over-under, and John Browning sailed for Europe to help work out any last-minute details. He died at the FN plant on the day after Thanksgiving.

One important feature of the over-under remained unfinished. Browning intended from the beginning that it should be a single-trigger gun, and he had been experimenting with an inertia-block system that would reliably shift the sears while preventing the involuntary pull from tripping the second lock. When he died, he hadn't yet found the mechanism that suited him.

The whole project got shelved in the aftermath of Browning's death. Except for a brief time at the beginning of his career, John Browning had always been an inventor, not a manufacturer, and had sold his early inventions outright. He received royalties on some later guns, but at the time of his death, all Browning guns still in production were manufactured and sold by other makers. He owned the rights to many of the sporting guns, however, including the Superposed, and his family subsequently organized Browning Arms Company to market them.

The first major Browning catalogue, issued in 1931, introduced the Superposed to the American market. It came in 12-gauge only, with 28-, 30-, or 32-inch barrels, ejectors, three different standard stock designs, double triggers, and a solid rib. The Standard Grade Superposed sold for $107.50, Pigeon Grade for $175, Diana Grade for $277, and Midas Grade for $374.

A ventilated rib cost $20 extra. For $30 more, you could get what the catalogue describes as the Browning Twin-Single trigger. The Twin-Single was Val Browning's first step toward designing what eventually would be the standard Superposed trigger. Essentially, it amounts to two single-trigger mechanisms in one gun, since either trigger will fire both barrels. The front one fires the under barrel first, then the over; the rear trigger simply reverses the order.

Val Browning didn't invent the concept, but he refined it a bit beyond any other. In most cases, single-double triggers have comprised a nonselective front trigger capable of tripping both locks, combined with a rear trigger that fires one barrel only. Such arrangements have been available in the past from Brno of Czechoslovakia, Simson of Germany, and in a trigger patented in 1962 by Fausto Massi, a gunmaker in Vicenza, Italy. If memory serves, the Browning system was used in a Spanish gun called the Laurona, which was briefly marketed in the United States about twenty-five years ago.

The Browning Twin-Single was not a bad trigger, all things considered. It rarely doubled, but it was extremely complicated and bloody hell to repair once it got out of whack. Val Browning continued to explore the inertia-block concept, and by 1939 came up with the single trigger that still is a part of the Superposed. It's one of the most reliable ever made.

Complexity always was in the nature of John Browning guns, and the Superposed is no exception, although it certainly is simpler than the various Browning autoloaders. The fore-end is a good example. Instead of fastening it with either an Anson, a Deeley, or the even simpler snap-type latch, Browning designed the Superposed so that the fore-end doesn't come off at all. Instead, it slides forward once the latch is released, allowing you to dismount the barrels from the frame. To remove the fore-end at all, you have to take out the screw that holds the wood in place and then drive out a friction-fitted pin to separate the fore-end iron from the barrel assembly. The 1931 catalogue makes a great to-do about the wonders of this arrangement, and subsequent Browning apologists have used up a lot of words trying to justify the design as providing some esoteric advantages.

The fact is that for all its sweet nature and wonderful handling qualities, the Superposed is a flawed design. Its complexity is unnecessary. Why John Browning chose to use a barrel lump and hinge pin instead of trunnions is anybody's guess. He certainly had good examples of the trunnion system in both the Boss and Woodward over-unders.

His underlug bolting system is similarly reactionary. That first catalogue devotes an entire page to arguing the merits of the hinge and bolt, eschewing both trunnions and mid-breech bolting as lacking the stamina to withstand long use. To anyone familiar with either the best English over-unders or the Remington Model 32 or the current best-quality Italian guns, it's not very convincing.

Which isn't to say that the Superposed is a bad gun. On the contrary, it's one of the greatest over-unders ever made. It always has been extremely well built;

it's handsome; and it's remarkably durable, which probably owes more to the quality of materials and workmanship that's gone into it than to any wear-resistant qualities inherent to the design. A Superposed will in time develop a loose hinge and a sloppy bolt, just like any other gun, but it'll stand up to a lot of abuse along the way.

The 1931 catalogue made one key point that no one could quarrel with: "Browning Superposed is the first over-under gun offered at a price which is not prohibitive." Even though $107.50 was far from pin money in the Depression years, the Superposed was a bargain. A lot of American-made guns were every bit as well built, but scarcely any, at that price, were as well finished. It wouldn't be accurate to say they sold like hotcakes, but Superposed guns did very indeed during the 1930s. By the time World War II brought production to a halt in 1939, about 17,000 had been built. The Lightning Model was introduced in 1935, and Val Browning's excellent single trigger became standard fare in 1939.

The Nazi *Blitzkrieg* swept over Holland and Belgium on May 10, 1940, and both countries surrendered eighteen days later. All of the arms factories at Liège, including FN, were quickly occupied and converted to producing weapons for the German military. A few Brownings were assembled from parts on hand, but none, of course, for export.

For a couple of years immediately following the war, the Belgian government required FN and other arms-makers to place top priority on re-equipping the Belgian army, which further postponed the production of sporting guns. FN built about 200 Superposed guns in 1948 and resumed production on a larger scale the following year. The 20-gauge Superposed first appeared in 1949. In 1950, magnum chambering became available, and the grading system for all guns changed from names to numbers, although the actual decoration remained much the same. Grade I offered the option of a solid or vent rib; grades II, III, IV, and V came with a vent rib as standard. The solid rib was dropped altogether in 1955, and a Grade VI gun was added in 1958.

In 1960, 28-gauge and .410-bore versions first appeared, and the grading system changed back to the original grade names. Grade VI, which apparently hadn't sold well, was discontinued.

Not all of the innovations applied to the Superposed were good ones. In 1961, with great fanfare, Browning announced the Broadway trap gun, which was a standard Superposed trap with a half-inch-wide rib. Some shooters liked it; others, myself included, thought it was an abomination. At the very beginning, John Browning reportedly described the over-under's advantage using the metaphor of a yardstick, arguing that one could sight down the narrow edge more easily than down the broad surface. In terms of "sighting," he was right, although a shotgun isn't meant to be "sighted." But a narrow rib does direct the eye more accurately than a wide one – and even while extolling the virtues of the Broadway rib, Browning also ordered it made with a narrow line of matting down the center, which has always struck me as a tacit admission that the extra width was useless. It was ugly besides. I've often wondered what John Browning would have thought of it.

And there's an important point here in more general terms. Browning himself described the over-under as more "useful" because of its "single sighting plane." He didn't invent that notion, but he certainly helped make it something of a cliché in American gun lore. I don't know when it got started (the single sighting plane is mentioned in the literature at least as far back as the early 1920s), but gun writers and the shooting public latched onto it as gospel, and it remains a common sentiment today.

Think about it for a moment, and it all turns to nonsense: No gun has more than one "sighting plane," no matter how many barrels it has or how they're arranged. Moreover, the idea of "sighting" has no more application to a shotgun than it does to the four food groups. Try to hit a moving target by sighting along the barrel and all you'll do is spray aimless lead. You have to watch the target, not the gun barrel; if the gun fits and if you mount it properly, the muzzles will be pointing where you look. No amount of blather about sighting planes is a substitute for gun fit. You won't shoot any better with a poorly fitting over-under than you will with any other gun that doesn't fit.

The 1960s were bittersweet years for the Superposed. Production and sales were high, but so were the prices, and they were getting higher every year, as European labor costs continued to rise. All of Browning's guns were in the same economic boat, and the company began looking to Japan as an alternative. Beginning in 1971 with the BT-99 single trap gun and the BSS double, Browning gradually shifted the bulk of manufacture from Europe to the Orient. The Japanese-made Citori over-under came on the market in 1973, the same year that FN began building a less expensive Browning over-under called the Liège.

The Liège proved a bummer. Its action wasn't nearly as good as the Superposed, and most of what had been done to reduce production cost also reduced the overall quality of the gun. It was discontinued in 1975.

By then even a Grade I Superposed cost well over $1000 – almost 300 percent more than it had cost just ten years earlier – and competition from cheaper guns was killing it in the marketplace. Browning pulled the plug in 1976. But not entirely. Even if the Superposed couldn't compete at $1000, there still was a place for it at the upper end of the market, and in 1977

Browning announced that the Superposed would henceforth be available on special order as a series called the Presentation Grades, highly decorated, gold-inlaid, fitted with decorative sideplates upon request – in short, custom built.

It remains available on that basis today. You can order a Superposed in the old grades – Pigeon, Pointer, Diana, and Midas – or as a completely custom-built gun decorated any way you want it. If you want to spend less, money, Browning also offers the B-125, which is assembled and finished in Belgium from parts made elsewhere.

It isn't as sleek as the best Italian over-unders, but the old Superposed is one of the world's great guns. There is a homey sort of charm about it that a lot of other, more expensive guns just can't match. I've owned a half-dozen or more of them over the years, and while I liked some better than others, they all handled well. Their triggers worked flawlessly, and they were all a pleasure to shoot. The last one, a Standard Grade built in 1938, got rebuilt as a skeet gun somewhere along the line, and it could break targets shot for shot with any gun I ever owned. It still does, in fact; I refitted the stock for Susan when she took up skeet a couple of years ago, and she broke twenty targets out of the first round she shot with it. Not bad for a beginner whose previous high score was about twelve. She could shoot just as well with any good gun that fit, but that argument wouldn't get you far if you tried to buy her Superposed.

During a visit to the Browning headquarters in Utah last fall, I spent a few minutes talking with Val Browning, John Browning's son and the man who designed the Superposed trigger. He's past ninety now, though you'd never guess it, and still spends an hour or two at the offices each day. When Paul Thompson, Browning's press-relations director, introduced us, he mentioned to Mr. Browning that I was particularly fond of the Superposed.

His eyes changed for a moment, as if he were looking back in time. Then he smiled at me and said, "You have good taste. I'm fond of it, too."

APPENDICES

WHEN THE GOOD GUNS GO AFIELD
Buying and Shooting an Older Gun

The newest addition to the clutter on my study wall is a photograph that Bill Habein made last October. I'm leaning, brushwhipped and bedraggled, against Bill's smokehouse, smiling the half-goofy smile of a man just back from a trip out of time. On a shelf beside me are five Minnesota grouse and a handsome shotgun.

It's a simple enough image, scarcely worth a second glance from an uninterested eye, but it talks to me in a voice resonant as fading thunder. It reminds me of a splendid day spent with a fine old friend in a place I dearly love. It reminds me, too, of the day I took a limit of grouse with six shots; I appreciate that, because I rarely shoot so well.

I appreciate it all the more because that old gun and I have gone a lot of miles together, burned a lot of powder, bagged a few birds, missed some, and generally had a hell of a good time no matter what happened. I found it in a gunshop a long time ago, scrubbed it of fifty years of neglect, restocked it myself to my dimensions, and in the process found a faithful companion. It's not the only gun I shoot, but it's the one I take when I want to shoot particularly well or when I'm in a slump.

There's a special appeal in hunting with a gun that has some history to it, one that knew the old days when the world was a simpler, wilder place, a gun that somebody took genuine pride in having built. I own some newer, high-tech pieces that are at least as artful, but I don't love them the way I love the old ones.

Still, no matter how emotionally cranked up you get at the idea of grand days afield with a fine old double, it's wise to remember that you're setting out to buy a used gun, and used guns have their weaknesses. Moreover, it's likely to be an old, used gun. Except for the Winchester 21, no great American doubles have been built for nearly forty years, and one even that new is a rare item. There are lots of best English guns around that date back to the turn of the century. So, generally speaking, the majority of guns you'll find will be of 1930s vintage or older. They can be wonderful things, but the further back you go, the more things you need to watch for.

Damascus barrels aren't nearly as common as they were when I started fooling with shotguns, but they're still around. And so are a few obtuse types who think they're all safe to shoot.

These barrels were made by twisting strips of iron, or alternating strips of iron and steel, into skelps and hammer-welding the skelps on a mandrel. The quality of the finished barrel depended entirely upon the skill of the man with the hammer. Most were perfectly safe to use – with the black-powder ammunition current at the time. But any flaw in the welding leaves a minute air pocket in the barrel wall.

259

Poorly made twist barrels can be full of them; moisture condenses in these and rust begins working from the inside out, leaving them riddled with unseen weak spots. The whole thing becomes a disaster just waiting to happen. Now, after so many years, some twist barrels aren't even safe with black powder, and a smokeless load can blow them to kingdom come. It takes a genuine expert to tell the difference.

Damascus barrels, particularly those on American guns, just aren't worth the risk, and they are a risk, regardless of what somebody might tell you about their being perfectly safe to shoot with the proverbial "light trap loads." Of those who persist in doing so, I can only say that the Foolkiller obviously has been busy elsewhere.

A twist barrel might not rupture on the first shot – or the fiftieth or the five-hundredth. But it will eventually. And when they go, they go with a bang, not a whimper. The most common place for a twist barrel to blow out is ten or twelve inches ahead of the chamber, since that's where the shot column is when a smokeless-powder load reaches peak pressure. It's also the place where your forward hand is holding the gun.

Some twist-barreled English guns were built and proved for some specific load of nitro powder. And you can send one back to the London or Birmingham proof house for reproving. (Actually, you can send any gun to one of the English proof houses, but it's not cheap and if the gun fails proof, you're out of luck.) If you absolutely must shoot a twist-barreled gun, have it reproved first, though the whole thing is far more trouble than almost any gun is worth.

The bottom line is simply not to consider twist barrels safe with any modern cartridge. I don't know about you, but I have no fingers to spare for a game of Damascus Roulette. It's a rigged game.

Another old wives' tale to watch for is the one about the classic American doubles made with false-Damascus barrels. Until about 1910 or thereabouts, twist barrels were the mark of a high-quality gun, and they were more expensive then steel tubes. To dress up an otherwise cheap gun, steel barrels sometimes were acid-etched with a Damascus-like pattern or wrapped in a sort of transfer paper that left the same sort of texture as real twist. These were poor-quality barrels to begin with, not even as strong as real twist.

In any case, none of the best American makers ever used false Damascus, and the tales of high-grade Smiths and Parkers with etched-steel barrels are just wishful thinking. If you see a Parker or Smith or Ithaca or Lefever of any grade with barrels that look like twist, that's exactly what they are. They're not the guns you're looking for if you're looking for guns to shoot.

A set of twist barrels that aren't pitted can be polished up and blued and thereby made to look like steel, even to a close examination. If you have any doubts about a particular gun, here's how to tell the difference: Take the fore-end off, buff some small area of the barrel down to bare metal, and put one or two drops of hydrochloric acid on the bare spot. Solid steel will show a uniform gray under the acid, but the pattern of a twist barrel will come up clearly, because the acid acts upon the component iron and steel in different ways. Simple as that.

Chances are, most of the barrels you'll see, steel or twist, will be on the long side. Thirty-inch tubes were the standard years ago, a holdover from black-powder days, when guns needed long barrels so the powder could burn completely and send the shot charge off at peak velocity. Old customs die slowly, and the thirty-inch standard persisted well into the nitro-powder era. Still, guns with 28-inch barrels are reasonably common, and they probably are the best choice nowadays. Factory-original short tubes – twenty-six inches or less – are hard to come by. Because they're scarce, they're also usually expensive.

In practical fact, even 30-inch barrels are no particular handicap, especially if you have the chokes honed out to dimensions appropriate for modern ammunition. Remember, a break-action gun with 30-inch tubes is about the same length overall as a repeater with a 26-inch barrel.

Balance and weight are the key factors. American guns with long barrels are likely to be a bit heavy for all-day hunting – but then, American guns generally are heavier than they need to be, regardless of how long the barrels are. A best English gun is built for optimal performance with a certain load, which in a 12-gauge game gun generally is an ounce of shot, and the overall weight is trimmed down to the minimum needed for safety, durability, and to dampen recoil. On a steady diet of heavy American loads, the typical English best will kick like hell, and the stresses eventually will damage the gun – not because it's inferior, but because it was built according to a principle different from ours.

Our guns, for the most part factory-made and therefore designed with Everyman in mind, were made to accommodate any load available at the time. To achieve that level of durability, they were overbuilt. There's much to be said for a gun that'll digest any old cartridge you stuff into it, but it requires a trade-off in weight and, to some extent, handling quality.

Proper balance goes a long way toward mitigating excess weight. In the classic ideal, a gun's weight should be perfectly balanced between the shooter's hands. If the majority of weight is in the stock, the barrels tend to feel whippy; if it's placed out front, the gun becomes nose-heavy. In my experience, very few shooters do their best work with a gun that's noticeably light in the muzzles. By the same token, there's a certain advantage in balance that's shifted forward a bit. The extra weight out front provides some inertia to help keep the barrels moving, a particular advantage in long-range shooting. That's why trap and waterfowl guns still are built with long barrels.

Actually, you can have any gun balanced any way you want it. You can shift the weight toward the muzzles by boring some wood out of the buttstock, which is how the English makers do it. You can move the balance point back by having the barrels struck thinner or by packing some lead into the buttstock.

Even though barrel length itself isn't a critical factor in dynamics, beware the American gun with odd-length tubes. Twenty-six, 28, 30, and 32 inches have always been standard barrel lengths in the American trade, and a gun with tubes of any other length most likely is a gun that's been sawn off. There are some exceptions, because most of the best makers offered odd-length barrels on special order, but they actually built very few guns that way. Don't be taken in by some bozo's claim that an otherwise ordinary gun with odd-length barrels was a special-order item. The odds are a zillion to one against it.

English and Continental guns often are different. The English have long been fond of 27-inch barrels. My John Wilkes has 29-inch tubes. On the Continent, barrels are measured metrically, in centimeters. Chances are, only guns built specifically for the American market will measure out in precise inches, but that isn't universally true, so the caveat out of hand against odd-length tubes doesn't apply to European guns.

But it does apply to any gun that's been sawn. No shotgun barrel is perfectly straight, least of all a double's. Those twin tubes have been carefully collimated to shoot to the same point of impact at a given distance – typically forty yards – and if you bob them, you're apt to end up with one that shoots where you look and one that doesn't. That, I know from sad experience, is frustrating.

Unfortunately, there's no infallible way to identify a gun that's been shortened, but there are some good clues. Odd-length barrels is one. Muzzles that aren't extremely close together, even touching, is another – although thinly-struck smallbore tubes often are well separated. The muzzles should be perfectly square with the center of the rib. As I said in the Parker chapter, weighing Parker barrels isn't a reliable test for chopped-off tubes. Neither, for that matter, is the absence of the little band of untextured steel at the muzzle-end of a Parker rib. The matting on most Parker ribs doesn't reach clear to the end, but it does on some factory-original guns.

If you're in doubt, ask to pattern the gun, and shoot about ten shots through each barrel. If both shoot to the same point of aim, there's no harm done either way, aside from having little or no choke – and that's not necessarily a bad thing, either.

Factory records for some of the best American doubles still exist, though all of them are to some extent incomplete. If you're considering a Winchester 21 or a Remington 32, you can send serial numbers to the factories and probably learn what length the barrels originally were. A.H. Fox work-order cards still exist, and Roe Clark can provide a description of the original factory specs for most Foxes. Details follow in the "Serial Numbers, Notes, and Sources" section.

Because the great American doubles were built during a time when shotshells were comparatively inefficient, most of them are choked more tightly than they now need to be. A lot of Continental guns, even new ones, suffer the same problem. You'd do well to consider having old, closely bored chokes honed out to more useful dimensions. Improved-cylinder and modified performance is about as tight as anyone needs for general upland work. I've had my favorite American guns reamed out to skeet and skeet, which is ideal for the shooting I do. They're no slouch in a duck blind, either. My John Wilkes is bored cylinder and half-choke, and that's a lovely combination. The old wheeze about blown patterns from cylinder-bored barrels is nonsense. If you do a lot of really close-in work, at woodcock or grouse or quail or whatever, no choke at all is a good way to go.

The fact is, modern cartridges are efficient enough that choke is far less important than it used to be. The only caution in having any choke work done is to find a first-rate 'smith and make sure he does the reaming from the breech-end. Chokes honed from the muzzles stand a good chance of ending up eccentric, and that can ruin the way a gun shoots.

You can learn a lot about the sort of care and treatment a gun has had just by looking at it. Dents and dings and bulges in the barrels are easy to spot, even if they've been repaired. Minor nicks aren't likely to cause any lasting harm, but deep dents create weak spots in the barrel walls. Repairing a dented barrel isn't a particularly hard job for a skillful gunsmith, but simply pressing out a dent doesn't necessarily make things as good as new. The steel has been worked twice in that spot, once when it was dented and again when the dent was removed, which affects the integrity of the steel. Moreover, if the gun was fired very much before the dent was pressed out, the friction of shot charges passing by has probably thinned the barrel wall at that spot, maybe a little, maybe a lot.

Smokeless powder loads reach peak pressure when the shot charge is within about fourteen inches of the chamber, and from there pressure drops off sharply. The nearer any dents are to the breech, the more cautious you should be about buying the gun as a shooter.

If the bores are clean, pitting is easy to spot. You can hide pits from at least a casual inspection by dumping talcum powder down the barrel and running a patch of some slick material through to smooth out the surface. No dealer of any decent reputation would do that, but there are some fast-buck artists around. Don't just glance down the bores; look closely.

A lot of old guns will show some pitting, and most have fairly rough-looking chambers. Before about 1930, the primers used in all centerfire ammunition contained potassium chlorate, which attracts moisture, and unless a gun was cleaned faithfully, primer residue quickly rusted the bores. Some manufacturers continued to use corrosive primers as late as 1940, so it's small wonder that lots of guns are pitted around the forcing cones and in the first few inches of bore.

Corrosive primers also eroded chambers, but even those of well-kept old guns usually aren't smooth and shiny, thanks to years of hot gases seeping back around the cartridges. So long as they aren't deeply pitted or furrowed, the roughness seems to do no harm.

Shallow, surface pitting is no great problem and can be polished out if the appearance troubles you. Deep pits, like deep dents, are bad news. And if even shallow pitting is polished out too enthusiastically, thin spots in the barrel walls are the result. It's a good idea to have any older barrels miked out by someone who has the proper gauges and knows where to measure. How critical any thin spots are depends upon how thin they are and where they occur. The closer to the muzzle, the less stress they have to bear, but thin barrels are easily dented. Get an opinion from a good barrel man if you're in doubt.

Chambers, too, can be a problem. Before the 1930s, American cartridges came in a bewildering variety of lengths, many of them shorter than today's 2¾-inch standard. Small-bore guns – 20s and 28s – often were chambered at 2½ inches. Sixteen-gauge shells were for many years standard at 2⁹⁄₁₆ inches, and 2⅝-inch 12-gauges were common. A lot of guns were bored with 2¾-inch chambers, but a lot of them weren't – and few makers bothered to stamp chamber length on the guns. Almost all A.H. Fox guns built in Philadelphia were chambered at 2⅝ inches; quite a few Parkers were, too. If you intend shooting heavy loads, you can have those chambers bored out.

Among English game guns, 2½-inch chambers always have been the standard, and a goodly number of ultra-lightweight guns are bored at two inches. As a general rule, DO NOT have them lengthened. Best English guns are built with a specific maximum load in mind, and boring the chambers deeper simply invites the use of cartridges hotter than the gun ever was intended to digest. That's asking for trouble. You can buy 2½-inch cartridges in this country without much trouble. Estate Cartridge Company of Conroe, Texas, makes them, and a number of gun dealers around the country import and sell British Eley shells.

Performance Shells, Inc., of Center Conway, New Hampshire, imports excellent English cartridges made in Birmingham and sold under the trade name Lyalvale Express. These are made in good plastic cases with one-piece poly shot-cup wads and are loaded with hard lead shot in American sizes. You can get them in 12, 16, and 20 gauges, and they are, to my mind, the best English shells you can get. Quite a few dealers now carry them.

If you must consider boring an English gun to 2¾ inches, send it to the maker or to some other English maker. Tell him what you have in mind, ask his advice, and take it. The gun will have to be reproved if it's rebored in England (and it certainly should be reproved in any case). The best advice still is to find 2½-inch cartridges and not to mess with the chambers.

Oversized chambers are less common than short ones, but you occasionally will find a gun that was bored to maximum tolerance and then some. Pits in the standing breech are a good clue; if a chamber is of significantly greater diameter than a cartridge case, gases can flow back around the case and erode the standing breech. It's not a particularly dangerous problem, but it's hard on guns.

Once you've found a good set of barrels, the next thing to look for is an action that locks tightly. A reliable bolting system is one of the toughest problems in designing a break-action gun, and at one time or another, makers have tried everything – underbolts, crossbolts, top hooks, cams, screws, and what have you. Most of them work about equally well, and none is immune to wear.

Actually, you can wear out a bolting system without ever firing a shot; all you have to do is slam it shut enough times. Unfortunately, one of the great myths among the misinformed is that you can judge the quality of a gun by how resoundingly it clangs when you slam the barrels up. All it really proves is that there's a powerful spring behind the bolt. The stronger the spring, the less slamming it takes to erode the bearing surfaces and produce a poor old gun that rattles like a bad set of false teeth.

The proper way to close a break-action gun is to hold the top latch with your right thumb, close the action and *ease* the latch over until the bolt takes hold. With a bit of practice, it can be done quickly and smoothly, and it won't slow you down in even the busiest shooting. But you seldom see anyone doing it, and that's why you need to look for worn-out bolts in a gun you might want to buy. Look carefully at where the top latch rests when the gun is closed. The farther to the left it is, the more worn the bolts.

Check for wear in the action knuckle: Close the action, take the fore-end off, hold the gun by the barrels, and rap the buttstock lightly with the heel of your hand. If you hear and feel some vibration, there's wear in either the hinge pin or the barrel lump or both.

Popular wisdom has it that gun that rattles when the action is open is either a poor-quality piece or worn out. If the barrels really flop around, then it probably is badly worn, but a bit of rattle isn't necessarily a bad sign. All it means is that the barrel lump is a shade narrower than the water-table slot. Some guns are filed to such close tolerances that there's no lateral play at all; others aren't, but that doesn't make them bad guns. And use naturally takes its toll. You'll find precious few old guns that don't show some wear and consequently some rattle.

If the action is on-face – if the breech end of the barrels is parallel to the standing breech and shows no appreciable gaps at top or bottom – and if it locks up tightly, then what's the difference if it clicks a bit with the fore-end off or when it's open? You aren't going to shoot it that way. Worn bolts and lumps and hinge pins, even if they're badly worn, don't mean that the gun is beyond hope.

Any gun can be tightened and refaced, though it's an easier job for some than for others. The old Lefever Arms and D.M. Lefever guns can be adjusted to compensate for a lot of wear. They even have screws that adjust the width of the barrel lumps. Later Parkers have a replaceable bearing surface at the bolting notch. Foxes and Smiths and new model Ithacas all use top-hook fasteners, and they're more difficult to tighten, but it can be done. A gun with a worn hinge often can be put right with a new hinge pin. A worn barrel hook can be renewed by having a new piece of steel brazed or soldered in and the arc refiled. Or it can swelled with a few lusty whacks from a ball-peen hammer, but that's like repairing a wristwatch with an impact wrench – and has about the same results. If you find a gun with dents in the barrel lump, leave it for the next guy.

Otherwise, give honest wear some judicious consideration, consult a good gunsmith if you're uncertain (because some tightening jobs cost more than some guns are worth), and remember that a gun that locks up soundly when you get it won't get any worse if you treat it kindly.

The most important part of any gun that you hope to shoot well is the stock. If it doesn't fit, you won't be happy with the gun for long, no matter how beautiful it is. Older American guns, especially those built before World War I, are likely to have some bizarre stock dimensions: two inches of drop at the comb and three inches or more at the heel. Later stocks tend to be straighter, but factory dimensions may not suit you.

You have several options in what to do about an ill-fitting stock. One is to ignore it and try to fit yourself to the gun rather than the other way around, but that's no good solution. Stocks can be bent, either using steam or hot oil, and that's an excellent choice. It's a job for a highly skillful stock man, though, not for the amateur. Another good choice, though often an expensive one, is a new stock altogether. In any case, make the gun fit.

Check the triggers by dry-firing with snap caps. The sears should break crisply and cleanly, and the second lock should require a bit more pressure than the first. One trigger – or one sear, if it's a single trigger – that pulls noticeably lighter than the other can mean a worn sear. Extremely stiff triggers are a sign of poorly fitted, poorly filed, or poorly designed sears. A heavy trigger-pull is a disaster if you hope to do any good shooting; it disrupts your swing, your timing, your concentration, everything. The same malady affects new guns, too. One of my shooting chums showed up at the gun club a few months ago with a brand-new 20-gauge Winchester Model 23, normally a well-built piece. Not this one. The trigger felt about the same with the safety off as it did with the safety on; the pull was so wretched that you could hang the entire weight of the gun on the trigger without tripping the sear. Naturally, none of us could hit anything with it, and it soon was on its way back to the factory.

Trigger-pull and stock fit are the queen bees in my shotgunning bonnet. No one can shoot at his best with a misfit stock or a bad trigger, and there's no reason to accept either.

Once you've checked the triggers, pay attention to what happens when you open the action. Most good guns have rebounding locks – the hammers fly forward, hit the firing pins, and then rebound slightly before coming to rest. That way, the pins aren't held protruding into the primers, and the action is easier to open. Some guns, notably A.H. Foxes, don't have rebounding locks; in these, the cocking mechanism is designed to withdraw the hammers in precise coordination as the barrels move on the hinge. These systems generally work fine, but they can get out of whack. A Fox that's hard to open needs adjustment.

Other guns have inertia-type firing pins, which work on the same principle as rebounding locks. When the hammer strikes the pin, it flies forward, hits the primer, and then rebounds back into the standing breech. Whatever the system, no gun should stick shut or drag when you open it. The problem can be as simple as broken or gummed-up firing pin springs, stretched pins, or clogged pin channels; or it can be as complex as a broken lock or mistimed cocking system.

If the gun has ejectors, they should release after the locks cock – and you can hear the locks cock if you listen closely. Both ejectors should release at the same instant and should throw the snap caps well clear. Sluggish ejectors can mean weak or broken springs, or they might simply mean that the gun needs a good cleaning. Dirt, congealed oil, and other such gunk can clog ejectors and make a good gun function poorly. Ejectors can be both difficult and expensive to repair, and some, notably Parker's, are notoriously hard to keep adjusted.

Any problems with triggers, locks, cocking systems, or ejectors need the attention of a good gunsmith.

A word about good gunsmiths: They're hard to come by. It's been my experience that many people who call themselves gunsmiths are little more than parts-changers; at best, they're mediocre craftsmen, and some are utterly inept. The remaining few are the ones to look for, and if you don't already know one, ask around and look at samples of the work before you entrust your guns to anyone. If you can't find a first-rate independent, you can't go wrong with the best custom shops – Griffin & Howe, Pachmayr, Paul Jaeger, and the ilk. In any case, find one you like, because if you insist upon shooting old guns, you'll need him sooner or later.

I realize that I've spoken freely here about altering classic shotguns, which according to some ways of thinking is a cardinal sin. I feel that way myself about a fine old American gun that has survived all these years in mint or near-mint condition. Even one in completely original condition that shows a bit of honest use probably should be preserved that way. But the fact is, the vast majority of old guns have been well used, if not always well treated, and most have been altered in some way over the years. Those guns are not collector's items, generally speaking, regardless of the attitude that would have any old double worth its weight in gold. They were built for use in the first place. No gun ever earned a lasting reputation sitting in a cabinet. The guns I'm talking about here are the ones that already have stood good service and are capable of delivering more. Those are the shooters.

Leave the mint-condition American classics for the collectors, but remember that there's nothing inviolable about a gun, certainly not one that's still in production, and not even a London best.

Pose the question of factory originality to an English gunmaker and he'll look at you as if you just grew another ear. Best English guns never were factory items to begin with; they were made for somebody, not for inventory. They were made exactly to their original owners' specifications, but you're looking for a gun to shoot, not for some way to memorialize the original owner. Moreover, best guns that change hands in England go back to the maker or to someone else to be fitted to the new owner and reconditioned. If the English best gun that you're looking to buy has been owned by more than one person, it's almost certainly been altered several times already, and there's no reason why you shouldn't do the same. That's what guns are for. The same caveats about good gunsmiths apply here, too, in spades. Best English guns are expensive, and the older ones were built by the finest craftsmen in the world, so be damn careful about who you allow to tinker with them.

How much you pay for the gun you like once you've found it depends upon how badly you want it. Like everything else really good, really good guns are expensive. On the other hand, really bad ones can be expensive, too. And you'll most likely have to pay a premium for certain names, which usually is more a function of reputation than of intrinsic quality. Parkers, for example, are fine guns, but they're grotesquely overpriced. So are Winchester 21s and L.C. Smiths. So are Purdeys and Hollands on the used-gun market. Foxes and Ithacas and Lefevers and Brownings and Perazzis and the like are seldom cheap, but they often are better values. You can buy stunningly fine best English guns by lesser-known makers at a fraction of what you have to pay for a Purdey or a Holland.

It's easy to drop too much money on any old gun out of sheer romance. It often happens because somebody is afraid he'll never find another, but the market for best guns actually is a healthy one. Not long ago, I talked with a rueful young man who'd bought a VHE Parker for just that reason, had it "restored" (often an overpriced proposition), custom cased, and suddenly found himself with upwards of $2500 invested in a gun worth less than half that amount. By then, he'd discovered that there are lots of Parkers for sale. He wanted to swap for a higher grade, and he was learning a hard lesson in the process.

The only appropriate advice in this is to do a bit of market research before you buy, figure in such after-market costs as repairs, alterations, and the like, and remember that you don't have to grab the first thing that comes along. It helps to harden your heart.

But not too much. If you think a gun is nothing more than a price tag or a tool, then it really doesn't matter what you shoot. But if you hunt for more than meat, appreciate fine craftsmanship, enjoy a gun that handles like a thing alive, and feel something greater than yourself when you see a lovely old artifact that speaks of history, then value and price are vastly different things.

HARD CHOICES
Best Guns and Steel Shot

This could be the shortest chapter in the history of books, because we can sum up the matter of using steel shot in a best-quality double in one word: never.

Waterfowlers are at the end of an era. Steel shot is here and here to stay. The change has been a long time coming, surrounded by controversy ranging from peevish to venomous, marked by opinions that range from reasonable to ridiculous. Human nature being what it is, mere legislation isn't likely to end the arguments.

But the legislation is in place, and steel shot is the law of the land. I've talked with a lot of wildfowlers who are trying to make sense out of the morass of conflicting opinion that has accrued to steel shot, and they're concerned about what it will do to their favorite duck guns.

It's a fair question and a wise one, for steel doesn't behave as lead does, either in the air or in the barrel. In the air at reasonable distances, steel is as effective as lead. In the barrel, it's more problematic, especially in older guns and particularly in old doubles.

Steel or iron shot is a great deal harder than lead, and that creates two distinct problems for guns. For one, steel pellets will quickly gouge furrows in a shotgun bore unless the column is enclosed in a collar or cup. It's not a new problem. Shortly after World War II, when lead for sporting use was still hard to come by, Winchester marketed Super Ferro shells, loaded with iron shot, at its franchised shooting ranges. That was long before shot collars were invented, and a lot of skeet and trap shooters soon found iron shot and even the best gun barrels to be an unhappy combination.

More recently, as ammunition companies set out to develop high-quality steel shot loads, researchers learned that conventional polyethylene shot cups, excellent for lead, weren't much better with steel than no cups at all. The steel pellets rubbed through the collar walls on the way down the barrel, mercilessly cutting up the bore. The answer is an exceptionally tough shot cup with extra-thick walls, and factory steel loads now have those. They're even available to handloaders.

But the other problem is one that can't be solved by ammunition technology, and it's the one that will bring an older gun to grief.

Because the pellets are so hard, a charge of steel shot resists compression. Instead of squeezing down on its way through the choke, as lead does, steel simply batters the choke cone, peening away the difference in diameter between the choke and the bore. Since something has to give, the barrel bulges until the choke has virtually been swaged away.

New, hard barrel steels can overcome this, but older, softer barrels can't. Even the best old barrels are malleable enough that steel shot will bulge them. The thinner the barrel walls and the steeper the angle of the choke cones, the sooner it happens.

Virtually all of the old, high-quality doubles have thinner tubes than you'll find on a single-barrel of the same vintage. They're struck thin to reduce weight, and even lead shot will bulge the chokes slightly. It takes thousands of rounds, and the result is almost imperceptible, but it happens.

Steel shot is far more dramatic. In the winter of 1972 – '73, Winchester-Western ballisticians tested the effects of lead, copper, and steel shot in six full-choke barrels, firing 5000 rounds in each. Lead and copper delivered almost identical results, enlarging barrel diameters by .0005 to .0014 inches. According to the test report, a bulge becomes visible after barrel diameter increases only about .001 inch. Steel loads expanded the test barrels six times that much, bulging them out by .0057 to .0065 inches. About half the bulging from steel shot occurred during the first 500 rounds.

All of the American gun- and ammunition-makers conducted similar tests and got similar results. None found that muzzles bulged by steel shot had any appreciable effect upon safety or pattern performance, but all of them caution specifically against using steel shot in older doubles.

Cosmetic damage to a single-barrel gun is one thing, but bulging the chokes of a double is quite another. A double's barrels are fastened together, usually with the muzzles touching and are further joined by a rib on top and a fillet underneath. Since bulging affects the entire circumference of a barrel, it's easy to imagine the stresses placed on the entire assembly – stresses that old doubles were never meant to absorb. The minimum risk is that the solder holding everything together will give way and the barrels, rib, and fillet will separate. That means a trip to the gunsmith and a hefty bill for resoldering everything and reblueing the barrels. And it means a nice old gun with permanently bulged muzzles. At worst, one or both barrels might even crack, though it's seldom happened.

There are some ways to reduce the risk. One is simply to open the chokes to a constriction of no more than .020 inches, which is about modified choke and which seems to be the point where steel loads quit bulging barrels. Any more choke than that is more handicap than advantage, anyway.

A few years ago, choke-tube guru Jess Briley of Houston, Texas, started making stainless-steel tubes specifically for steel shot. Others now make them, too. Briley's are about three inches long, have slightly thicker walls than conventional tubes, and handle steel quite well so long as constriction is kept to the .020-inch maximum. The catch here is that only guns with relatively thick barrel walls are candidates for this treatment.

A more radical solution is to have a set of new, hard-steel barrels made for your favorite fowling piece. A number of gunsmiths around the country can do the work, but it won't come cheap.

None of these approaches completely eliminates the possibility of some damage to an old gun. Iron has considerably less mass than lead and therefore requires about half again more pellets to make up an equal shot charge by weight. In order to make room for them in the cartridge, shot cups for steel loads have no cushioning properties, and the set-back from a steel load is sharper than from lead. More recoil means more pounding of solder joints, more stress on the standing breech, the internal parts, and the stock. After years of use, the solder that holds ribs and fillets and fore-end lugs can crystallize and break, even with lead-shot loads. It's happened to me with an L.C. Smith, a Fox, an Ithaca, and a Browning Superposed, none of which has ever had a steel load shot through it.

If you must shoot steel in an old gun, there is one likely candidate: an A.H. Fox HE Grade, also known as Super-Fox. If there's any American double that will stand up to the pounding, a Super will. With a set of Briley's tubes installed, it would be super, indeed. The Parker Reproductions Steel Shot Special is likewise an excellent choice.

A number of new or nearly new doubles also will handle steel nicely. Remington's Model 3200 Magnum, introduced about 1975 and now out of production, was made with steel shot in mind, but Remington does not recommend using steel in any other version of the 3200. Ruger's excellent Red Label over-under is approved for steel, as are some of the Winchester Model 101s and 23s. Browning Arms cautions against using steel shot in the Superposed, but the Citori over-under and the B-SS side-by-sides built after 1977 will handle it without a whimper.

Most of the best European makers, especially those with an eye already on the American market, will set up a new gun for steel shot if you ask them to. Holland & Holland, for example, offers optional steel-shot barrels for its Northwood and Cavalier boxlocks. Others will make up extra-thick barrels on request.

Traditions in gunning die particularly hard. The steel-shot controversy is a hot item, but disagreements really are no more vehement than those that once raged over the relative merits of black and smokeless powder or of twist and fluid-steel barrels. Time is the only sieve that finally will sift out the truth. Regardless of where you stand on the issue, steel shot is a reality, and the wise shooter will use it only in an adequate gun. It's going to make me sad to leave my old Ithaca and Parker duck guns behind, but I'd feel worse if I tore them up. They deserve better than that.

SERIAL NUMBERS, NOTES,
AND SOURCES

Iwish old guns could talk. I wish they could tell me about the places they've been, the countrysides they've been carried through, the birds and the dogs and the days they've seen, how they got from there to here. I'd like to know something about the men who've owned them, whether they were duffers or good shots, mean spirits or good men; I'd like to know if they got as much pleasure as I do just from owning and shooting a fine gun.

I get much the same feeling, holding a nice old gun, that I get when I find a stone tool or a blade or a projectile point that someone made thousands of years ago. Chances are, the last person who held this thing was the person who made it, and I feel something that reaches across all those ages, something of the pride he must have taken in his craftsmanship, something of the satisfaction he must have felt in using his skills to make his way in the world.

To me, the pleasure in a gun is never quite complete until I've learned something of its history, even if it's no more than having a rough idea of when it was built. Sometimes that's as much as we can ever learn for sure, but it's a place to start. If we can fix the origin of a gun in space and time, then a broader sense of history and a healthy imagination can supply much of the rest.

The serial number obviously is the most direct link to the origin of any gun, but whether the number leads to a written record or simply into the dark firmament of history is a chancy thing. Some gunmakers have kept excellent records; others haven't. Even well-kept records have been subject to all the vicissitudes of time and events: changes of company ownership, floods, fires, wars, acts of God, mischance, careless bookkeeping, and overzealous housecleaning.

Happily, though, some serial number information is available for virtually all of the guns I've discussed here. Some of it is abundant and quite specific, some of it approximate, virtually all of it more or less accessible. None of it, however, is perfectly complete.

For those of you interested in researching the origins of your favorite guns, I offer the following as a point of departure.

Parker

As the last maker of original Parker guns, Remington Arms owns the old Parker Brothers records. Remington has steadfastly refused to allow any independent researcher access to them, for reasons that aren't clear – or at least not clear to me. After more than fifty years of storage, it's possible that the records are now in poor condition.

Parker serial number tables are available, however. There's one in Larry Baer's book, *The Parker Gun* (Beinfeld, 1980), and one is available from Ron Moulton, 1740 Colorado Avenue, Turlock, California 95380. Moulton bought out the old Lightner Library collection of catalogue reprints several years ago; contact him for a price list and ordering information.

A. H. Fox

The only systematic Fox records extant are work-order cards that show, among other things, when guns were shipped from the factory. These are stored in the Savage Arms archives and are not available to the public, but Roe Clark, a former Savage executive, will provide information from the cards on specific guns. Send serial numbers and $7 per gun to:

S. Roe Clark
Route 1, Otis Stage Road
Blandford, Massachusetts 01008

A.H. Fox Gun Company assigned serial numbers in blocks organized by grade and gauge, as follows:

A – F Grades, 12-gauge	1 – 50000
Sterlingworth, 12-gauge	50000 – 200000
A – F Grades, 20-gauge	200000 – 250000
Sterlingworth, 20-gauge	250000 – 300000
A – F Grades, 16-gauge	300000 – 350000
Sterlingworth, 16-gauge	350000 – 400000
Single Trap guns	400000 –

Some years ago, Roe Clark prepared a Fox serial number chronology. It's based on the work-order cards and therefore indicates shipping dates, not actual dates of manufacture. It also is to some degree an extrapolation and not a card-by-card analysis. Since Fox often did not ship guns in the same order they were built, there are many out-of-sequence numbers. Still, Roe's chronology is extremely useful; copies are available from Ron Moulton (see Parker for the address).

L. C. Smith

Thanks to William Brophy, who rescued the original Hunter Arms records, quite a lot of production and serial number information is available. Every student of the American gun should have a copy of Brophy's book, *L.C. Smith Shotguns* (Beinfeld, 1977). It is an admirable piece of research, with excellent illustrations, serial number tables, even some shipping records.

Lefever

Although virtually no original Lefever Arms or D.M. Lefever Company records still exist, my old friend Bob Elliott has extrapolated a serial number table for Lefever Arms guns based on certain known dates in Lefever history. Although the dates naturally are to some extent approximate, Bob's work unquestionably is the best information we're ever likely to have on Lefevers.

You'll find the serial number table – and a world of good information on Lefevers – in the book that Bob and Jim Cobb wrote, titled *Lefever: Guns of Lasting Fame*. It, too, is a must for any gun-fancier. For a copy, contact:

Robert Elliott
14077 FM 849
Lindale, Texas 75771

Ithaca Gun Company several years ago provided serial number tables for the Ithaca-built Lefevers: the Nitro Special, A Grade, and single-barrel. As with the table for Ithaca guns, there are some discrepancies and anomalies that cannot be resolved.

LEFEVER NITRO SPECIAL

NUMBER	YEAR	NUMBER	YEAR
100000 – 101599	1921	299250 – 299999	1935
101600 – 119899	1922	325000 – 327299	1935
119900 – 158699	1923	327300 – 336399	1936
158700 – 185399	1924	336400 – 345099	1937
185400 – 214399	1925	345100 – 345899	1938
214400 – 233007	1926	345900 – 347099	1939
233100 – 252699	1927	347100 – 353099	1940
252700 – 272999	1928	353100 – 354999	1941
273000 – 297199	1929	355000 – 356299	1942
297200 – 298699	1930	356300 – 357299	1946
298700 – 298749	1933	357300 – 361199	1947
298750 – 299249	1934		

LEFEVER A GRADE

NUMBER	YEAR	NUMBER	YEAR
300000 – 300654	1934	301050 – 301699	1935
300655 – 301007	1935	301700 – 302099	1936
301008 – 301023	1936	302100 – 302399	1937
301024 – 301037	1937	302400 – 302465	1938
301038 – 301045	1938	302466 – 302496	1939

LEFEVER SINGLE BARREL

NUMBER	YEAR	NUMBER	YEAR
1 – 8505	1927	22300 – 23099	1936
8506 – 15759	1928	23100 – 23499	1937
15760 – 20280	1929	23500 – 23799	1938
20281 – 20799	1930	23800 – 24579	1939
20800 – 21799	1931	24580 – 24604	1941
21800 – 21899	left open	24605 – 24607	1941
21900 – 22299	1935		

Ithaca Gun Company

On the whole, Ithaca's records are orderly and relatively complete – or at least they were when Ithaca declared bankruptcy in 1986. The Bureau of Alcohol, Tobacco and Firearms now has all Ithaca records and does not allow public access to them. I have no idea why. Your tax dollars at work.

Fortunately, Ithaca prepared a serial number table some years ago and granted permission to reprint it. Unfortunately, there are some inconsistencies that probably never will be resolved. The man who prepared it is no longer living, and Ithaca has never been able to clarify the anomalies.

BAKER MODEL

NUMBER	YEAR	NUMBER	YEAR
1 – 2447	1880 – 1885	7004 – 8787	1888
2448 – 4104	1886	8788 – 10534	1889 (January-August)
4105 – 7003	1887		

CRASS MODEL

NUMBER	YEAR	NUMBER	YEAR
17235 – 21999	1892	30223 – 33026	1898
22000 – 25421	1893	33027 – 38399	1899
25422 – 26759	1894	38400 – 46627	1900
25760 – 27762	1895	46628 – 61609	1901
27763 – 28713	1896	61610 – 76599	1902
28714 – 30222	1897	76600 – 94108	1903

LEWIS MODEL

NUMBER	YEAR
94109 – 105999	1904
106000 – 119320	1905
119321 – 123677	1906

MANIER MODEL

NUMBER	YEAR
130000 – 138145	1906
138146 – 151283	1907
151284 – 151770	1908

FLUES MODEL (including single trap and Auto & Burglar guns)

NUMBER	YEAR	NUMBER	YEAR
175000 -182031	1908	289300 – 299799	1918
182032 – 192499	1909	299800 – 315399	1919
192500 – 205399	1910	315400 – 343335	1920
205400 – 216499	1911	343336 – 356513	1921
216500 – 230099	1912	365514 – 361849	1922
230100 – 242599	1913	361900 – 372099	1923
242600 – 256699	1914	372100 – 390499	1924
256700 – 268199	1915	390500 – 398352	1925
268200 – 276899	1916	398353 – 398365	1926
276900 – 289299	1917		

NEW ITHACA DOUBLE (including Auto & Burglar guns)

NUMBER	YEAR	NUMBER	YEAR
425000 – 425299	1925	464828 – 464850	1939
425300 – 439199	1926	464851 – 464899	1940
439200 – 451099	1927	464900 – 465199	1938
451100 – 454530	1928	465200 – 465999	1939
454600 – 457299	1929	466000 – 466999	1940
457300 – 458399	1930	467100 – 467146	1941
458400 – 459139	1931	467147 – 467199	1946 (Specials)
459140 – 459162	1932	467200 – 468099	1941
459163 – 459195	1933	468100 – 468699	1946
459196 – 459637	1935	468700 – 468794	1947
459638 – 459649	1936	468795 – 468799	1948
459650 – 460799	1935	468800 – 469949	1947
460800 – 462899	1936	469950 – 469979	1948
462900 – 464699	1937	470000 – 470099	1948
464700 – 464827	1938		

MAGNUM 10-GAUGE DOUBLES

NUMBER	YEAR
500000 – 501010	1932 – 1942

KNICKERBOCKER MODEL SINGLE TRAP

NUMBER	YEAR
400000 – 402789	1922 – 1944

As this is going to press, my friend Frank Conley is working on a book about American single trap guns – the most systematic work that's ever been done on the subject. His chapter on Ithaca singles will include detailed serial number tables right up to the last gun, completed in 1982. Keep an eye out for this book; it's going to be a dandy.

ITHACA DOUBLES BUILT FOR WELLS FARGO

This table was prepared by the late Ithaca historian John McMorrow.

YEAR	MONTH	ITHACA SERIAL NUMBERS	NUMBER OF GUNS BUILT	WELLS FARGO NUMBERS
1909	February	182707 – 182747	41	unk.
		182900 – 182938	39	unk.
		183021 – 183045	25	unk.
		183060 –	1	unk.
	March	184178 – 184189	12	unk.
	April	184248 – 184282	35	unk.
		184757 – 184759	3	unk.
		185000 – 185024	25	unk.
	May*	185452 – 185481	30	438 – 467
	June	186512 – 186517	6	unk.
1911		211325 – 211372	48	unk.
1912	March	219800 – 219847	48	269
	June	223300 – 223347	48	unk.
	November	228942 – 228966	24	368
1913	January	230300 – 230314	15	unk.
	March	233137 – 233172	36	unk.
	November	241054 – 241061 } 241100 – 241106 }	53	484 – 9
1914	August	251875 – 251879 } 251887 – }	6	unk.
	September	253041 –	1	unk.
	November	255400 – 255424	25	unk.

YEAR	MONTH	ITHACA SERIAL NUMBERS	NUMBER OF GUNS BUILT	WELLS FARGO NUMBERS
	December	255977 – 255999 ⎫ 256500 – 256524 ⎭	48	unk.
1915	June	262627 – 262636 ⎫ 262638 – 262643 ⎭	15	562 – 576
		262672 –	1	577
		262682 – 262699	18	578 – 583
		262773 – 262774	2	584 – 585
	July	263167 – 263176	10	586 – 595
		263178 –	1	596
		263180 – 263187	8	597 – 604
		263191 – 263194	4	606 – 609
		263199 –	1	605
	September	265369 – 265390 (except 269384)	30	unk.
1916	October	275246 – 275247	2	unk.
1917	March	279565 – 279588	24	unk.
	April	281187 – 281198		
		281202 – 281209	20	unk.
	May	281259 – 281285	27	unk.
	June	282886 –	1	unk.

*10-gauge hammer guns, Quality A, 24-inch twist barrels

Except for the thirty 10-gauge hammer guns made in May 1909, all of the doubles that Ithaca built for Wells Fargo Express Company were Field Grade 12-gauge hammerless guns with fluid-steel barrels. Those built in 1909 were made with 26-inch barrels, all others with 24-inch barrels.

Remington Model 32

At the moment, it's extremely difficult to obtain any historical information from Remington Arms. Remington's archivist died several years ago, and Remington Arms has not seen fit to fill the position. Dick Dietz, public relations director, is a helpful chap, but his staff is small and unable to spend time looking up serial numbers.

The situation may change in the future. For now, all you can do is try your luck:

Richard F. Dietz
Remington Arms Company, Inc.
2498-5 Nemours
Wilmington, Delaware 19898

Winchester Model 21

Winchester production records are fairly complete although not entirely free of gaps, thanks to a fire at the factory years ago. There are, moreover, some inconsistencies in the Model 21 number sequence, dating from the years when the 21 was a production gun. As in most factories, frames were machined in quantity, numbered, and stored. In actual production, the gunsmiths simply selected frames at random and started building guns, so even though frames were numbered in sequence, guns weren't always completed in the same order.

Winchester never has put together a systematic serial number table for the Model 21, but individual guns usually can be traced. Winchester records now are stored at the Buffalo Bill Historical Center. Contact:

> Gael Oswalt
> Buffalo Bill Historical Center
> Box 1000
> Cody, Wyoming 82414

European Guns

Historical information on European guns is in some ways more accessible and at the same time more problematic. Small shops tend to keep more precise records than large factories, and the fact that best European guns have always been built to order also helps ensure that written records are made on each gun. On the other hand, Europe has suffered the most destructive wars in history, and that has taken a certain toll in addition to all the other mishaps that paperwork is heir to.

Language differences can be a problem, although generally not an insurmountable one, since English is one of the major languages of world trade. In some cases, easiest access to European makers is through their American agents.

So, if you own a gun by one of the current makers I've discussed here and want to know something of its history, or if you want information on ordering a new gun, the following contacts will get you started:

> James Purdey & Sons
> Audley House
> 57 – 58 South Audley Street
> London W1Y 6ED, England
>
> Holland & Holland, Ltd.
> 31 Bruton Street
> London W1X 8JS, England
>
> Thomas Boss & Company
> London, England

> John Dickson & Son
> Edinburgh, Scotland
>
> John Wilkes
> 79 Beak Street
> London W1, England
>
> William Evans, Ltd.
> 67a St. James's Street
> London SW1 A1PH, England

William Powell & Son
35 Carrs Lane
Birmingham B4 7SX, England

Westley Richards & Company, Ltd.
40 Grande Road, Bournbrook
Birmingham B29 6AR, England

W&C Scott
Tame Road, Witton
Birmingham B6 7HS, England

Georges Granger guns may be
ordered through:

Bill Dowtin
Route 4, Box 930A
Flagstaff, Arizona 86001

For Darne and Bruchet guns,
contact the American importer
for Bruchet:

Wes Gilpin
Loren Thomas, Ltd.
P.O. Box 18023
Dallas, Texas 75218

Or:

Paul Bruchet
25 Rue des Armuriers
42100 St. Etienne, France

For information on Vouzelaud
guns, contact:

Waverly Arms
2025 Heron Court
Suffolk, Virginia 23433

The best Spanish gunmakers are now only beginning to become active in the American market, and so far as I know, none is represented by an exclusive American agent. Paul Jaeger, Inc., a division of Dunn's, Inc. of Grand Junction, Tennessee, imports made-to-order Arrieta guns in two models. William Larkin Moore & Company (see the Italian section, below, for the address) imports some Garbi guns. You also may contact the makers directly:

Armas Garbi
Urki, 12-14, EIBAR
Guipuzcoa, Spain

Manufacturas Arrieta, S.L.
Barrio Uransandi
Apartado 93, ELGOIBAR
Guipuzcoa, Spain

Pedro Arrizabalaga, S.A.
Errekatxu, 5, EIBAR
Guipuzcoa, Spain

Grulla Armas
Apartado 453, Avenida Otaola, 12
20600 EIBAR
Guipuzcoa, Spain

Makers of best-quality Italian guns are well-represented in the United States by independent importers or, in the case of Beretta, by an American subsidiary. For Beretta, contact:

Beretta USA Corporation
17601 Beretta Drive
Accokeek, Maryland 20607

For Piotti, Rizzini, Ferlib,
and others, contact:

William Larkin Moore & Company
31360 Via Colinas, No. 109
Westlake Village, California 91361

For Perazzi guns, contact:
Perazzi USA
1207 South Shamrock Avenue
Monrovia, California 91016

Many fine Italian gunmakers either are not represented by American agents or are represented only on a limited basis. LT Imports of Chicago (312-254-4275) will place special orders for Marocchi guns. Ivo Fabbri builds only a few guns each year, on special order, and has no agents anywhere.

You can contact these or any of the Val Trompian makers through the Brescia gunmakers guild. Language difference isn't a problem, since the guild employs a translator:

> Carla Conti Gussago
> Via Matteotti 214
> 25063 Gardone VT
> Brescia, Italy

German and Belgian guns, too, are well represented in the United States. Merkel and Francotte guns are available through:

> Armes de Chasse
> P.O. Box 827
> Chadds Ford, Pennsylvania 19317

Armes de Chasse also imports Chapuis side-by-side guns and rifles and W&C Scott guns.

Ernest Dumoulin guns are imported by:

> Midwest Gun Sport
> 1108 Herbert
> Zebulon, North Carolina 27597

For Krieghoff and Shotguns of Ulm, contact:

> Krieghoff International
> P.O. Box 549
> Ottsville, Pennsylvania 18942

Production information on Browning guns is available from a number of sources. George Madis has compiled an excellent little guide titled "Browning Dates of Manufacture, 1824 to the Present" (Art and Reference House, Brownsboro, Texas, 1988).

Guns, of course, are available though the many Browning dealers around the country. For other information, contact:

> Browning Arms Company
> Route One
> Morgan, Utah 84050

In addition to the sources I've already mentioned, best-quality American and European guns are available through a multitude of dealers, large and small. It would be impossible to list them all, but here are a few of those most active in the best-gun market. Many of these dealers publish periodic gun lists.

Bedlan's
1318 East Street
Box 244
Fairbury, Nebraska 68352

W.M. Bryan & Company
P.O. Box 12492
Raleigh, North Carolina 27605

Buckhorn Quality Firearms
2496 South Stemmons
Lewisville,Texas 75067

Cape Horn Outfitters
212 East Morehead
Charlotte, North Carolina 28202

Champlin Firearms, Inc.
Woodring Municipal Airport
P.O. Box 3191
Enid, Oklahoma 73702

Stephen Cobb
RD 1
Bedminster, New Jersey 07921

Criswell's Ltd.
Box 277
Yorba Linda, California 92686

Game Fair Ltd.
99 White Bridge Road, No. 105
Nashville,Tennessee 37205

Griffin & Howe
36 West 44th Street
Suite 1011
New York, New York 10036

Hallowell & Company
340 West Putnam Avenue
Greenwich, Connecticut 06830

Bill Hanus Birdguns
P.O. Box 80
Pinos Altos, New Mexico 88053

Paul Jaeger, Inc.
Highway 57E
Grand Junction, Tennessee 38039

Jaqua's Fine Guns
900 East Bigelow Avenue
Findlay, Ohio 45840

Thomas J. Koessl
7615 Maple Road
Baileys Harbor, Wisconsin 54202

New England Arms Company
Box 278, Lawrence Lane
Kittery Point, Maine 03905

Northwoods Firearms
Meredith, New Hampshire 03253

The Orvis Company
10 River Road
Manchester, Vermont 05254

Pachmayr Ltd.
1875 South Mountain Avenue
Monrovia, California 91016

Puglisi Gun Emporium
1336 Commonwealth Avenue
Duluth, Minnesota 55808

Quality Arms
Box 19477
Houston, Texas 77224

Safari Outfitters Ltd.
71 Ethan Allen Highway
Ridgefield, Connecticut 06877

James Wayne Firearms
2608 North Laurent
Victoria, Texas 77901

Theodore C. Wood
RD 2
Salem, New York 12865

Woodcock Hill
P.O. Box 363
Benton, Pennsylvania 17814

If you're in England, you'll also find an excellent selection of guns at:

J.C. Field and Stream
604 Fulham Road
London SW6 5RP

EPILOGUE
Middle Ground

As I write this, it's the middle of March 1989. A few days ago, the President of the United States imposed what is described as a temporary embargo on the importation of semiautomatic assault weapons. Or, more accurately, the president has consented to suspending imports; it was first announced by someone whose working title seems to be Drug Czar. An ambiguous title, at best, since I can only assume that there are czarlike characters on both sides of the drug issue.

If that were the only ambiguity in all this, the whole thing would be less problematic. Unfortunately, it's more complicated than that. Most real issues are.

Some difficult questions need attention. Not the least of them is this:

Where should a man of gentle sensibilities stand on an issue that has some validity on either side?

No decent, civilized man or woman can possibly find wanton slaughter or crime-related warfare to be acceptable behavior in any social structure, least of all in our own. The problem is that many of us who are decent and civilized find a sincere and wholly innocent satisfaction in owning and using firearms. The two are not mutually exclusive, despite the carping of those whose intellectual capacities are too limited to encompass the fact that one can be a decent, moral human being and still love guns. To those people, guns confer no innocent pleasures. Those people argue that society, if not mankind itself, will somehow be improved if all guns of all kinds are taken away. Their aim is to disarm America, and they make no bones about saying so.

The other side has its own extreme. In that view, firearms ownership is a divine ly invested prerogative not to be questioned by any concern nor interfered with at any cost.

I think both opinions are utter nonsense. One is based on ignorance, the other on paranoia. I cannot see either extreme as anything more than the effluvium of overactive mouths powered by underactive minds. Nothing is ever as simple as the lunatic fringes would have it be.

Anyone who has read more than two paragraphs of my work knows that my interest in guns is historical, technical, and artistic. On the practical side, the gun appeals to me as a tool for sport, for both game and target shooting. I see it as an artifact deeply interwoven with social and economic history and with the aesthetic components of human nature.

I have not the slightest interest in military weaponry and wouldn't know an AK-47 from a Kalashnikov or an Uzi from an impact wrench. To me, it's all ugly, graceless machinery, no more interesting or appealing than the mechanism inside a toilet tank.

I'm even less inclined to support the interests of those who would use such weaponry, whether against a schoolyard full of children or in defending one criminal enterprise against incursion from another. At that level, it isn't even a firearms issue. At that level, the use of firearms is only the symptom of far deeper social and personal ills.

But it's a firearms issue nonetheless, in part because our national insistence upon oversimplification will make it so. And it's a political issue as well as a moral dilemma, for much the same reason.

If it were simply a question of whether to remove firearms from the hands of criminals and sociopaths, the answer would be easy. But we have ample evidence to prove that making firearms inaccessible by legal means is no solution. Gun control cannot even adequately treat the symptoms, much less cure the real disease. In that regard, one can mount a compelling argument for the position that any concession in the matter of firearms ownership only diminishes the rights of the wrong people.

That clearly is true in the case of sporting guns, but considerably less clear when assault weapons are the issue. To my mind, there is a vast difference between sporting arms – including those of autoloading designs – and military weapons. Do assault rifles have a legitimate sporting use? Not in my opinion. No matter how or where I tug at the corners, I cannot stretch my personal definition of sport to include a machine meant solely to belch out umpteen rounds of ammunition in a few milliseconds. That kind of firepower is not only incompatible but is indeed antithetical to my view of sport.

But is suspending the importation of such weapons the thin end of the wedge, as some have argued? Will it lead to a permanent ban on private ownership of military weapons? And what if it does? Will that make our society any safer or will it simply open the way for those who would ban the private ownership of firearms altogether?

I have no regard for military weapons nor for the paramilitary factions that insist upon owning them. But should I defend the weapons' existence, even though I disagree with the whole concept behind them, and should I defend the right of private individuals to own them, even though I disagree with the purpose of such ownership – all because the right to own sporting guns is extremely important to me?

At the moment, I have more questions than answers. So do a lot of people I've talked with over the past days, people who love guns as much as I and who equally deplore their misuse. Where should we stand?

My best suggestion is that we should beware the simple solution, whatever it may be. There are no simple answers to complex questions. The real answer lies somewhere in the middle, where it's hard to hear the voices of reason because so much hysterical shrieking is coming from the poles. But if we do not find that middle ground, if we allow ourselves to be forced toward one extreme or the other, then whatever happens will surely come back to haunt us.

INDEX

INDEX

286

INDEX

288